SK

The Complete Visitors Guide

Angela Nicholson
MA (Hons), FSA Scot

Keith Nicholson
BSc (Hons), MSc, PhD, CChem, MRSC, MInstEnvSc, FAEG

Thistle*Press*

Quality guides to Scotland

© Angela Nicholson, 1994

Cover photograph
The Needle of The Quiraing with the
Trotternish Ridge in the background.
Walk No. 26
© Keith Nicholson, 1994

ISBN   0 9520950 1 7

British Library Cataloguing-in-Publication
Data.
A catalogue record for this book is
available from the British Library.

Published by
Thistle*Press*,
Insch, Aberdeenshire,
AB52 6JR, Scotland.

CONTENTS

Part 1
Practical Information

Part 2
Touring Guide

Part 3
Walks Guide

Part 4
Landscape, Geology & The Skye Volcano

HOW TO GET THERE

By Car

For the motorist, there are three main access routes to the Isle of Skye. From the south, follow the A82 to just beyond Fort William and then take the A830 which branches west along Loch Eil to the scenic coastline of Arisaig and Morar. The A830 terminates at Mallaig and here the ferry to Armadale on Skye may be joined (see below).

From the north, those travelling down through Gairloch and Torridon may take the A890 which branches south-westwards at Achnasheen. This road passes through the magnificent mountain scenery of Glen Carron and along the shore of Loch Carron before joining the A87 just short of Kyle of Lochalsh. At Kyle, there is a frequent ferry service to Kyleakin on Skye (see below).

From Inverness, the motorist can follow the scenic A82 southwards along the shore of Loch Ness to Invermoriston. Here, the A887 branches westwards through Glen Moriston and Glen Shiel to terminate at Kyle of Lochalsh where the ferry to Kyleakin can be joined. The road passes close to the breathtaking peaks of the Five Sisters and is definitely one for lovers of grand mountain scenery. This approach also gives the motorist the choice of branching west at Shiel Bridge to follow the narrow road up and over the Mam Ratagan Pass to Glenelg where the tiny Kylerhea ferry may be joined (see below). Although much improved in recent years, this road is still mainly single track and a steep ascent and descent is involved. If you have time to spare however, this is certainly the most leisurely way to approach Skye and the scenery is spectacular.

By Rail

If you are journeying by rail, there are two scenic lines to choose from. THE WEST HIGHLAND LINE connects Glasgow and Mallaig via Fort William. From Glasgow, the train heads north-west through Dumbarton and along the Gare Loch and Loch Long before heading north to Crianlarich. From here, the track crosses the starkly beautiful Rannoch Moor and then bends westwards to Fort William. The line continues along the shore of Loch Eil and upon reaching the picturesque coastal village of Arisaig, bends northwards through Morar to Mallaig. Most trains include a trolley service of cold snacks and hot and cold drinks. Cyclists should check with Scotrail in advance of travel as carriage space for cycles is very limited and prior reservations are required. Not all trains connect with the Armadale ferry - check before departure. For detailed information on the timetables and fares which apply to the West Highland Line, telephone Glasgow (041) 204 2844

(24 hours), Fort William (0397) 703 791 or Mallaig (0687) 2227.

THE KYLE LINE connects Inverness with the Kyle of Lochalsh. From the highland capital, the track runs westwards along the Beauly Firth and turns north to Dingwall, where it splits into two. The western branch heads inland to Achnasheen and then bends south-westwards through Glen Carron towards Loch Carron. Here, the line hugs the water's edge and as the loch opens up, there are spectacular views of the Applecross mountains. The final stretch runs south along the coast, with stunning views of Skye, before terminating at Kyle of Lochalsh. Again, most trains include a trolley service of cold snacks and hot and cold drinks. During the summer months there are special Hebridean Heritage and Atlantic Heritage trains which operate a dining car service. The Hebridean Heritage train also carries a special Observation Car with on-board commentary for which an extra charge is payable. Cyclists should check with Scotrail in advance of travel as carriage space is very limited - prior reservations are required. A new service recently introduced on the Kyle Line is the "Young Explorer Train" - a train comprised entirely of the traditional coaching stock which has much more room for cycles, backpacks and climbing gear etc (cycle reservations are still required, however). Young Explorer Trains run between June and September only. For detailed information on the timetables and fares which apply to the Kyle Line, telephone Inverness (0463) 238 924.

By Bus

A number of companies operate excellent bus services to Skye.

CITYLINK. For full details, telephone Glasgow (041) 332 9191. Service as follows:
Glasgow-Fort William-Isle of Skye: Service No. 516. Runs daily. Route on Skye: Kyleakin Jetty, Broadford Post Office, Sconser (Ferry Road End), Sligachan (Road End), Portree Square, Uig Pier (not all runs).

HIGHLAND BUS & COACH. For full details, telephone Portree (0478) 612 622 or Inverness (0463) 710 555. Service as follows:
Inverness-Portree: Service No. 970. Operates Monday-Saturday and also Sunday when Inverness Technical College is in session. No service on 25/26 December and 1/2 January. Route on Skye: Kyleakin, Broadford Post Office, Sconser, Sligachan, Portree Square.

SKYE-WAYS operate three runs and can also arrange through tickets in conjunction with other major coach operators throughout the U.K. For full details, telephone Kyle (0599) 4328 or Inverness (0463) 710 119. Services are as follows:
Glasgow-Fort William-Kyle: Service No. 915. Runs daily. Passengers must change to Service No. 917 at Kyle of Lochalsh. On Skye, the bus stops at the

following places: Kyleakin Ferry Terminal, Broadford Post Office, Sconser, Sligachan, Portree Square.

Glasgow-Fort William-Isle of Skye: Service No. 916. Runs daily. No change required. Route on Skye as above.

Inverness-Isle of Skye: Service No. 917. Runs daily. Route on Skye as above, but Monday-Saturday terminates at Uig Pier.

The Ferry Crossings

At present, all visitors to Skye must undertake a short sea crossing to reach the island. There are three ferry routes to choose from:

Kyle of Lochalsh-Kyleakin: This short 5 minute journey has long been the most popular ferry crossing to Skye. Operated by Caledonian MacBrayne, two RO/RO ferries, MV Loch Dunvegan and MV Loch Fyne, run daily, including Sundays, at frequent intervals between 0730 and 2145. Thereafter, sailings are made at half hourly intervals throughout the night (except between 0200 and 0300), subject to demand. Drivers, passengers and bicycles are carried free of charge. Vehicle reservations are not required - simply turn up and drive on to the ferry. This service can get quite busy in the summer months, but CalMac do an excellent job in ensuring that everything runs smoothly and delays are kept to a minimum. Unfortunately, with the new Skye Bridge due to open in 1995, this valuable service will cease to exist - the Government will not allow CalMac to operate in competition with the bridge. For full details, telephone Kyle (0599) 4482.

Mallaig-Armadale: This 30 minute ferry crossing is also operated by Caledonian MacBrayne and is popular with travellers arriving by rail on the West Highland Line and those driving up the west coast through Oban and Fort William. MV Iona runs Monday-Saturday, with Sunday sailings from late June to late August only. Vehicles are conveyed from Easter to mid-October only and reservations are required. In winter a passenger-only service operates. Bicycles are carried free of charge. A self-service restaurant and bar facilities are located on board. For full details and reservations, telephone Mallaig (0687) 2403 or Armadale (04714) 248.

Glenelg-Kylerhea: If you are seeking a quiet and rather unusual approach to Skye, the Glenelg to Kylerhea ferry is the one for you. The 5 minute sailing across the beautiful Kylerhea narrows follows the route of the original Skye ferry, used by the cattle-drovers of old. The crossing is made by a unique six-car turntable ferry operated by skipper Roddy MacLeod - keep an eye out for the seals which love to play in the frothy surf of the narrows. The ferry runs frequently as required during the following times: early April to late May - Monday-Saturday 0900-1800, no Sunday service; late May to late August - Monday-Saturday 0900-2000, Sunday 1000-1700; late August to late September - Monday-Saturday 0900-1800, Sunday 1000-1700. For full details, telephone/fax (059 981) 302.

GETTING AROUND THE ISLAND

MAPS

For hillwalkers, fishermen and others requiring detailed map coverage of the countryside, the Ordnance Survey 1:50,000 Landranger series is excellent value. Two maps cover most of the area detailed in this guide - Sheet 23: North Skye and Sheet 32: South Skye. The eastern extremity of the island around Kyleakin is covered by Sheet 33: Loch Alsh, Glen Shiel & surrounding area.

By Bus

The island is well served by public transport. Bus routes are operated by the following companies:

HIGHLAND BUS & COACH, Park Road, Portree, Isle of Skye. Telephone Portree (0478) 612 622 for full details. Services as follows:

Portree-Kyleakin: Service No. 50. Monday-Saturday only. Route: Portree Square, Sligachan, Sconser Ferry Road End, Broadford, Kyleakin. Returns by same route.

Armadale-Kyleakin: Service No. 51. Monday-Saturday only. Route: Ardvasar Post Office (1st run of day only), Armadale Pier, Teangue Post Office, Isle Oronsay, Drumfearn Road End, Broadford, Kyleakin. Returns by same route.

Portree-Armadale: Service No. 52. Monday-Saturday only. Route: Portree Square, Sligachan, Sconser Ferry Road End, Broadford, Drumfearn Road End, Isle Oronsay, Teangue Post Office, Armadale Pier, Ardvasar Post Office (last run of day only). Returns by same route.

Portree-Elgol: Service No. 150. Monday-Saturday only. Route: Portree Square, Sligachan, Sconser Ferry Road End, Broadford, Torrin, Elgol. Returns same route.

NICOLSONS BUS SERVICES, Borve, by Portree, Isle of Skye. Telephone (047 032) 240 for full details. Services as follows:

Kilmaluag-Portree via Staffin: Contract No. 531. Monday-Friday, plus Saturday from June to September. Route: Kilmaluag (Balmacquien Road End), Flodigarry Hotel Road End, Staffin House Hotel, Culnaknock Road End, Torvaig Road End, Portree Square, Portree High School. Returns by same route.

Kilmaluag-Portree via Uig: Contract No. 532. Monday-Friday, plus Saturday from June to September. Route: Kilmaluag (Balmacquien Road End), Duntulm Hotel, Kilmuir School, Uig Pier, Uig Police Station, Earlish Road End, Kingsburgh Road End, Kensaleyre Church, Borve Junction, Portree High School, Portree Square. Returns by same route.

Glendale-Portree via Dunvegan & Edinbane: Contract No. 533. Monday-Friday, plus Saturday from June to September. Route: Glendale (Lower Milovaig Road End), Colbost (Borreraig Road End), Lonmore, Dunvegan Hotel, Dunvegan Castle, Fairy Bridge, Edinbane Hospital, Arnisort Church, Bernisdale Post Office, Skeabost Hotel, Portree High School, Portree Square. Returns by same route.

Dunvegan-Portree via Sligachan: Contract No. 534 Part 1. Monday-Friday only. Route: Dunvegan Hotel, Lonmore, Vatten School, Harlosh Post Office, Feorlig Junction, Ose Post Office, Ullinish Hotel, Struan Post Office, Drynoch Road End, Sligachan Hotel, Portree High School, Portree Square. Returns by same route.
Portree Local Service: Contract No. 534 Part 2. Monday-Friday only. No service on Portree public holidays. Route: Portree Square, Sluggans (Industrial Estate), Portree Square.

SKYEWAYS, Ferry Pier, Kyle of Lochalsh, Ross-shire. Telephone Kyle (0599) 4328 for full details. Services as follows:
Kyleakin-Armadale: Service No. 700. Monday-Saturday only. Route: Kyleakin Ferry Terminal, Broadford Post Office, Isle Ornsay Road End, Armadale Pier. Returns by same route.
Portree-Kyleakin: Service No. 701. Monday-Saturday only. Route: Portree Square, Sligachan (Bus Shelter), Sconser (Ferry Terminal), Broadford (Hospital Road End), Kyleakin (Ferry Terminal). Returns by same route.
Portree-Armadale: Service No. 702. Monday-Saturday, May-September only. Route: Portree Square, Sligachan (Bus Shelter), Sconser Ferry Terminal, Broadford (Hospital Road End), Isle Ornsay (Road End), Armadale Pier. Returns by same route.
Uig-Kyleakin: Service Nos. 701/916/917. Departs from Uig Monday-Saturday only. On Sundays, departs from Portree. Route: Uig, Portree, Sligachan, Sconser, Broadford, Kyleakin. Returns by same route.

SUTHERLAND'S BUS SERVICE, Carbost, Isle of Skye. Telephone Carbost (0478) 640 280/210/286 for full details. Service as follows:
Portree-Fiscavaig/Glenbrittle: Summer service operates Monday-Friday only, from late May to late September. Route: Portree Square, Sligachan, Carbost, Fiscavaig, Glenbrittle (certain runs also call at Sconser Pier). Returns by same route.
Winter Service operates rest of year, Monday-Friday only. Route: Portree Square, Portree High School, Sligachan, Drynoch Junction, Carbost Post Office, Portnalong, Fiscavaig (certain runs also call at Sconser Pier). Returns same route. Transport to Glenbrittle can also be arranged - contact Sutherland's on the above number.

See also the Citylink, Highland Bus & Coach and Skye-Ways services detailed in the "How To Get There" section above.

By Postbus

In addition to delivering the mail, the postbus carries passengers and for a modest fee can pick you up or drop you off at several points on the postal round. The Isle of Skye is served by three postbuses:
Elgol-Broadford Postbus: Runs Monday-Saturday. For full details, contact Broadford Post Office. Tel. (0471) 822 201. Route: Glasnakille, Elgol Pier Hill Top, Elgol Post Office, Drynan Road End, Strathaird, Faolin, Torrin Post Office, Kilbride Road End, Swordale, Broadford Post Office, Broadford Hospital (certain runs only), Broadford School (on school days only). Returns by same route.

Dunvegan-Glendale Postbus: Runs Monday-Saturday. For full details, contact Glendale Post Office. Tel. (047 081) 266. Morning Route: Glendale Post Office, Fasach, Borreraig, Colbost, Skinidin Post Office, Dunvegan Post Office, Glendale Post Office. On Monday and Wednesday mornings, also calls at Ramasaig. Afternoon Route: Glendale Post Office, Colbost, Skinidin Post Office, Dunvegan Post Office, Skinidin Post Office, Colbost, Fasach, Glendale Post Office, Milovaig, Neist Point, Glendale Post Office.

Dunvegan-Waternish Postbus: Runs Monday-Saturday. For full details, contact Dunvegan Post Office. Tel. (047 022) 201. Route: Gillen, Knockbreck, Waternish Post Office, Fairy Bridge, Dunvegan Post Office, Fairy Bridge, Waternish Post Office, Hallin Post Office, Carnach, Knockbreck School, Geary, Gillen.

Advice To Motorists

Many of the roads on the Isle of Skye are single track with passing places. Please note that it is an *offence* to hinder traffic which is travelling behind you. Pull into the nearest passing place on your left or stop opposite one on your right and allow following traffic to overtake. Similarly, use passing places to permit on-coming traffic to pass.

ACCOMMODATION   DIRECTORY

Ullinish Lodge Hotel

Ullinish Lodge Hotel and Restaurant, Struan, By Portree, Isle of Skye, IV56 8FD. Tel: 047 072 214. After Spring '94: 0470572 214.

The Ullinish Lodge is an eighteenth century house of considerable character which has been tastefully converted to achieve the friendly and welcoming ambience of a family home providing the facilities which guests are now entitled to expect, whilst retaining much of its' original character.

Visited by Doctor Johnson and James Boswell in 1773 who were appreciative of the Lodge's magnificent setting on the shores of Loch Bracadale overlooking Loch Harport to the breathtaking Cuillin mountains.

The Ullinish Lodge offers 27,000 acres within which can be found a wealth of ancient monuments, endless walking amidst tranquil unspoilt scenery, rough shooting, brown trout lochs and salmon rivers. A short 9 mile drive brings you to the historic Dunvegan Castle set in its' own botanical gardens.

After your day out, return to the Lodge and enjoy the full facilities provided in your room prior to enjoying our home cooked cuisine offering a balance of meat, game, fish and shellfish all provided from the wealth of Scotland's land and sea. Then relax by the open fire in our lounge with your coffee and perhaps one of our finest malt whiskies.

Resident Proprietors: John and Claudia Mulford. Fully Licenced. Non residents welcome. Restaurant from 7pm. Booking essential.

Rooms: 8 all with private facilities and colour television. Open Easter-end October. B&B from £25-£35. Please telephone for further details and full colour brochure.

STB Commended 3 crown.   *Taste of Scotland recommended.*

Breakish

Taigh Aiseig   Bed & Breakfast

Our newly renovated crofthouse is situated in a peaceful location overlooking a sandy beach. Our rooms, with private facilities & colour T.V., command spectacular views of the Cuillins & nearby islands. Central for touring all parts of Skye - 4 1/2 miles from Kyleakin (first turning on right after Kylerhea turn-off).

Mrs Sikorski, "Taigh Aiseig",
Breakish, Isle of Skye, IV42 8PZ.
Tel: (0471) 822 606.

Broadford   *Fairwinds*

Bungalow peacefully situated overlooking river and mountain. Five minutes from village centre. 2 Doubles and 1 Twin Room (1 Double ensuite). Tea making facilities, wash basins, central heating, guests' lounge with colour television.
(2 Crowns Commended).
Bicycles available for hire, daily and weekly rates. Ideal centre for walking.

Mrs J. Donaldson,
Fairwinds, Elgol Road, Broadford,
Isle of Skye, IV49 9AB.
Tel. Broadford (0471) 822 270.

Breakish Self Contained Flat

Situated in this pleasant crofting community, on the outskirts of Broadford, in a large garden. Convenient to road with seashore close by. Tastefully converted apartment, well decorated and furnished. Excellent base for exploring the magnificent scenery of the island or western highlands. Ample opportnuity for walking, climbing and relaxing. Downstairs: Lounge. Upstairs: Kitchen and Dining area 3 Bedrooms - 1 Double and 2 Twins; Bathroom with toilet and shower. Services: Gas fire in Lounge with meter. Central heating and electric included in rent, also all linen and towels. Colour TV, Fridge/Freezer and Microwave. Utility room with auto washer and coin operated tumble dryer. Parking for 3 cars. Shops 1/2 mile, Restaurant/Pub 1/4 mile.
Mrs Seonaid R. Nicolson, Scorrybreac,
Scullamus, Breakish, Isle of Skye,
IV42 8QB. Tel. 0471 822 525

BRAES   by PORTREE
GEDINTAILOR
SELF-CATERING HOUSE

Charming, homely, comfortable, generously equipped house sleeping 7. Spectacular panoramic views across islands to mainland peaks. Secluded, sheltered position within easy walk of sandy beach. 6 miles from Portree on B883. Endless activities on land and sea in beautiful surroundings.

Details: Major J.D. Bengough, White Lodge, Church Street, Sidbury, Devon, EX10 0SB. Tel. (0395) 597214.

Carbost
Self-Catering Bungalow

Well-equipped house in quiet
village with views over sea-loch and
to the Cuillin Hills. Ideal centre for
hill-walking or climbing. Sleeps six
in four bedrooms. Electric heating
with one open fire.

Further details and brochure available
from Miss M. Steele, 29 Dubford Place,
Bridge of Don, Aberdeen, AB23 8FW.
Tel. (0224) 823 154.

Dunvegan

This modern bungalow is situated four
miles from Dunvegan, on a working
family farm; has beautiful views of
Rhum and Canna, and many lovely
walks on the nearby hills. It has one
double and two twin rooms (all with hot
and cold) and a Visitors' lounge.

Mrs Ann Macdonald,
Cnoc Nan Craobh, Orbost Farm,
Dunvegan, Skye IV55 8ZB.
Tel. (047 022) 225.

Carbost
Self-Catering Cottage

Ideal walking/climbing centre. 1/2 mile
from village (Distillery, Inn).
Comfortably modernised well-equipped
old schoolhouse sleeping 8 (3
bedrooms). Open fires, electric
heating, washer/dryer, drying room,
telephone. Large schoolroom is
wonderful wet weather refuge.

Enquiries to Mrs Peppe, Glendrynoch
Lodge, Carbost, Skye, IV47 8SX.
Tel. 0478 640218

Dunvegan
(2 self catering cottages)

Creagan Breac is a byre converted to
spacious cottages. Picture windows
embracing superb views, Cuillins,
MacLeod's Tables and moorland.
Electric, washbasins in bedrooms -
pets welcome - parking.

2 Crown Award.

Details from Mrs J. Robinson, Bridge
Cottage, Broughton Mills, Broughton-
in-Furness, Cumbria, LA20 6AY.
Tel. 0229 716402.

Lochview Bed & Breakfast
By Dunvegan

Situated on peaceful lochside, a minute's walk from shore. Enjoy the sun setting on the loch, before it sinks behind MacLeod's Tables; relax and unwind by the welcoming open fire in the residents' lounge, with tea and coffee-making facilities. Full Scottish or vegetarian breakfast. Single/double/twin/private facilities.

Bookings or just more information from
Mrs C. Inglis, Lochview, Harlosh, by Dunvegan, Isle of Skye, IV55 8ZH. Tel. (047 022) 293.

Orbost Farmhouse
nr Dunvegan

Working family hill farm with farmhouse nestling at foot of hills with a short walk to beach. Superb location for relaxing, walking or touring. The two tastefully decorated bedrooms (with shared bathroom) include sinks and tea/coffee facilities. Pleasant residents' lounge with coal fire. Breakfast includes farm fresh eggs & home-made jams.

Orbost Farmhouse, nr Dunvegan, Isle of Skye, IV55 8ZB. Margaret MacDonald Tel: 047 022 479

Luib by Broadford
Luxury Loch-side Bungalow

Beautiful views across Loch Ainort to the Red Cuillins from the verandah. Entrance to beach from garden. Consists of Double and Twin Bedrooms, Shower room, Bathroom, fully equipped Kitchen, comfortable Lounge with open or electric fires, T.V., Central heating. Sleeps 5. Easy access from main road. Car parking.

SORRY NO PETS.
Prices from £100.

Details from Mrs G. Willett, Laimhrig, Luib, by Broadford, Isle of Skye, IV49 9AN. Tel. (0471) 822 686.

Orbost House
(near Dunvegan)
2 Self-Catering Apartments

Unique property containing two self-catering apartments, one sleeping up to 6 and the other 7. Situated in 2 acres of lawn and trees, overlooking sea, mountains and island of Rum. Ten minutes walk from safe, sandy beach. All electric. Ideal for walking, fishing, sub-aqua, archaeology, climbing and bird-watching.

From £150-220/week.

Telephone for brochure: 047 022 389. Mrs Sandy Kozikowska, Orbost House, Dunvegan, Isle of Skye, IV55 8ZB.

PORTNALONG

Ivanhoe   B & B

At "Ivanhoe" a warm welcome awaits you.   Situated above Fiscavaig Bay with spectacular views over Loch Bracadale to MacLeod's Tables.   Ideal for shore or moorland walks.   4 miles from the famous Talisker Distillery. Central heating throughout.   T & C facilities in bedrooms.   Quiet and peaceful.

Mrs P. Wood, Ivanhoe, 19 Fiscavaig, Portnalong, Isle of Skye, IV47 8SN. Tel. (0478) 640 360.

STAFFIN
Tigh Cilmartin

Old manse set in peaceful location at north end of the Trotternish ridge close to Quiraing. Beautiful views and only 15 minutes walk from sea and beach.

B&B from £12.

Details from Debbie Poole, Tigh Cilmartin, Staffin, Isle of Skye, IV51 9HY. Tel 0470 562331.

Skeabost House Hotel

At the head of Loch Snizort stands Skeabost House Hotel, a romantic Victorian hunting lodge surrounded by 12 acres of flourishing woodlands and well tended gardens.   This friendly family run hotel has earned a reputation for comfort and cuisine. Free golf and salmon fishing on the River Snizort.

Bookings and enquiries:
Tel. 0470 53 2202, Fax: 047053 2454.

Treaslane   Skeabost
B & B   *by Portree*

Comfortable accommodation in traditional crofthouse, refurbished to high standard (S.T.B. Highly Commended 2 Crowns). Situated 9 miles from Portree on the main Portree-Dunvegan road (A850). Two double rooms (one ensuite, one with private facilities), lounge with panoramic views over Loch Snizort. Warm welcome assured.

Neil & Mary Cameron, "Hillcroft", Treaslane, Skeabost Bridge, by Portree, Isle of Skye, IV51 9NX. Tel. 047082 304.

HOTEL, SELF-CATERING AND B & B DIRECTORY
Please quote this guide when contacting the following advertisers.

ARDVASAR, SLEAT (Self-Catering Cottages) STB 4 Crown Commended. 1 mile from Mallaig/Armadale Ferry, area of natural scenic beauty overlooking Sound of Sleat and Knoydart hills, close to sea, shops and pub. Cottages fully furnished, linen supplied. Contact Mr & Mrs Shone, 4 Calligarry, Ardvasar, Sleat, Isle of Skye, IV45 8RU. Tel. (04714) 278.

BRAES AREA (Self-Catering House) Gedintailor, Braes, by Portree. Charming, homely, comfortable, generously equipped house sleeping 7. Spectacular, panoramic views across islands to mainland peaks. Secluded, sheltered position within easy walk of sandy beach. 6 miles from Portree on B883. Endless activities on land and sea in beautiful surroundings. Details from Major J.D. Bengough, White Lodge, Church Street, Sidbury, Devon, EX10 0SB. Tel. (0395) 597 214. *Display Advert*

BREAKISH (B & B) Our newly renovated crofthouse is situated in a peaceful location overlooking a sandy beach. Our rooms, with private facilities & colour T.V., command spectacular views of the Cuillins & nearby islands. Central for touring all parts of Skye - 4 1/2 miles from Kyeakin (first turning on right after Kylerhea turn-off). Details from Mrs Sikorski, Taigh Aiseig, Breakish, Isle of Skye, IV42 8PZ. Tel. (0471) 822 606. *Display Advert*

BROADFORD (B & B) "Fairwinds". Bungalow peacefully situated overlooking river and mountain. Five minutes from village centre. 2 Doubles and 1 Twin Room (1 Double ensuite). Tea making facilities, wash basins, central heating, guests' lounge with colour television. 2 Crowns Commended. Bicycles available for hire, daily and weekly rates. Ideal centre for walking. Details from Mrs J. Donaldson, Fairwinds, Elgol Road, Broadford, Isle of Skye, IV49 9AB. Tel. (0471) 822 270. *Display Advert*

BROADFORD (B & B) "Ptarmigan". Friendly family home in idyllic setting 15 metres from water's edge. Enjoy bird and otter spotting from your bedroom window. All rooms on ground floor with panoramic views across Broadford Bay. Minutes walk from local restaurants and pubs. All bedrooms en-suite and triple glazed with remote control colour TV, video, period radio, teamaker, hairdryer, binoculars. Payphone available. Access, Visa and American Express welcome. Open all year round. One Twin and two Double rooms. Mrs D. MacPhie, Ptarmigan, Broadford, Isle of Skye, Inverness-shire, IV49 9AQ. Tel. (0471) 822 744. Fax: 0471 822 745. *Display Advert*

BROADFORD (B & B) Secluded bungalow 200m off main road on outskirts of Broadford village. 2 Twins (1 ensuite), 1 Double, 1 public bathroom, 1 public shower room. Full Scottish breakfast. Details from Mrs Fiona MacKay, Strathnaver, Harrapool, Broadford, Isle of Skye, IV49 9AQ. Tel. (0471) 822 406.

BROADFORD (Self-Catering Apartment) Self-catering apartment, within easy walking distance of shops & restaurants. One bedroom with single & double bed. Upstairs lounge, with view of Red Cuillins - double sofabed - T.V. Well equipped kitchen - toilet/shower room. Towels & linen provided. Suit 4 adults. Details from Mrs Sandra Parry, 2 Harrapool, Broadford, Isle of Skye, IV49 9AQ. Tel. (0471) 822 498.

BROADFORD (Self-Catering Cottage) 5 miles north of Broadford; close to the shore with spectacular views over Loch Ainort to the islands of Raasay and Scalpay and the Red Cuillin. The fully equipped cottage has been fully modernised and provides very comfortable accommodation for 4. STB 4 Crowns Commended. Details from Mrs Catherine MacKinnon, "Myrtle Bank", Portnalong, Isle of Skye, IV47 8SL. Tel. (0478) 640 346.

BROADFORD AREA (Self-Catering Annexe) Floreat Annexe is a semi-detached house in a peaceful setting with wonderful views over the loch. There are three bedrooms sleeping six. Every effort has been made to make your stay pleasant. Details from Mrs E.R. Cleave, Floreat, Ard Dorch, Broadford, Isle of Skye, IV49 9AJ. Tel. (0471) 822 531. *Display Advert*

BROADFORD AREA (Self-Catering Bungalow) Astbury Cottage is a luxury loch-side bungalow situated at Luib near Broadford. There are beautiful views across Loch Ainort to the Red Cuillins from the verandah. Entrance to beach from garden. Consists of Double and Twin Bedrooms, Shower room, Bathroom, fully equipped Kitchen, comfortable Lounge with open or electric fires, T.V., Central heating. Sleeps 5. Easy access from main road; car parking. Sorry no pets. Prices from £100 per week. Details from Mrs G. Willett, Laimhrig, Luib, by Broadford, Isle of Skye, IV49 9AN. Tel. (0471) 822 686. *Display Advert*

BROADFORD AREA (Self-Catering Cottage) Cottage on sea loch at Heaste, 5 miles from Broadford. Sleeps 8. £180-£200 per week. For further details, telephone Victoria Gibson on (041) 337 2456.

BROADFORD AREA (Self-Catering Flat) Self contained flat in the pleasant crofting community of Scullamus. Large garden, close to seashore and convenient to road. 3 bedrooms sleeping six, lounge, kitchen/dining area and bathroom with shower and toilet. Fully equipped including all linen and towels, colour T.V., Fridge/Freezer and Microwave, utility room with auto washer and coin operated tumble dryer. Central heating and electric included in rent; gas fire in lounge with meter. Parking for 3 cars; Shops 1/2 mile; Restaurant/Pub 1/4 mile. Details from Mrs Seonaid R. Nicolson, Scorrybreac, Scullamus, Breakish, Isle of Skye, IV42 8QB. Tel. (0471) 822 525. *Display Advert*

CALLIGARRY, ARDVASAR (Self-Catering Bungalows) Situated in the south end of Skye, these 2 modern 2-bedroomed bungalows are purpose-built on a working croft with magnificent views across the Sound of Sleat to the Knoydart hills on the mainland. Very comfortably furnished and fully equipped including bedlinen and towels. Details from Mrs J. MacLure, 10 Aird, Ardvasar, Sleat, Isle of Skye, IV45 8RN. Tel. (04714) 205.

CARBOST (Self-Catering Bungalow) Well-equipped house in quiet village with views over sea-loch and to the Cuillin Hills. Ideal centre for hill-walking or climbing. Sleeps six in four bedrooms. Electric heating with one open fire. Further details and brochure available from Miss M. Steele, 29 Dubford Place, Bridge of Don, Aberdeen, AB23 8FW. Tel. (0224) 823 154. *Display Advert*

CARBOST (Self-Catering Cottage) Ideal walking centre, 1/2 mile from village (Distillery, Inn) and within easy reach of the Cuillins. Comfortably modernised and very well-equipped old schoolhouse sleeping 8 (3 bedrooms). Open fire, electric heating, washer/dryer, drying room, telephone. Large schoolroom is wonderful wet weather refuge. Enquiries to Mrs Peppe, Glendrynoch Lodge, Carbost, Skye, IV47 8SX. Tel. (0478) 640 218. *Display Advert*

CARBOST/PORTNALONG (Self-Catering Cottages, Flat & Independent Hostels)
STB 3 Crown Commended cottage at Carbost, flat & cottage at Portnalong, sleeping 4,4 & 6. No smoking, no pets. Views of mountains & loch. Also available Croft Bunkhouse & Bothy, fully equipped Independent hostels sleeping 14 & 6, only £5.00 person/night. Details: P. Thomas, 7 Portnalong, Isle of Skye, IV47 8SL. Tel. (0478) 640 254.

DUNVEGAN (Hotel) The Tables Hotel & Restaurant is centrally situated in the village overlooking Loch Dunvegan with panoramic views of MacLeod's Tables mountains. One mile from Dunvegan Castle. A relaxed, informal atmosphere with imaginative food (including vegetarian), good wines and peat fire. An excellent base for hill walking, fishing, rambling, birdwatching or just exploring the island. The Tables Hotel & Restaurant, Dunvegan, Isle of Skye, IV55 8WA. Tel. (047 022) 404. Proprietors: Mr & Mrs A. Macdonald. *Display Advert*

DUNVEGAN (Self-Catering Cottages) Dunvegan Castle holiday cottages. We have four properties available for let on a self-catering basis. Each property has its own idyllic setting and unique character and is furnished and equipped to the highest standard. Scottish Tourist Board 4 Crown Commended. Tel. (047 022) 206 for information pack. *Display Advert*

DUNVEGAN (Self-Catering Cottages) Creagan Breac is a byre converted to two spacious cottages. Picture windows embracing superb views, Cuillins, MacLeod's Tables and moorland. Electric, washbasins in bedrooms - pets welcome - parking. 2 Crown Award. Details from Mrs J. Robinson, Bridge Cottage, Broughton Mills, Broughton-in Furness, Cumbria, LA20 6AY. Tel. (0229) 716 402. *Display Advert*

DUNVEGAN AREA (B & B) Cnoc Nan Craobh is a modern bungalow situated four miles from Dunvegan, on a working family farm, with beautiful views of Rhum and Canna, and many lovely walks on the nearby hills. It has one double and two twin rooms (all with hot and cold) and a Visitors' lounge. Details from Mrs Ann Macdonald, Cnoc Nan Craobh, Orbost Farm, Dunvegan, Isle of Skye, IV55 8ZB. Tel. (047 022) 225. *Display Advert*

DUNVEGAN AREA (B & B) Lochview is peacefully situated by the lochside, a minute's walk from shore. Enjoy the sun setting on the loch, before it sinks behind MacLeod's Tables; relax and unwind by the welcoming open fire in the residents' lounge, with tea and coffee-making facilities. Full Scottish or vegetarian breakfast. Single/double/twin/private facilities. Bookings or just more information from Mrs C. Inglis, Lochview, Harlosh, by Dunvegan, Isle of Skye, IV55 8ZH. Tel (047 022) 293. *Display Advert*

DUNVEGAN AREA (B & B) Working family hill farm with farmhouse nestling at foot of hills with a short walk to beach. Superb location for relaxing, walking or touring. The two tastefully decorated bedrooms (with shared bathroom) include sinks and tea/coffee facilities. Pleasant residents' lounge with coal fire. Breakfast includes farm fresh eggs & home-made jams. Details from Margaret MacDonald, Orbost Farmhouse, nr Dunvegan, Isle of Skye, IV55 8ZB. Tel. (047 022) 479. *Display Advert*

DUNVEGAN AREA (Self-Catering Apartments) Orbost House is a unique property containing two self-catering apartments, one sleeping up to 6 and the other 7. Situated in 2 acres of lawn and trees, overlooking sea, mountains and Island of Rum. Ten minutes walk from safe, sandy beach. All electric. Ideal for walking, fishing, sub-aqua, archaeology, climbing and bird-watching. From £150-220/week. Telephone for brochure: (047 022) 389. Mrs Sandy Kozikowska, Orbost House, Dunvegan, Isle of Skye, IV55 8ZB. *Display Advert*

DUNVEGAN AREA (Self-Catering Cottage) Situated in Colbost. Fully equipped (except linen) comfortably furnished two-bedroom cottage in 1/4 acre garden. Sleeps four. £100-£210 per week. Area ideal for outdoor life - hill walking, sea angling etc. Dogs welcome. Particulars from L. Shurmer, Skinidin, Dunvegan, Isle of Skye, IV55 8ZS. Tel. Dunvegan 380.

EDINBANE (Self-Catering Houses) 2 modern semi-detached houses, fully equipped, including linen. Each sleeps 6, shower, colour T.V., fridge, microwave, dishwasher etc. Ideal area for touring. Quiet peaceful setting. Boat may be available, pets welcome, STB 3 Crown Commended, open all year. £100 to £300 per week. Mr R. MacFarlane, 15 Edinbane, By Portree, Isle of Skye, IV51 9PR. Tel/Fax 047 082 270.

GLENDALE (B & B) Warm friendly welcome at our modern crofthouse on working croft in lovely glen with view to Outer Hebrides. One double, two twin rooms. Home baking and cooking. Optional evening meal. Vegetarian food available. Attractions: walking, fishing, birdwatching, museums, Dunvegan Castle. French/German spoken. Pets by arrangement. Details from Janet Kernachan, 4 Lephin, Glendale, Isle of Skye, IV55 8WJ. Tel. (047 081) 376.

GLENDALE (Self-Catering Cottage) Very well equipped croft cottage in 8 acres of own ground. Sleeps 5. Facilities for walking, fishing, boating and horse riding arranged locally. Many local craft centres and places of interest including Dunvegan Castle about 7 miles away. Rates from £180-£230 per week include electricity. Details from Mrs K. Painting, 13 Ferndale Road, Banbury, Oxon, OX16 0RZ. Tel. (0295) 252 120.

HARLOSH (Self-Catering Flat) STB Commended 3 Crowns. Self-contained flat, fully equipped. Sleeps 3. Beautiful views: Atlantic to south, MacLeod's Tables to west, Cuillin Hills to east. Five miles south of Dunvegan. £120-£160 per week. Mrs E.M. Jones, Strathardle, Harlosh, Dunvegan, Isle of Skye, IV55 8ZG. Tel. (047 022) 360.

KILMORE (B & B) One Double, one Twin, one Single. Working croft, 3 miles north of Armadale Pier on A851 overlooking Sound of Sleat, opposite Loch Nevis Taxi Service & Private Tours to all parts of island. Rates per person £14-£15 per night. Pets welcome. Telephone Julie MacDonald on (04714) 272. 3 Kilmore, Sleat, Isle of Skye, IV44 8RG.

LOWER MILOVAIG (Self-Catering Cottage) Charming traditional cottage with commanding view of Loch Pooltiel, Dunvegan Head & the Outer Hebrides. Recently completely renovated. Comfortably furnished. Sleeps 4. Colour T.V. Bed linen provided. £90-£200 p.w. Contact: Nick Carter, 10 Lower Milovaig, Glendale, Isle of Skye, IV55 8WA. Tel. (047 081) 367.

LUIB (Self-Catering Cottage) Lochside cottage with uninterrupted views across Loch Ainort to the Red Cuillin Hills. Comfortably furnished. Fully equipped kitchen, electric heating by £1 coin meter. Ex linen. 3 bedrooms sleeping 5-6. £100-£200 per week. Winter weekends Friday-Monday £50, Monday-Friday £70. Contact Mrs A. Horne, 10 Marybrown Walk, Garelochhead, Helensburgh, G84 0BQ. Tel. (0436) 810 632.

ORD (B & B) Fiordhem, our home, is a unique stone cottage, idyllically situated 20 feet from the lochside, commanding breathtaking views of the Cuillins and providing unparalleled opportunities for studying the abundant wildlife. Otters and seals frequent the waters over the garden wall. The perfect holiday base. You are welcome to share it with us. 3 Double/Twin, all private facilities. Open March to October (then by arrangement). Details from Mrs B. La Trobe, Fiordhem, Ord, Isle of Skye, Inverness-shire, IV44 8RN. Tel. (04715) 226. *Display Advert*

PORTNALONG (Self-Catering Cottage) Modernised, extended former crofthouse with spacious sittingroom, large kitchen with dining area, 2 bedrooms sleeping 4, bathroom and shower-room. Comfortably furnished, fully equipped including bed linen, it is all electric, electricity on 50p meter. Quiet area. £90-£140 weekly. Jan-Dec. Mr Daniel MacLeod, 19 Portnalong, by Carbost, Isle of Skye, IV47 8SL. Tel. (0478) 640 249.

PORTNALONG AREA (B & B) At "Ivanhoe" a warm welcome awaits you. Situated above Fiscavaig Bay with spectacular views over Loch Bracadale to MacLeod's Tables. Ideal for shore or moorland walks. 4 miles from the famous Talisker Distillery. Central heating throughout. T & C facilities in bedrooms. Quiet and peaceful. Details from Mrs P. Wood, Ivanhoe, 19 Fiscavaig, Portnalong, Isle of Skye, IV47 8SN. Tel. (0478) 640 360. *Display Advert*

PORTREE (Hotel) Set in its own grounds overlooking Portree Harbour and the Cuillin mountain range, the Cuillin Hills Hotel provides comfort, luxury and high quality service for the discerning customer. Our restaurant and bar offer a wide selection of menus using fresh local produce wherever possible. Cuillin Hills Hotel, Portree, Isle of Skye, IV51 9LU. Tel. (0478) 612 003, Fax: 0478 613 092. *Display Advert*

PORTREE (Hotel) Centrally situated in picturesque Somerled Square, the Portree Hotel is ideally located for touring the island. Its 24 en-suite bedrooms have colour televisions, tea/coffee facilities, telephones, hairdryers and clock radios. Wide choice of menus - 5 places to eat! Portree Hotel, Somerled Square, Portree, Isle of Skye, IV51 9EH. Tel. (0478) 612 511, Fax: 0478 613 093. *Display Advert*

PORTREE (Guesthouse) Springfield Guest House. A family run guest house 5 minutes walk from the shops and buses. Overlooking playing field, close to swimming pool. H & C in all rooms, tea & coffee making facilities, private car park. Springfield Guest House, Home Farm Road, Portree, Isle of Skye. Tel. (0478) 2505. *Display Advert*

PORTREE (B & B) 10 minutes walk from Portree centre. Overlooking Portree Bay. One Double room, one Twin room, each with T.V., teamaking facilities, H&C, central heating. Mrs J.A. MacCallum, "Woodlands", Viewfield Road, Portree, Isle of Skye, IV51 9EU. Tel. (0478) 612 980.

PORTREE (B & B) 19th century house, central heating throughout, situated in quiet residential area 1/2 mile from centre of Portree. All bedrooms have wash basins, tea and coffee making facilities. B&B £15 per person per night. Mrs C. Murray, "Conusg", Coolin Hills Gardens, Portree, Isle of Skye, IV51 9NR. Tel. (0478) 612 426.

PORTREE AREA (B & B) 1 Single, 1 Double, 1 Twin/Family with H & C, tea tray, C.H. 2 bath/shower rooms. T.V. lounge. We are situated at Achachork, 2 miles north of Portree on the A855, an ideal base for touring the very beautiful north of the island. The house has a commanding view of Portree and the Cuillins. Terms from £13.00 per person Bed & Scottish Breakfast. Mrs J.C. MacDonald, 10 Achachork, Portree, Isle of Skye, IV51 9HT. Tel. (0478) 612 213.

SCONSER (B & B) Comfortable family house. One twin room, two double (one en-suite). Tea/coffee and central heating. Situated on the shores of Loch Sligachan, one mile from the hotel. An ideal central location for climbing, hill-walking or touring by car. Reduced rates for longer stay. Contact Neil & Susan MacLean, "Sgurr Mhairi", 29 Sconser, Isle of Skye, IV48 8TD. Tel. (0478) 650 334.

SCONSER (B & B) We do Bed & Breakfast, with evening meal if required, in a warm & friendly atmosphere. For our guests there is a comfortable lounge with panoramic views across Loch Sligachan. Our breakfasts are multi-choice and very filling. 2 Double rooms, 1 Twin room, all have Tea/Coffee making facilities. Details from Morag Nicolson, Sgoirebreac, Sconser, Isle of Skye. Tel. (0478) 650 322.

SCONSER (Self-Catering Flat) On main Kyleakin/Portree road with panoramic loch and hill views. Ideal touring, climbing, walking and fishing base. All linen, electricity and gas included in price (£120-£250 per week). STB 3 Crowns Highly Commended. Details from Mr & Mrs Jagger, Loch Aluinn, 7 Sconser, By Kyle, Isle of Skye, IV48 8TD. Tel. (0478) 650 288.

SCONSER (Self-Catering Cottage) The cottage nestles in the foothills of the famous Cuillin mountains on the bank of Loch Sligachan. It is furnished to a high standard with all bed linen provided & electric blankets. Sleeps 4. T.V., washing machine & fridge all provided. Prices from £100-£260 per week. Phone for brochure. Morag Nicolson, "Sgoirebreac", Sconser, Isle of Skye, IV48 8TD. Tel. (0478) 650 322.

SKEABOST (Hotel) At the head of Loch Snizort stands Skeabost House Hotel, a romantic Victorian hunting lodge surrounded by 12 acres of flourishing woodlands and well tended gardens. This friendly family run hotel has earned a reputation for comfort and cuisine. Free golf and salmon fishing on the River Snizort. Skeabost House Hotel, Skeabost Bridge, Isle of Skye. Bookings and enquiries, tel. (0470) 532 202, fax: 047053 2454. *Display Advert*

SKYE (Self-Catering Cottages/Chalets/Farmhouses) Mackay's Agency - specialists in holiday property letting with cottages, farmhouses and chalets throughout Scotland. We have an excellent selection of self-catering properties throughout Skye. Enjoy the independence of your own holiday home from £25 per person per week. Full colour brochure available: Tel. (24 hrs) 031-226-4364 or write to: Mackay's Agency, 30 Frederick Street, Edinburgh, EH2 2JR. Please mention this guide when you write/phone. *Display Advert*

SLIGACHAN (Self-Catering Cottage) Stunning position close to Cuillins and only 1/2 mile from hotel (wet-weather centre). 4 bedrooms sleeping 8, kitchen, sitting room, bathroom, shower, drying room. Comfortably modernised and well-equipped. Open fires, electric heating, washer/dryer, telephone. Enquiries to Mrs Peppe, Glendrynoch Lodge, Carbost, Isle of Skye, IV47 8SX. Tel. (0478) 640 218. *Display Advert*

STAFFIN (B & B) "Graceland" B & B, overlooking Staffin Bay with the Torridon mountains in the distance. A lovely walking area. One Double room and one Family room. £13 per person per night. Rooms have vanity units, colour T.V., coffee & tea making facilities. Mrs Betty Nicolson, "Graceland", Staffin, Isle of Skye, Inverness-shire, IV51 9JZ. Tel. (047 062) 313.

STAFFIN (B & B) Tigh Cilmartin is an old manse set in a peaceful location at the north end of the Trotternish ridge, close to the Quiraing. Beautiful views and only 15 minutes walk from sea and beach. B&B from £12 per person per night. Details from Debbie Poole, Tigh Cilmatin, Staffin, Isle of Skye, IV51 9HY. Tel. (0470) 562 331. *Display Advert*

STAFFIN (Self-Catering Flat) Holiday flat in the Staffin area of Skye. The flat is fully equipped. Sleeps 2-3. It has a magnificent view over Staffin Bay and is only a 15 minute walk from the Quiraing Hills which have some of the most beautiful walks in the British Isles. Mrs M. MacDonald, Sea Breeze, Glasphein, Staffin, Isle of Skye, Inverness-shire, IV51 9JZ. Tel. (047 062) 236.

STAFFIN (Self-Catering Cottages) Gairloch View Holiday Cottages are situated on the north coast of the island with magnificent sea views overlooking Gairloch and nestling below the famous Quiraing. Ideal for hillwalking, sightseeing, fishing, birdwatching or just relaxing. Cottages are fully equipped, STB 4 Crown Highly Commended. Price includes heating, electric, linen and towels. £120-250/week. Details from Mrs M. MacDonald, 13 Storr Road, Portree, Isle of Skye, IV51 9LX. Tel. (0478) 612 765. *Display Advert*

STRATHAIRD (Guesthouse - Self-Catering Annexe) Strathaird House. Our comfortable family run guesthouse is close to Elgol, Loch Coruisk, and the Cuillin mountains. Enjoy good food and a library by the fireside within the rambling house. A self-catering annexe is also available. Bookings to: Mr & Mrs Kubale, Strathaird House, Strathaird, Isle of Skye, IV49 9AX. Tel: (04716) 269. *Display Advert*

TREASLANE (B & B) Comfortable accommodation in traditional crofthouse, refurbished to high standard (STB Highly Commended 2 Crowns). Situated 9 miles from Portree on the main Portree-Dunvegan road (A850). Two double rooms (one ensuite, one with private facilities), lounge with panoramic views over Loch Snizort. Warm welcome assured. Neil & Mary Cameron, "Hillcroft", Treaslane, Skeabost Bridge, by Portree, Isle of Skye, IV51 9NX. Tel. (047 082) 304. *Display Advert*

ULLINISH (Hotel) Ullinish Lodge is an 18th century country house beautifully set overlooking the Cuillin mountains and Loch Harport. It is ideally situated for exploring the ancient monuments on Skye, walking the scenic hills or just touring around Skye. The hotel offers a 27,000 acre estate on which to enjoy ancient monuments, trout and salmon fishing, and rough shooting. There is a large lounge with an open fire, and a pleasant restaurant featuring a wide range of finest Scottish produce. Friendly welcoming staff to see to your every need, and fully licenced bars containing a wide selection of highland refreshments. Rooms: 8 all with private facilities including colour television. Open Easter-end October. B&B from £25-£35. Full details and colour brochure on request. Restaurant booking advisable. STB Commended 3 crown, Taste of Scotland Recommended. Dogs Welcome. Ullinish Lodge Hotel and Restaurant, Struan, By Portree, Isle of Skye, IV56 8FD. 047 072 214. After Spring '94 0470572 214. *Display Advert*

CAMP AND CARAVAN SITES

The island of Skye contains an excellent selection of camp and caravan sites, all set amidst spectacular scenery.

LOCH GRESHORNISH CARAVAN & CAMPING SITE Open Easter-October. Situated by the shores of Loch Greshornish 1 mile from Edinbane on the A850 Portree/Dunvegan road. Showers, drying facilities, hair dryers. Razor points. A.A. Rec. Shop 1 mile from site. Prop. Joyce MacDonald. Loch Greshornish Caravan and Camping Site, Edinbane, Isle of Skye, IV51 9PS. Tel. Edinbane 230.

Dunvegan: Dunvegan Caravan Site, Dunvegan, Isle of Skye, Inverness-shire, IV55 8WF. Tel. (047 022) 206. This 2 acre grassy site is situated about 1/2 mile east of the village of Dunvegan on the A850 Portree road. Several food shops and hotels with restaurant facilities are located in Dunvegan village within reasonable walking distance of the site. Petrol is also available in the village. **Facilities:** 30 pitches for tents and caravans. Hard standing for caravans and camper vans. Toilet block with hot water, showers and electric shaver points. Laundry and drying room facilities. Pets are accepted by arrangement and there are chemical toilet disposal facilities. The site is open from April to September inclusive.

Dunvegan: Kinloch Camp Site, Millburn House, Dunvegan, Isle of Skye, Inverness-shire. Tel. (047 022) 210. Operated by Peggy and Colin Campbell, this attractive grassy site is set right by the shore, overlooking Loch Dunvegan. You can choose your own pitch. A peaceful location yet close to the facilities in Dunvegan village. To find the site, head north into Dunvegan on the A863. Take the small road which branches left immediately before the bakery. The campsite lies a short distance down this road, on the right. **Facilities:** Toilets, cold water. The site is open from April to October inclusive.

Edinbane: Loch Greshornish Caravan and Camping Site, Edinbane, Arnisort, by Portree, Isle of Skye, Inverness-shire, IV51 9PS. Tel. (047 082) 230. This attractive 5 acre grassy site is set right by the coast overlooking Loch Greshornish at Arnisort 9 miles east of Dunvegan on the A850. Shop and hotel restaurant facilities are to be found some 1 1/2 miles from the site in the little village of Edinbane. Petrol is also available in Edinbane. **Facilities:** 130 pitches for tents and caravans. Toilet block with hot water, showers and electric shaver points. Drying room facilities. Pets are accepted by arrangement and chemical toilet disposal facilities are available. The site is open from April to October inclusive.

Glenbrittle: Glenbrittle Campsite, Glenbrittle Farm, Glenbrittle, Isle of Skye, Inverness-shire, IV47 8TA. Tel. (0478) 640 404. This 6 acre grassy site is situated at the south end of Glen Brittle, close to the magnificent Cuillin mountains. From the Sligachan Hotel, take the A863 and after 5 1/2 miles, turn left onto the B8009. After c.1 3/4 miles, turn left onto the unclassified Glenbrittle road and follow it to the end. The campsite has a glorious location right by the shore, looking out onto Loch Brittle. Its position at the foot of the Cuillin hills makes it an excellent choice for climbers and walkers alike. An on-site shop sells food, a selection of camping gear, O.S. maps and a good selection of books and guides. The shop is open Mon, Wed, Fri, Sat 0900-2100; Tue, Thu 0900-1200 and 1400-2100; Sun 0900-1000, 1200-1400 and 1800-2100. **Facilities:** 209 pitches for tents and caravans. Toilet block with hot water, showers, hairdryers and electric shaver points. Drying facilities are available and there is an on-site payphone. The site is open from April to September inclusive.

Portree: Torvaig Caravan and Camping Site, Portree, Isle of Skye, Inverness-shire, IV51 9HS. Tel. (0478) 612 209. This 3 acre grassy site is situated about 1 mile north of Portree on the A855 Staffin road. The sloping site is shielded from the road by mature conifers. Excellent shopping and restaurant facilities are located nearby in Portree. Petrol is also available in Portree. **Facilities:** 160 tent and caravan pitches. Toilet block with hot water, showers and electric shaver points. Pets are accepted by arrangement and there are chemical toilet disposal facilities. Gas cylinder exchanges/refills are also available. The site is open from April to October inclusive.

Sligachan: Sligachan Campsite, Sligachan, Isle of Skye, Inverness-shire, IV47 8SN. Tel. (0478) 650 204. This 4 acre mixed grass and hardstanding site is situated opposite the Sligachan Hotel by the main A850 Portree road. The site is located on the low-lying ground at the head of Loch Sligachan and is ideally placed for those who wish to explore the Cuillin via Glen Sligachan. Excellent bar and restaurant facilities are available in the adjacent Sligachan Hotel. The hotel also does take-away meals. Public pay phones and a bus stop are located adjacent to the site. **Facilities:** 110 tent and caravan pitches. Toilet block with hot water, showers and electric shaver points. Laundry facilities and payphone available. Pets are accepted by arrangement. The site is open from Easter to October inclusive.

Staffin: Staffin Caravan and Camping Site, Staffin, Isle of Skye, Inverness-shire, IV51 9JX. Tel. (047 062) 213. This 2 acre grass and hardstanding site is situated off a minor road at the south end of Staffin village on the A855 some 16 miles north of Portree. The site, although sheltered, has an attractive elevated position with views to the sea. Shop and restaurant facilities are located nearby within Staffin village. **Facilities:** 80 pitches for tents and caravans. Toilet block with hot water, showers and electric shaver points. Gas cylinder refills/exchanges are available and there is a special games area. Pets are accepted by arrangement. The site is open from mid-April to October inclusive.

Uig: Uig Caravan and Camping Site, Uig, Isle of Skye, Inverness-shire, IV51 9XU. Tel. (047 042) 360. This 2 1/2 acre mixed grass and hardstanding site is situated right by the shore in the little village of Uig, some 16 miles north-west of Portree on the A856. Several food shops and restaurants are located within easy walking distance in Uig village. Petrol is also available in Uig. **Facilities:** 40 pitches for tents and caravans (electric hook-ups are available). Toilet block with hot water, showers and electric shaver points. Laundry facilities. Small shop. Pets are accepted by arrangement. The site is open from April to October inclusive.

Camping is also possible at Portnalong, adjacent to the Taigh Ailean Hotel. Enquire at the hotel. Mountain bikes and fishing rods for hire. Tel. (0478) 640 271.

YOUTH HOSTELS
Armadale: Armadale Youth Hostel, Ardvasar, Sleat, Isle of Skye, IV45 8RS. Tel. (04714) 260. Grade 2, sleeps 42. Lying close to Armadale Pier where the ferry from Mallaig docks, this hostel is well placed for those who wish to explore Sleat - the tranquil "Garden of Skye".

Broadford: Broadford Youth Hostel, Broadford, Isle of Skye, IV49 9AA. Tel. (0471) 822 442. Grade 2, sleeps 78. This hostel lies outwith the main Broadford village area, yet is still within easy walking distance of village facilities and shops.

Glenbrittle: Glenbrittle Youth Hostel, Glenbrittle, Isle of Skye, IV47 8TA. Tel. (047 842) 278. Grade 2, sleeps 46. Set in a rural location in remote Glen Brittle at the foot of the Cuillin mountains, this hostel is ideally placed for hill walkers and climbers.

Kyleakin: Kyleakin Youth Hostel, Kyleakin, Isle of Skye, IV41 8PL. Tel. (0599) 4585. Grade 1, sleeps 78. Depending on how busy the hostel is, family rooms may be available by prior arrangement. Located at the heart of the small village of Kyleakin, this hostel is within easy walking distance of Kyleakin Pier, where the ferry from Kyle of Lochalsh docks. Shops and services are located within Kyleakin village.

Uig: Uig Youth Hostel, Uig, Isle of Skye, IV51 9YD. Tel. (047 042) 211. Grade 2, sleeps 60. Depending on how busy the hostel is, family rooms may be available by prior arrangement. Set within the village of Uig, this is the only youth hostel in the north of Skye and is well placed for exploring the Trotternish peninsula. Shops and services are located in Uig village. The hostel lies within walking distance of the pier where ferries to Tarbert on Lewis and Lochmaddy on North Uist can be joined.

INDEPENDENT HOSTELS
There are several independent hostels on the Isle of Skye, each privately owned and operated with a minimum of rules. No membership is required to use these hostels. Accommodation is in small bunkrooms or dormitories and fully equipped kitchens and hot showers are available. Some hostels also have drying and/or laundry facilities. The type of bedding provided varies from place to place, so please check with the individual establishment prior to arrival.

THE CROFT BUNKHOUSE & BOTHY, PORTNALONG   Fully equipped Independent hostels sleeping 14 & 6.   Only £5.00 person/night.   Details: P. Thomas, 7 Portnalong, Isle of Skye, IV47 8SL.   Tel. (0478) 640 254.

SKYEWALKER INDEPENDENT HOSTEL, PORTNALONG   Comfortable, centrally heated hostel for individuals or groups - self-catering or part/full board.   £5.50 per night includes showers, linen etc.   Shop & post office on site.   Tearooms open to residents & non-residents.   Bike hire.   Friendly family run hostel.   Skyewalker Independent Hostel, Fiskaig Road, Portnalong, Isle of Skye.   Tel. (0478) 640 250.

Breakish: Fossil Bothy, 13 Lower Breakish, Isle of Skye, IV42 8QA.   Tel. (0471) 822 644 weekdays, (0471) 822 297 all other times.   Sleeps 8.   It is essential to telephone first to ensure availability.   Situated in a secluded position right by the seashore, in the scattered township of Lower Breakish, c.2 1/2 miles east of Broadford.   Free use of bicycles.   Within walking distance of the main Kyleakin-Portree bus route.   Open Easter-October, but advance group bookings are accepted throughout the year.

Dunvegan Area: Uiginish Lodge Self-Catering Hotel: Self-catering accommodation is also available at the Uiginish Lodge Hotel, by Dunvegan.   Tel. (047 022) 445.   Open from April to October inclusive.   Reception open 0900-2000.   Uiginish Lodge is a former hunting lodge, located on the shore of Loch Dunvegan.   Double, twin and family bedrooms with h & c are available for overnight or long term stays.   Kitchens and living rooms are available for use at all times and there are also showers and laundering facilities.   Linen and equipment are provided.   Continental breakfasts are available by arrangement.

Elgol: Blaven Bunkhouse, Blaven, by Elgol, Isle of Skye.   Tel. (0471) 822 397.   Bunkhouse sleeps 10.   Situated in a peaceful rural location on the shores of Loch Slapin some 9 miles south of Broadford by the A881 to Elgol.   On the Broadford to Elgol bus route.   The bunkhouse is open 24 hours a day.   Duvets are provided and bed linen can be hired.   There is a T.V. lounge and laundry/drying facilities are available.   Cooked meals are available by arrangement and daily deliveries are made by a local shop.

Kyleakin: Skye Backpackers Guest House, Kyleakin, Isle of Skye, IV41 8PH.   Tel. (0599) 4510.   Sleeps 36.   Breakfast available by arrangement.   The hostel is situated within the small village of Kyleakin, within easy walking distance of several shops, the Kyle of Lochalsh-Kyleakin ferry connection and bus services to Portree.   The guest house is open all year.

Portnalong: The Croft Bunkhouse and Bothy, 7 Portnalong, Isle of Skye, IV47 8SL.   Tel. (0478) 640 254.   Bunkhouse sleeps 14, bothy sleeps 6.   Family rooms available.   Situated in a peaceful rural location in the scattered crofting community of Portnalong.   Within easy walking distance of a small food shop, the Taigh Ailean Hotel (licensed bar and hot food) and the Portree-Fiscavaig/Glenbrittle bus route.   Bike hire available.   The hostel and bothy are open all year.

Portnalong: Skyewalker Independent Hostel, The Old School, Portnalong, Carbost, Isle of Skye, IV47 8SL. Tel. (0478) 640 250. Sleeps 30 (in 6 and 8-bedded rooms). Family rooms available. Drying room facilities. Showers and bed linen included in charge. The hostel contains disabled showers and toilets and wheelchair ramps at all entrances. Situated at the heart of the tiny community of Portnalong. Close to a small food shop, the Taigh Ailean Hotel (licensed bar and hot food) and the Portree-Fiscavaig/Glenbrittle bus route. Meals available by arrangement. The hostel is open all year.

Portree: Portree International, Tourist Hostel & Conference Centre, Dunvegan Road, Portree, Isle of Skye, IV51 9HG. Tel. (0478) 613 732. Sleeps 50 in 10 bedrooms. The hostel is situated in Portree, the largest town on the island. Payphone, television and laundry facilities for guests' use. Linen is available on request. Cafe, shop, licensed bar and games room on site. Pets accepted by prior arrangement. Credit cards accepted. The hostel is open all year.

Staffin: Dun Flodigarry Hostel, Staffin, Isle of Skye. Tel. (047 052) 212. Sleeps 66. Small shop on site. Meals available by arrangement. Laundry and drying rooms, showers, sleeping sheet and tea and coffee included. For an additional small charge, the hostel's mini-bus is available for transport. This hostel is situated in the north of the island, in the quiet rural community of Flodigarry. It is ideally placed for exploring the fascinating rock formations around the Quiraing. Within easy walking distance of the Kilmaluag-Portree bus route. The hostel is open all year. Access and Visa accepted.

Uig Area: The Byre Bunkhouse, Glen Hinnisdal, nr Uig, Isle of Skye. Situated in a beautiful rural location in Glen Hinnisdal, 4 1/2 miles south of Uig.

SKYE TELEPHONE NUMBER CHANGES
Some Skye telephone numbers will change while this guide is available. See General Tourist Services for full details.

FISHING

The Isle of Skye offers some fine brown trout fishing as well as spate river salmon and sea-trout fishing. The best trout fishing is to be found in the Storr Lochs, which are situated a few miles north of Portree. These fresh water lochs are managed by the Portree Angling Association and are stocked regularly to provide excellent sport. The Association also manages a number of other fine waters in the north of the island. Many of the rivers on Skye have runs of sea-trout and salmon at reasonable prices and the River Hinnisdal just south of Uig is one of the finest. Excellent salmon fishing is also to be found on the Rivers Snizort and Ose. In addition, there are a variety of other lochs and rivers scattered throughout the island which provide good sport. Whether you are looking for easily accessible roadside waters or remote hill lochs set amidst spectacular scenery, Skye has something for everyone.

When out fishing, please bear in mind the following points. Always wear a life-jacket when out in a small boat. When walking in the hills, follow the Country Code and check that you will not be interfering with stalking activities. If you are walking to isolated hill lochs, equip yourself sensibly - follow the recommendations for walkers given in the Walks section.

LOCH/RIVER PERMITS

Broadford River - (O.S. 32/640236). Permission: Broadford Hotel, Broadford. Tel. (0471) 822 204/205.

Kilmaluag River - (O.S. 23/435742). Salmon, sea-trout and brown trout. Bank fishing. No set sessions. No restrictions. Permission: Jansport, Wentworth Street, Portree. Tel. (0478) 612 559.

Kilmartin River - (O.S. 23/489674). Salmon, sea-trout and brown trout. Bank fishing. No set sessions. No restrictions. Permission: Jansport, Wentworth Street, Portree. Tel. (0478) 612 559.

Lealt River - (O.S. 23/515604). Salmon and sea-trout. Morning or afternoon sessions. No restrictions. Permission: Jansport, Wentworth Street, Portree. Tel. (0478) 612 559.

Loch An Iasgaich - (O.S. 32/673143). Brown trout. Permission: Feareann Eilean Iarmain. Tel. (04713) 332.

Loch Barabhaig - (O.S. 32/684098). Brown trout. Permission: Feareann Eilean Iarmain. Tel. (04713) 332.

Loch Cleap - (O.S. 23/467663). Brown trout. Bank fishing. No boat fishing. Fly fishing only. Permission: Jansport, Wentworth Street, Portree. Tel. (0478) 612 559.

Loch Cleat - (O.S. 23/447673). Brown trout. Bank fishing. No boat fishing. Fly fishing only. Permission: Jansport, Wentworth Street, Portree. Tel. (0478) 612 559.

Loch Connan - (O.S. 23/388430). Brown trout. Permission: Ullinish Lodge Hotel, Struan, by Portree. Tel. (047 072) 214.

Loch Corcasgil - (O.S. 23/452643). Brown trout and ferox. Permission: Jansport, Wentworth Street, Portree. Tel. (0478) 612 559.

Loch Corlarach - (O.S. 23/234520). Brown trout. Permission: MacLeod Estates, Dunvegan Castle. Tel. (047 022) 206.

Loch Coruisk - (O.S. 32/485205). Brown trout. Permission: Strathaird Estates, Strathaird. Tel. (04716) 238.

Loch Cuithir - (O.S. 23/476597). Brown trout. Permission: Jansport, Wentworth Street, Portree. Tel. (0478) 612 559.

Loch Duagrich - (O.S. 23/400399). Brown trout. Permission: Ullinish Lodge Hotel, Struan, by Portree. Tel. (047 072) 214.

Loch Dubhar-sgoth - (O.S. 23/456640). Brown trout. Permission: Jansport, Wentworth Street, Portree. Tel. (0478) 612 559.

Loch Dhughaill - (O.S. 32/613082). Brown trout. Permission: Clan Donald Visitor Centre, Armadale. Tel (04714) 305/227.

Loch Droighinn - (O.S. 23/456712). Brown trout. Permission: Jansport, Wentworth Street, Portree. Tel. (0478) 612 559.

Loch Fada - (O.S. 23/458697). Brown trout. Bank fishing. No boat fishing. Fly fishing only. Permission: Jansport, Wentworth Street, Portree. Tel. (0478) 612 559.

Loch Hasco - (O.S. 23/456702). Brown trout. Bank fishing. No boat fishing. Fly fishing only. Permission: Jansport, Wentworth Street, Portree. Tel. (0478) 612 559.

Loch Langaig - (O.S. 23/462708). Brown trout. Bank fishing. No boat fishing. Fly fishing only. Permission: Jansport, Wentworth Street, Portree. Tel. (0478) 612 559.

Loch Leum Na Luirginn - (O.S. 23/447676). Brown trout. Bank fishing. No boat fishing. Fly fishing only. Permission: Jansport, Wentworth Street, Portree. Tel. (0478) 612 559.

Loch Mealt - (O.S. 23/505650). Brown trout and Arctic char. Bank fishing. No boat fishing. Fly fishing only. Permission: Jansport, Wentworth Street, Portree. Tel. (0478) 612 559.

Loch Na Creitheach - (O.S. 32/513205). Brown trout. Permission: Strathaird Estates. Tel. (04716) 238.

Loch Na Sguabaidh - (O.S. 32/560233). Brown trout. Permission: Strathaird Estates. Tel. (04716) 238.

Loch Ravag - (O.S. 23/380450). Brown trout. Permission: Ullinish Lodge Hotel, Struan, by Portree. Tel. (047 072) 214.

Loch Sneosdal - (O.S. 23/413692). Brown trout. Permission: Jansport, Wentworth Street, Portree. Tel. (0478) 612 559.

Loch Suardal - (O.S. 23/240510). Brown trout. Permission: MacLeod Estates, Dunvegan Castle. Tel. (047 022) 206.

Lochan Dubh - (O.S. 32/659126). Brown trout. Permission: Feareann Eilean Iarmain. Tel. (04713) 332.

River Brogaig - (O.S. 23/471679). Salmon, sea-trout and brown trout. Bank fishing. No set sessions. No restrictions. Permission: Jansport, Wentworth Street, Portree. Tel. (0478) 612 559.

River Conon - (O.S. 23/399637). Spate river salmon and brown trout. Permission: Jansport, Wentworth Street, Portree. Tel. (0478) 612 559.

River Hinnisdal - (O.S. 23/397573). Salmon and sea-trout. North bank. Permission: The Ferry Inn, Uig. Tel. (047 042) 242.

River Ose - (O.S. 23/317408). Spate river salmon and sea-trout. Permission: Ullinish Lodge Hotel, Struan, by Portree. Tel. (047 072) 214.

River Rha - (O.S. 23/396643). Spate river salmon and brown trout. Permission: Sligachan Hotel, Sligachan. Tel. (0478) 650 204.

River Sligachan - (O.S. 32/487300). Sea-trout and salmon. Permission: Sligachan Hotel, Sligachan. Tel. (0478) 650 204.

River Snizort - (O.S. 23/420483). Spate river salmon and sea-trout. Permission: Ullinish Lodge Hotel, Struan, by Portree. Tel. (047 072) 214. Also Skeabost House Hotel, Skeabost Bridge. Tel. (047 032) 202.

The Storr Lochs - (O.S. 23/500505). Brown trout. Bank and boat fishing. Fly fishing only. Permission: Jansport, Wentworth Street, Portree. Tel. (0478) 612 559.

Torrin Estate Lochs - (O.S. 32/577208). Brown trout. Numerous lochs on the Torrin Estate, Strathaird. Permission: Torrin Post Office, Torrin. Tel. (0471) 822 232.

Local Advice: The Secretary of the Portree Angling Association is happy to give advice on the various waters managed by the club.   Contact: Neil Cameron, "Hillcroft", Treaslane, by Portree, IV51 9NX. Tel. (047 082) 304.

Tackle Hire: TAIGH AILEAN HOTEL, Portnalong. Tel. (0478) 640 271.
THE GUN AND TACKLE ROOM, Uiginish Lodge Hotel, By Dunvegan. Tel. (047 022) 445.

Tackle Purchase: DUNVEGAN SPORTS & FISHING TACKLE, Dunvegan.   Tel. (047 022) 234.
THE GUN AND TACKLE ROOM, Uiginish Lodge, by Dunvegan. Tel. (047 022) 445.
JANSPORT, Wentworth Street, Portree. Tel. (0478) 612 559.

SEA ANGLING

The rugged coastline of Skye is incised by many deep unpolluted sea lochs which offer plenty of possibilities for the angler. Mackerel, coalfish and pollock can be caught from the rocks, while from a boat, many deep-water species are within range: haddock, herring, skate, cod, ling, plaice, wrasse and conger eel.

M.V. MACLEOD OF MACLEOD, the personal vessel of the Chief of Clan MacLeod, can be chartered for evening fishing trips. Sea-angling is also available from the side of Loch Dunvegan. For further details, telephone MacLeod Estates on (047 022) 206.

SKYECREWS CHARTERS offer skippered sea-angling trips on board their 32' Aquastar "Banrigh Nan Tonn" which sails from Struan Jetty south of Dunvegan. Fishing gear and bait are available on board for those who do not have their own equipment. For further details contact Peter Walker (047 022) 492 or Peter Bates (047 022) 373.

UIGINISH LODGE, by Dunvegan can arrange sea-angling and game fishing trips. Tel. (047 022) 445.

Further information on local sea-angling facilities can be obtained from the following:
SKYE SILVER, Colbost, by Dunvegan Tel. (047 081) 263.
LOCH BAY TEAROOM, Stein, Waternish. Tel. (047 083) 235.

TOURIST SERVICES & ATTRACTIONS

TOURIST INFORMATION CENTRES

There are three Tourist Information Centres on Skye which carry a range of local maps, books and leaflets. Staff can offer free advice on the local area and can also locate vacant accommodation and make bookings for you. A small fee may be charged for this "Book-A-Bed-Ahead" service. Bookings are normally accepted up to 24 hours in advance.

Broadford: Tel. (0471 822) 361. Located next to the petrol station by the main A850 in Broadford village. Open April-October, Monday-Saturday 0930-1900, Sunday 1000-1400.

Portree: Tel. (0478) 2137. Located upstairs in Meall House, Bank Street in the town centre. Open all year, Monday-Saturday 0930-1900 (High Season 0900-2000). When the office is closed, an electronic window display provides information on accommodation and visitor attractions in the area.

Uig: Tel. (047 042) 404. Open April-October, Monday-Saturday 0930-1900.

Display advertisements mentioned in the Service Directory below appear in the relevant section of the Touring Guide.

ART GALLERIES

THE DUN STUDIO, BORVE Professional Artist John Bathgate. Paintings inspired by the Scottish landscape in oils, watercolours and mixed media. Commissions undertaken. Open 10am-7pm daily. Open all year. The Dun Studio, 30 Borve, By Portree, Isle of Skye, IV51 9PE. Tel. (0470) 532 402. *Display Advert*

THE LITTLE GALLERY, PORTNALONG The Little Gallery was established in 1983 at Portnalong overlooking Loch Harport on the west coast of Skye. It is the sole outlet for the fine detailed etchings by Jean Thomas of the Cuillin, birds and animals. The gallery also has available original watercolours by Jean Thomas and other invited artists. There is a good selection of original greetings cards and notelets. Open daily, 9.30-6.00. The Little Gallery, 7 Portnalong, Isle of Skye. *Display Advert*

ORBOST GALLERY, BY DUNVEGAN Orbost Gallery shows work by professional artists in both oil and watercolour. Wood engravings printed on the gallery's Columbian press are also on sale. The gallery stocks artists' materials, makes picture frames and provides a restoration service. Open Easter to October, 10am to 6pm or by appointment. Orbost Gallery, Dunvegan, Isle of Skye, IV55 8ZB. Tel. (047 022) 207. *Display Advert*

BAKERY

BROADFORD BAY STORES AND BAKERY Hand made bread, rolls, scones etc. Filled rolls, groceries, postcards, cards, hardware, gifts and souvenirs also available. Open Mon-Fri 7am-5pm; Sat 7.30am-4pm. Broadford Bay Stores & Bakery, Broadford, Isle of Skye. Tel. (0471) 822 224.

BANKS

Broadford: BANK OF SCOTLAND. Tel. (0471) 822 211.
Portree: BANK OF SCOTLAND, Somerled Square. Tel. (0478) 612 338.
CLYDESDALE BANK, Somerled Square. Tel. (0478) 612 050.
THE ROYAL BANK OF SCOTLAND, Bank Street. Tel. (0478) 612 822.

BOAT HIRE/CRUISES

BELLA JANE BOAT TRIPS, ELGOL   See the seals and enjoy the beautiful scenery. 2 hr trips from Elgol jetty to Loch Coruisk run 7 days a week from 1st April to 31st October (weather permitting). To check if boat is running please ring Donald S. MacKinnon on 04716 244. Bella Jane can also be chartered for longer cruises to Loch Coruisk and other destinations, including the Islands of Rhum, Canna, Eigg etc. Bookings taken all year round. Fully equipped, licensed and insured for 12 passengers. Large heated wheelhouse and toilet on board. Refreshments can be provided on request. All enquiries welcome, tel. (04716) 244 (evenings best). *Display Advert*

DUNVEGAN CASTLE LOCH CRUISES & SEAL BOAT TRIPS   Come aboard the M.V. MacLeod of MacLeod for a spectacular and exhilirating cruise through Loch Dunvegan. Professional crew, fully insured and D.O.T. licensed. Private charters by arrangement or enjoy a fascinating traditional boat trip to the nearby seal colony. A favourite with children and adults alike. Boats leave the jetty at frequent intervals throughout the day. Telephone (047 022) 206 for further details. *Display Advert*

SLEAT MARINE SERVICES, ARDVASAR (Yacht Cruising)   Charter a yacht of 34 to 40 feet length overall (6 to 8 berths) to cruise the West coast and Islands of the Hebrides. Yachts are available self sail to experienced crews or with a qualified Skipper for the less experienced. Minimum charter period 7 days. Sleat Marine Services, Ardvasar, Isle of Skye, IV45 8RU. Tel. (047 14) 216/387 (workshop). *Display Advert*

CAR HIRE

Broadford: SUTHERLANDS GARAGE. Tel. (0471) 822 225.
Portree: EWEN MACRAE, Dunvegan Road. Tel. (0478) 2554/2002.

CRAFTS/SOUVENIRS

A' BHUTH BHEAG, PORTREE   Antiques and old gold and silver jewellery, china, brass ware, plated ware, old tools, fishing gear, books, prints and paintings and the famous Isle of Skye Tartan cloth in worsted and tweed. Open 9am-5.30pm, Mon-Sat. A' Bhuth Bheag, Wentworth Street, Portree, Isle of Skye. Tel. (0478) 612 443.

CURLEW CRAFTS STUDIO, FISCAVAIG   A family run Craft Studio displaying original hand-painted China, unique turned and carved woodware, Cushion covers, Aprons, Knitting bags and many other fabric items all produced on the premises. Open Daily 10 a.m. to dusk. Curlew Crafts Studio, 22 Fiscavaig, Portnalong, Isle of Skye, IV47 8SN. Tel: (0478) 640 269. *Display Advert*

RAGAMUFFIN, ARMADALE We have a dazzling collection of Scottish knitwear - hand knits, fair isles, shetlands, designer knits and a glorious range of original clothes made in the workshop & locally. We also have jewellery, pottery, gloves & hats, hand painted badges & sheep that baa, books & bags & much more.......RAGAMUFFIN, ARMADALE, SLEAT, ISLE OF SKYE, IV45 8RS. Tel: (047 14) 217. *Display Advert*

THE ST. KILDA CONNECTION, DUNVEGAN The St. Kilda Connection offers a selection of handloomed sweaters produced from natural wool and finest quality yarns. Subtle soft dyes reflecting the mood of the landscape are contrasted with the vibrant colours and intricate patterns of other styles. Also available are: capes, wraps, coats, scarves, ties, waistcoats, gloves, hats, socks, rugs, handpainted glass, handmade leather goods with Celtic designs, designer woollens, cottons, tee-shirts, plus many other gifts. Exceptional quality at affordable prices. Browsers welcome. *The St. Kilda Connection.* You'll find us on the corner of the road leading to Dunvegan Pier. *Display Advert*

SKYE SILVER, COLBOST Established 1974. The original silver and gold jewellery from Skye. Visit our shop at Colbost near Dunvegan - full of delightful jewellery and other gifts to bring back memories of your visit to our island. Friendly mail-order service available - please send S.A.E. for our free, full-colour brochure. Seven miles from Dunvegan on the B884 to Glendale. Open 7 days a week, 10.00am to 6.00pm. Skye Silver, The Old School, Colbost, Dunvegan, Isle of Skye. Tel. Glendale (047 081) 263. *Display Advert*

SLEAT TRADING, ARMADALE PIER (Crafts - Souvenirs - Outdoor Gear) We stock a comprehensive range of waterproof and outdoor clothing, camping equipment, fishing tackle, maps, books - old and new, Highland prints, games, cards, kites, wine, honey, pottery, T-shirts and sweatshirts. Sleat Trading, Armadale Pier, Sleat, Isle of Skye, IV45 8RS. Tel. (04714) 265. *Display Advert*

THE WORKSHOP, BRAES The Workshop offers a wide choice of turned goods made mostly from local and native woods, as well as handmade furniture at reasonable prices. Showroom open weekdays from Easter to mid September. Commissions undertaken. The Workshop, Braes, Portree, Isle of Skye, IV51 9LL. Tel. (0478) 650 226. *Display Advert*

EATING OUT

MACLEOD'S TABLE RESTAURANT, DUNVEGAN Open seven days a week serving everything from morning coffee, snacks, and sandwiches to hot meals, lunches and afternoon tea. Lots of home cooking and good Scottish Fayre. June, July, August: open until 9.30pm for evening meals. Locally caught seafood and other produce complimented by an interesting selection of wines, all at affordable family prices. Tel. (047 022) 310. *Display Advert*

THE OYSTERCATCHER, STAFFIN A warm welcome awaits you 16 miles north of Portree. Views overlooking the Minch and up to the mighty Quiraing. Teas, coffees, home baking and light snacks. A restaurant menu offering traditional Scottish cooking. Vegetarian food. A special menu for children. A selection of all that is best in Scottish and local crafts. The Oystercatcher Restaurant, Tea Room and Crafts. Telephone (047 062) 384. *Display Advert*

THE SEAGULL RESTAURANT AND COFFEE HOUSE, BREAKISH   Just six miles from the Kyle-Kyleakin Ferry on the main road to Broadford and Portree.   Local fish and seafood, Scottish meat and a variety of vegetarian options - a place to unwind in peace.   Open Easter-October Daily 12 noon - 10pm.   Telephone (0471) 822 001.
Display Advert

FUEL

BRACADALE FUELS can deliver bags of peat, logs, coal and kindling at very reasonable prices to heat your holiday cottage.   Tel. (047 072) 291.

GUIDED WALKS

BADGERS NICE 'N' EASY WALKS.   Rambles, walks and tours.   Full or half day.   Transport can be arranged to and from your destination.   Tel. (04716) 228 for further details.
CUILLIN GUIDES.   Tel. (047842) 289.   J. Akroyd.
PINNACLE RIDGE.   Tel. (04714) 239.   Colin Threlfall.

MUSEUMS/EXHIBITIONS

AROS: SKYE'S HERITAGE CENTRE, PORTREE   All the ingredients for a perfect day out.   Exhibition: Audio-Visual Show: Forest Walks: 80-seat Restaurant: Shop.   Open every day 9am - 6pm (9pm High Season).   The Aros Centre, Viewfield Road, Portree, Isle of Skye.   Tel. (0478) 613 649.   Fax 0478 613 100.   *Display Advert*

BORRERAIG PARK EXHIBITION CROFT, BY GLENDALE   Here awaits a unique gallimaufry of mulitifarious indigenous exhibits for your delight and edification.   Also see our selection of the finest quality knitwear and crafts produced with pride on Skye.   Scenic location 8 miles from Dunvegan, 3 miles from Glendale.   Ample parking.   Open all year.   Tel. 0470 511 311.   *Display Advert*

COLBOST FOLK MUSEUM, GLENDALE   The museum contains implements and furniture of bygone days, has a peat fire burning throughout the day, and is typical of living conditions in the 19th century.   A replica of an illicit whisky still can also be seen to the rear of the Colbost Folk Museum.   Open daily including Sundays 10am-6.30pm.   *Coaches Welcome*   Colbost Folk Museum, 4 miles from Dunvegan on the B884 Glendale Road (adjacent to the Three Chimneys Restaurant).   Telephone Dunvegan 296.   *Display Advert*

DUNVEGAN CASTLE   Skye's most famous landmark.   Any visit to the enchanted Isle of Skye must be deemed incomplete without savouring the wealth of history offered by Dunvegan Castle.   Licensed restaurant; two craft and souvenir shops; castle water gardens; audio-visual theatre; clan exhibition; items belonging to Bonnie Prince Charlie; loch boat trips; famous seal colony; pedigree highland cattle herd; loch cruises.   Open 21st March - 29th October.   *Romantic and historic Dunvegan Castle - the home of the chiefs of MacLeod for nearly 800 years.*
Display Advert

GIANT ANGUS MACASKILL MUSEUM, DUNVEGAN The tallest Scotsman, and the tallest recorded "true" (non-pathological) giant, was Angus MacAskill (1825-63), born on the island of Berneray, in the Sound of Harris, in the Western Isles. He stood 7ft 9in (236cm), weighed 425lbs and died in St Ann's, on Cape Breton Island, Nova Scotia, Canada - *Guiness Book of Records*. The Museum contains a life-size model of Angus MacAskill. Open daily, Monday-Saturday 9.30am-6.00pm; Sunday 12.30-5.00pm. *Coaches Welcome* The Giant Angus MacAskill Museum, situated in the centre of Dunvegan near the public car park. Telephone Dunvegan 296. *Display Advert*

LUIB FOLK MUSEUM, NEAR BROADFORD Situated in the heart of the Cuillins and depicts living conditions in the early 20th century. Bonnie Prince Charlie Exhibition "Over The Sea To Skye" - The Trail Of The Fugitive. Open daily (including Sundays) 9am-6pm. *Coaches Welcome* Luib Folk Museum, located at Luib, on main Broadford-Sligachan road (15 miles Kyleakin; 35 miles Dunvegan; 40 miles Colbost). Telephone Broadford (0471) 822 427. *Display Advert*

SKYE SERPENTARIUM, BROADFORD (Reptile Exhibition & Shop) The only one of its kind in Scotland. On show are snakes, lizards, frogs & tortoises. Regular handling sessions take place. During summer reptile eggs may be seen hatching. The shop sells T-shirts, books, toys and even baby snakes. Listed in The Scotsman as one of Scotland's top ten undiscovered gems of tourist attractions. Open Easter-October. Catherine & Alex Shearer, Skye Serpentarium, The Old Mill, Harrapool, Broadford, Isle of Skye, IV49 9AQ. Tel. (0471) 822 209.

OUTDOOR CLOTHING

CIOCH DIRECT, ULLINISH CLOTHING FOR OUTDOOR ENTHUSIASTS. We make fleece and waterproof equipment especially for walkers, climbers, skiers and paragliders. Large choice of made to measure garments using the latest high performance fabrics. Please call at Cioch Direct, 4 Ullinish, Struan, off the A863 between Sligachan and Dunvegan or ring Helen at (0470) 572 307.

PETROL

SUTHERLANDS, BROADFORD 24 hour shopping & fuel. Shop for groceries, soft drinks, confectionery, papers, magazines, film, coal, logs, kindlers, gifts, postcards, books, toys. Also car repairs, sales and rentals. Car rental: free collection from Kyleakin and airstrip. Transport from and to other locations can be arranged. Sutherlands, Broadford, Isle of Skye. Tel. (0471) 822 225. *Display Advert*

Armadale: SKYE FERRY FILLING STATION. Tel. (04714) 249. Open Mon-Sat 0830-1830.
Borve: THE FERRYWAY. Open Monday-Sunday until 2100.
Broadford: SUTHERLAND'S GARAGE. Tel. (0471) 822 225.
Dunvegan: ATHOLL FILLING STATION. Tel. (047 022) 487. Open Mon-Sun. DUNVEGAN GARAGE. Tel. (047 022) 234.
Edinbane: EDINBANE STORE.
Isleornsay: TIGH OSDA EILEAN IARMAIN. Tel. (04713) 332.

Kyleakin: KYLEAKIN FILLING STATION, The Chalet. Tel. (0599) 4431. Open
Monday-Saturday 0800-2130; Sunday 0930-2130.
Portree: EWEN MACRAE, Dunvegan Road. Tel. (0478) 612 554. Open Monday-
Sunday 0800-2100.
PORTREE FILLING STATION, Viewfield Road. Tel. (0478) 612 251. Open
Monday-Saturday 0800-2100; Sunday (April-Nov only) 0930-1730.
Staffin: BP FILLING STATION.
Struan: R.J. MACKINNON & SON, The Garage. Tel. (047 072) 204.
Uig: THE PIER GARAGE. Tel. (047 042) 261. Open Monday-Saturday 0900-1800.

24 HOUR CAR BREAKDOWN & RECOVERY SERVICE
Breakish: STAGS BREAKDOWN & RECOVERY SERVICE, 27 Lower Breakish (by
Broadford). Tel. (0471) 822 631.
Broadford: SUTHERLAND'S GARAGE. Tel. (0471) 822 225.
Portree: EWEN MACRAE. Tel. (0478) 2554/2002.

TAXI SERVICES
ARDVASAR TAXIS, Mountview, 2 Calligarry, Armadale. Tel. (04714) 361. Tours.
CALEY TAXIS, Portree. Tel. (0478) 612 797.
CLAN MACDONALD TAXIS, 3 Kilmore, Sleat. Tel. (04714) 272. Taxis and private
hire. Historic Clan tours by arrangement.
GUS'S TAXIS, Staffin Road, Portree. Tel. (0478) 613 000. 24 hour service. Tours.
IAIN HUNTER, 11 Viewfield Square, Portree. Tel. (0478) 612 140. Is;and tours.
A.D. MACDONALD, 1 Urquhart Place, Portree. Tel. (0478) 612 521.
SKYE TAXIS, 17 Riverbank, Broadford. Tel. (0471) 822 730.
UIG TAXIS, Uig. Tel. (047 042) 342/418. 24 hour service. Island tours.
WATERLOO PRIVATE HIRE, 16 Waterloo, Breakish. Tel. (0471) 822 630/822 247.
Island tours by arrangement.

USEFUL TELEPHONE NUMBERS
Doctor: Broadford - Tel. (0471) 822 460
Dunvegan - Tel. (047 022) 203
Ferindonald - Tel. (04714) 283
Portree - Tel. (0478) 612 013
Uig - Tel. (047 042) 202
Dentist: Portree - Tel. (0478) 612 582
Police Stations: Ardvasar - Tel. (04714) 222
Broadford - Tel. (0471) 822 222
Dunvegan - Tel. (047 022) 333
Portree - Tel. (0478) 612 888
Uig - Tel. (047 042) 222
Weather Forecast: 6 day weather forecast for the Highland region - Tel.
(0898) 654 601. Also, Met. Office Weathercall for the Highland region - Tel.
(0898) 500 425.

Skye Telephone Number Changes: Some Skye telephone numbers will change while this guide is available. Certain three figure numbers will become six figures by prefixing with a new code. The area code will then change to 0470. Areas affected are as folows:

DUNTULM: 3 figure numbers will be prefixed by 552.
DUNVEGAN: 3 figure numbers will be prefixed by 521.
EDINBANE: 3 figure numbers will be prefixed by 582.
GLENDALE: 3 figure numbers will be prefixed by 511.
SKEABOST BRIDGE: 3 figure numbers will be prefixed by 532.
STAFFIN: 3 figure numbers will be prefixed by 562.
STRUAN: 3 figure numbers will be prefixed by 572.
UIG: 3 figure numbers will be prefixed by 542.
WATERNISH: 3 figure numbers will be prefixed by 592.

TOURING GUIDE

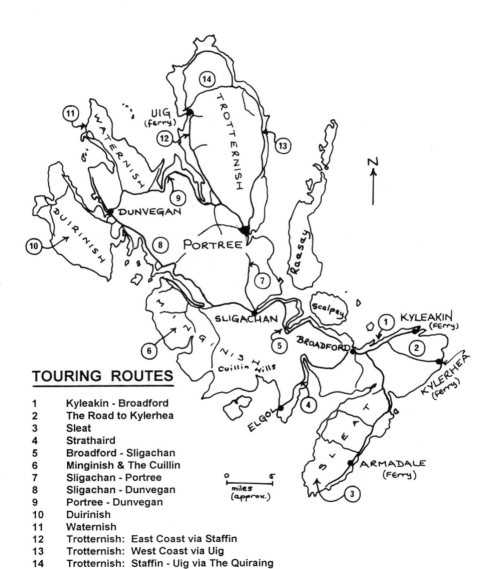

TOURING ROUTES

1   Kyleakin - Broadford
2   The Road to Kylerhea
3   Sleat
4   Strathaird
5   Broadford - Sligachan
6   Minginish & The Cuillin
7   Sligachan - Portree
8   Sligachan - Dunvegan
9   Portree - Dunvegan
10   Duirinish
11   Waternish
12   Trotternish: East Coast via Staffin
13   Trotternish: West Coast via Uig
14   Trotternish: Staffin - Uig via The Quiraing

KYLEAKIN TO BROADFORD

The ferry crossing from Kyle of Lochalsh to Kyleakin has long been the most popular way to approach the Isle of Skye. This short sea journey allows the tourist to pause for thought and take in the breathtaking beauty of Eilean a Cheo - the Misty Isle. On rainy days, with the clouds well down on the Cuillin mountains, its easy to appreciate how this name came about. If the crossing is made on a sunny day however, the majestic peaks of the Cuillin rising above the sparkling waters of the Kyle will be a scene long remembered.

Sadly, this beautiful ferry crossing will soon cease to exist when the new toll bridge comes into operation in 1995 as the Government will not allow Caledonian MacBrayne to run their ferries alongside. The bridge construction work can be seen as you cross the Kyle, marring one of the most famous views in Scotland.

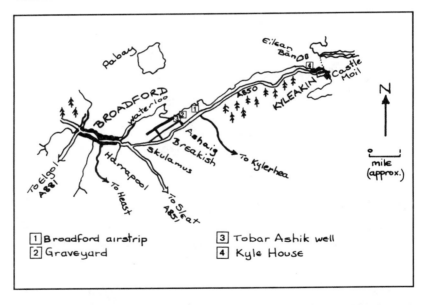

1 Broadford airstrip
2 Graveyard
3 Tobar Ashik well
4 Kyle House

Ferries have provided a much-needed lifeline to the remote west coast and islands of Scotland for many years. The first mention of a ferry boat at Kyle Akin occurs in the early 17th century when records show that one Lauchlan MacKinnon was granted charters in 1616 and 1627 allowing him to place a ferry on the water. The islands really only began to open up in the early 19th century with the coming of the steamships. The first recorded steamship sailing to Skye was made in late 1822 by the paddle steamer "Highlander" which was stationed at Tobermory on Mull. Up until the First World War, several companies operated steamships in the west coast waters, the most famous being MacBrayne's which started life as David Hutcheson & Co. From 1879 onwards, the company's activities were carried out by founding partner David MacBrayne. At the height of their operations, MacBrayne's made frequent passenger and cargo sailings to several places on Skye including Portree, Kyleakin, Armadale, Broadford, Glendale and Dunvegan. The arrival of the ferry was always an event of great importance to the islanders for the boats brought not only passengers but also supplies, mail and news.

As the ferry draws near to Kyleakin, there is a good view into the old harbour area. Brightly coloured fishing boats are often to be seen here, although the fishing industry has declined greatly in recent years.

KYLEAKIN
The little village of Kyleakin or Haakon's Strait is said to be named after the 13th century Norwegian king, Haakon whose unconquered fleet of 100 brown-sailed galleys passed through the Kyle on the way to the Battle of Largs in 1263. The ensuing Norwegian defeat at the hands of King Alexander III was of great historical significance not only to the Isle of Skye, but to the Hebrides as a whole. It loosened the Norse grip on the Western Isles which were eventually ceded to the Scottish Crown in 1266.

In the early 19th century, Alexander MacDonald, son of the first Lord MacDonald, had ambitious plans to enlarge the tiny village of Kyleakin and to rename it "New Liverpool". It was to become a model town, complete with two-storey houses quite unlike the traditional one-storey black-houses common throughout the island at the time. This grandiose scheme met with many problems in the early stages, not least of which was finding sufficient employment opportunities for the enlarged population and the whole idea eventually fell through. Lord MacDonald did however establish the first shop on the island at Kyleakin and was also responsible for carrying out the Gothic alterations at Armadale Castle on Sleat.

It is worth climbing up to the village War Memorial to take in the spectacular views over the Kyle. The path lies just to the right of the Castle Moil Restaurant and takes about 5 minutes each way. There is a view indicator board just beyond the memorial which points out features of interest.

Castle Moil
The seaward approach to Kyleakin is dominated by the guant ruin of Castle Moil which sits atop a rocky promontory overlooking the Kyle. In the

latter part of the middle ages, the castle was known as Dun Akyn or Haakon's Fort, a name which, like Kyleakin itself, derives from the visit of King Haakon's fleet. The castle was built by the MacKinnons of Strath and it remained that clan's ancestral seat for many years. The architectural details of the tower house indicate a construction date in the late 15th or early 16th century and this appears to be borne out by historical evidence which records that the castle was the meeting place of rebellious Highland chiefs following the death of James IV at Flodden in 1513. The radiocarbon dating of a piece of wood recovered from the site during renovation provides further evidence, suggesting a high probability of a construction date sometime between 1490 and 1513. The last person to live in the castle was Neill, the nephew of the 26th MacKinnon chief. Young Neill was brought up by his aunt Jane following the death of his father at the Battle of Coire na Creiche in the Cuillin in 1601. The castle subsequently fell into disrepair and became known as Caisteal Maol, the Bare Castle. A large part of the structure was blown down in a fierce storm in February 1949 and the castle was damaged further during the severe gales of February 1989. Happily, the remains were recently consolidated by Skye and Lochalsh District Council and Historic Scotland.

Legend has it that Castle Moil was built by a Norwegian Princess who was the wife of a MacKinnon chief. The Princess became known as "Saucy Mary" because she extracted tolls from passing vessels by hanging an enormous chain across the narrow Kyle. Only ships from her native land were exempt and those who refused to pay up were denied passage. For access to the castle, see the Walks section.

KYLEAKIN

Bike Hire: BIKES OF SKYE, The Pier. Tel. (0599) 4795. Mountain bikes, tourers, trainers and runabouts for full day, half day and evening hire. Panniers and tents are also available for hire. Cycles and accessories for sale.
CASTLE MOIL RESTAURANT. Tel. (0599) 4164.

Cruises: CASTLE MOIL SEAL CRUISES. Cruise the waters of Lochalsh on board M.V. Argus. The boat visits the seal colony on Eilean Dubh and offers plenty of opportunities for bird-watching. Toilet facilties and bar on board. Cruises depart from the ferry slip at 1000, 1200, 1400, 1600 and 1930. Reduced rates for children. Book on board or at the Pier Coffee House, Kyleakin. Tel (0599) 4641. M.V. Argus is also available for charter. Tel. (059 984) 235 for details.
CALEDONIAN MACBRAYNE offer day cruises during the summer months to the Crowlin Islands and Loch Duich via Kyle of Lochalsh. Contact the Kyleakin Ferry Terminal for full details on (0599) 4482.

Early Closing: Thursday.

Eating Out: CASTLE MOIL RESTAURANT. Tel. (0599) 4164. All day breakfasts, salads, seafood, steaks, grills, vegetarian burgers, baked potatoes, sandwiches, tea and coffee. Open Monday-Saturday 0900-2130; Sunday 1000-1500 and 1800-2100. Self service 0900-1700; table service 1700-2130. Access and Visa accepted. The King Haakon Lounge Bar holds a ceilidh night on Thursdays.

(Continued)

CROFTER'S KITCHEN. Tel. (0599) 4134. Licensed restaurant. A wide range of hot meals, locally caught fish and shellfish, ploughman's lunches, salads, soup, baked potatoes, vegetarian options, snacks, morning coffee and afternoon teas. A selection of Highland wines and Isle of Skye whisky to accompany your meal. Children's menu available. Open daily, including Sunday, 1000-2100. Access and Visa accepted.

KINGS ARMS HOTEL. Tel. (0599) 4109. Morning coffee, lunches, dinners, bar lunches and suppers.

KYLEAKIN HOTEL. Tel. (0599) 4445. Restaurant and bar meals served daily 0730-2200. Menu includes soup, fish & chips, salads, steak, vegetarian options and various sweets. Specialising in fresh local seafood. Children's meals are available.

PIER COFFEE HOUSE. Tel. (0599) 4641. A choice of soup, sandwiches, rolls, burgers, baked potatoes, fish & chips, pies and various main meals. Tea, coffee, ice-cream.

Petrol: KYLEAKIN FILLING STATION. Tel. (0599) 4431. By left of A850, just outside Kyleakin. Small licensed shop sells groceries, sweets, Sunday papers and hires out videos. Open Monday-Saturday 0800-2130; Sunday 0930-2130.

Shopping: CAMERONS. Tel. (0599) 4519. Newsagent. Souvenirs, gifts, groceries, photographic film, ice-cream.

CASTLE MOIL GIFT SHOP. Various souvenirs and a good selection of Scottish books. Ice-cream.

THE CROFTERS KITCHEN. Tel. (0599) 4134. A small shop area at this restaurant stocks a selection of souvenirs, postcards, O.S. maps and guide books.

MACDIARMID OF SKYE. Knitwear.

Toilets: At the pier.

Eilean Ban

As the A850 leaves Kyleakin, there is a good view right to the white lighthouse on Eilean Ban, built in 1857. The light is now fully automated but was once tended by keepers whose families lived in cottages on the island. Eilean Ban, the White Island, is so-called because of its wide stretches of beautiful white sands. These were described by the writer John Buchan in his book "Prince of the Captivity". This small (12 acre) island was once the home of Gavin Maxwell, author of "Ring of Bright Water". Maxwell bought the island in 1963 with the intention of turning it into a zoo for indigenous west Highland wildlife. He knocked the two keepers' cottages into one and went to live there in 1968 after his house at Sandaig south of Glenelg on the mainland was destroyed by fire. Sadly, ill-health prevented him from realising his dream and he shortly moved to Kyle House just outside Kyleakin. He died at Broadford Hospital on 7 September 1969. Maxwell's otter Teko is buried on the island beneath a boulder. Maxwell's partner, John Lister-Kaye, subsequently wrote a book about their plans, named after the island. Eilean Ban is now owned by the National Trust For Scotland and is being used as a stepping stone for the new bridge from the mainland which will come ashore just outside Kyleakin village.

On The Road To Broadford

The A850 continues close to the coast and traverses a fairly flat landscape which is rather untypical for Skye. Ahead there is a magnificent panorama of the Red Hills and the Black Cuillin, the Trotternish peninsula and the island of Raasay. Before long, the well-signposted minor road to the Kylerhea otter sanctuary and the Glenelg ferry is passed on the left. To the right of the road at this point lies Broadford airstrip, the only strip on the island, constructed by the 37th Engineer Regiment and opened in 1972. At the western end of the runway is a small graveyard which contains the graves of those who died when the cruiser HMS Curacao was cut in half by the liner Queen Mary, while acting as her escort on 2 October 1942.

Ashaig

The road now passes through an area known as Ashaig which has associations with the early Celtic missionary St Maelrubha. Maelrubha lived from 642 to 722 and was a disciple of St Columba. He is responsible for spreading Christianity throughout the western Highlands of Scotland. Tradition has it that the saint used Ashaig as a ferrying place and regularly preached by the shore near the point where the Abhainn Ashik enters the sea. It is said that Maelrubha kept his book of scriptures in a recess in the rocks and hung the church bell from the branches of a nearby ash tree.. This area was also once famous for the spring water from Tobar Ashik well.

The Island Of Pabay

Lying just offshore at this point can be seen the small island of Pabay, the Priest's or Monk's Isle. This island contains limestone bands of the Upper Lias formation which are extremely rich in fossils. The famous 19th century geologist Hugh Miller visited the island on his way home after a holiday in the Hebrides. Miller later noted, "He would be a happy geologist who, with a few thousand to spare, could call Pabba his own...though limited in area, the petrifications of its shores might of themselves fill a museum." Pabay also contains the remains of an ancient chapel and burial ground. It was once the haunt of pirates and other men of dubious character who were anxious to avoid the attentions of the law.

The Gaelic Revival

By this time the visitor will probably have noticed that all the road signs on the island are bi-lingual, with the Gaelic names shown in green. Gaelic is the indigenous language of the Highlands and Islands and was once spoken throughout much of Scotland. Following the 1745 Jacobite Rising, the Government tried to stamp out Gaelic language and culture and their repressive policies towards the language continued until relatively recent times. The first step towards rectifying the situation came in 1891 with the formation of An Comunn Gaidhealach, a society set up to protect the Gaelic language. Then in 1918 a clause was inserted in the Education Act stating that Gaelic would be taught in schools in Gaelic-speaking areas. Despite these measures, it still seemed for many years that the language was on the brink of extinction. Happily, in recent years there has been a great revival of interest in the Gaelic language, fuelled by Gaelic-medium education in primary schools and by children's playgroups (croileagan) and youth groups (sradagan). This revival has been particularly strong on Skye which has always been considered to be at the heart of the Gaidhealtachd or Gaelic community.

Breakish

The road now pulls away from the coast and passes through a succession of scattered settlements which were once thriving fishing and crofting communities. First comes Upper Breakish or Breacais in the native Gaelic. The houses of Lower Breakish lie downhill to the right, close to the shore. These townships are said to derive their name from the Gaelic "a'bhreac" which means small-pox, a reference to the dreadful plagues which swept through Skye in the 17th and 18th centuries.

BREAKISH

Eating Out: THE SEAGULL RESTAURANT & COFFEE HOUSE, Upper Breakish. Tel. (0471) 822 001. Licensed restaurant, by left of A850. Open daily Easter until October, from 1200-2200. Outwith this period phone for opening hours. Coffee, tea, snacks and cakes are available throughout the day. Additionally, a lunch menu is served from 1200-1500 and dinner from 1800-2200. The restaurant specialises in locally caught fish and seafood and other choices include Scottish venison, lamb and beef and at least two vegetarian main courses. Children are welcome. Evening reservations accepted. The restaurant also has a range of crystals, gemstones and minerals from around the world on display and for sale.

The Outskirts Of Broadford

The countryside becomes noticeably more populated as Broadford is approached. First of all, the visitor reaches Skulamus, where the A851 leaves the A850 to travel southwards down the Sleat peninsula. Then, a small road on the right leads to the curiously named township of Waterloo. This settlement derives its name from the many soldiers who settled here on their return from the Battle of Waterloo. It is said that in all 1,500 Skye men fought at Waterloo. Next comes Harrapool where a minor road branches south to climb up and over the moorland to the remote community of Heast. Finally the visitor arrives at Broadford itself, clustered around the wide sweep of Broadford Bay.

Eating Out: THE HEBRIDEAN HOTEL. Tel. (0471) 822 486. By left of A850 as you enter Harrapool. Tea, coffee, snacks.

THE ROAD TO KYLERHEA

The single track road to Kylerhea branches south-east from the A850 4 miles west of Kyleakin and is undoubtedly the most spectacular route on and off the island. The faint of heart should note however that there are some daunting twists and steep gradients to be negotiated and consequently this route is unsuitable for caravans.

The first section climbs steadily, following the gorge of the Abhainn Lusa to the right, and passing a large expanse of forestry on the left. The narrow road makes its way through Glen Arroch and over the high moor, crossing the watershed at the pass known as Bealach Udal. Beyond the pass, the road begins a steep descent down Kylerhea Glen, flanked on the right by Ben Aslak and on the left by Sgurr na Coinnich. This section gives good views across the narrows of Kyle Rhea to the Glenelg mainland opposite.

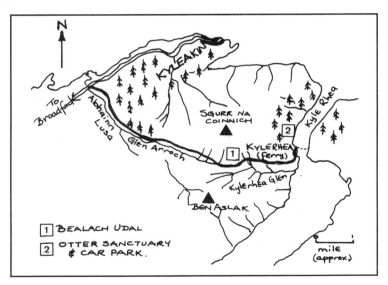

As you continue, spare a thought for the 19th century traveller known as "Nauticus" who ascended this steep pass on tricycle in the summer of 1880. "Nauticus" was near the end of an incredible 2,462 mile journey around Scotland when he was ferried across from Glenelg to Kylerhea. It is said that his arrival caused quite a commotion on Skye as the islanders had never before set eyes on a tricycle and indeed had encountered few bicycles. "Nauticus" had great difficulty in pushing his heavy machine to the top of the

Bealach Udal. In the account of his travels published in 1884 he writes, "...the gradient was such as to make me fear that I should have to take my tricycle to pieces and carry it up bit by bit." Having attained the bealach, there were futher problems. He continues, "Having mounted, I was just commencing to move, when a sudden squall burst upon me, and in a second I was being whirled along by a furious gust of wind. To my horror, I discovered that I was being carried at railway speed down a steep pitch, with only a low wall between me and a frightful precipice; moreover the road twisted in and out in a succession of sharp corners. It was an anxious moment! Had I lost my head for a second nothing could have saved me."

At the foot of the glen lie the scattered houses of Kylerhea. Towards the end of the road, a small track forks left up a steep hill to the Kylerhea Otter Sanctuary which contains one of Europe's most thriving otter populations. The right fork terminates at the Glenelg Ferry slipway.

Kylerhea Otter Haven

The remote Kylerhea shoreline provides an ideal habitat for one of Britains's rarest mammals, the otter. Here you will have a unique opportunity to view this fascinating creature in its natural surroundings. Elsewhere in Britain, due largely to the destruction of habitat and disturbance by man, the otter is rarely seen and is usually a nocturnal animal. At Kylerhea however, thanks to the inaccessibility of the shoreline, the otters appear mainly during the day and are often to be seen swimming amongst the kelp close to the shore, particularly at half tide. The tumbled rocks along the Kylerhea shoreline provide ideal sites for the otters' shelters or "holts" and the narrows contain an abundant supply of food as shoals of fish are almost continually on passage. The thriving otter population at Kylerhea is cared for by the Forestry Commission, with advice from the Vincent Wildlife Trust, the leading researchers on otters. The Commission has undertaken a number of conservation projects in the area to protect and enhance the precious Kylerhea habitat. Many broadleaved trees have been planted to provide additional cover for the mammals and freshwater pools have been established to encourage frogs to breed - one of the otter's favourite foods. In 1988 the Forestry Commission erected a special observation hide to enable visitors to observe the local wildlife without disturbance. This has proved hugely successful and the hide is now visited by around 14,000 people each year. Thanks to generous public donations a second hide is now planned close to the shore to enable scientists to gather more information on conservation and management.

Otter Haven Trail: To reach the public hide at KYLERHEA OTTER HAVEN entails a pleasant walk along a forest road and a short section of well made path. The return trip can easily be made within an hour (plus time in the hide). Stout footwear is advisable. Although bumpy, access is possible for wheelchairs with assistance. Vehicular access is available to the hide for severely disabled visitors. Telephone the Forest Office at Balmacara on (059 986) 321 for details. Please remember that the otter is a protected species and that it is an offence to intentionally disturb one or to knowingly approach its place of shelter. Visitors must not stray from the designated paths or approach the shoreline. Dogs are not permitted and must be left behind in your car. In addition to otters, you may see a variety of other wildlife including seals, falcons, sea eagles, golden eagles, cormorants, herons and red-breasted mergansers. Information on identification is displayed in the hide and it is a good idea to bring along a pair of binoculars. If you do not wish to visit the hide, there are several picnic tables adjacent to the small carpark which have a delightful view over the Kyle Rhea narrows. Here you can listen to a tape of otter calls which runs on solar batteries.

As you gaze across the water to the mainland opposite, the buildings of the remote Eilanreach Estate can just be made out to the south of Glenelg. For a time this was home to the author Gavin Maxwell who wrote about life with his pet otter Mij in "Ring of Bright Water". Maxwell lived by the shore at Sandaig until 1968 when his house was destroyed by fire.

While scanning the Kyle, you should also keep an eye out for the resident sea serpent. This frightening beast was seen in August 1872 by the Rev. John MacRae, minister of Glenelg and his friend Rev. David Twopeny from Kent. The two men had just set out in a small cutter for a pleasure cruise down the Sound of Sleat when they suddenly spied a dark mass beneath the waves. Then several black lumps rose one after another out of the water, all in a row. The two Reverends saw the serpent again on the following day and it was later seen by the ferrymen on either side of the Kyle as it passed through the narrows on the evening of 21 August. Several people claim to have seen the beast since.

The Kylerhea Ferry
From the otter sanctuary, it is worth continuing on foot down to the Kylerhea slipway to watch the operations of the unique 6-car turn-table ferry. Before the Highland Railway was extended from Strome Ferry to Kyle of Lochalsh in 1897, this was the main ferry crossing to the Isle of Skye. There was once an inn on either side of the channel here where weary travellers could rest on their way to and from the island. The vehicular ferry service was begun as an experiment in the summer months of the early 1930's. Strict petrol rationing during the Second World War brought the venture to a close for a while. The service was re-started in 1946 and then closed again in 1948 due to lack of support. Today, business is healthy and looks set to increase when the new toll bridge brings the Kyle of Lochalsh-Kyleakin ferry service to

an end in 1995, as many visitors still entertain the romantic notion of going "over the sea" to Skye.

The Kylerhea-Glenelg Drove Road

Kylerhea lies on the route taken by the cattle drovers of old and it was at this point, the narrowest stretch of water between Skye and the mainland, that the cattle were made to swim across at slack tide. The first droves were carried out as early as 1502 when MacDonald of Kingsburgh began exporting the black cattle reared on the fertile basaltic pastures of his Trotternish lands. The Skye cattle were driven south and traded in the Lowlands for barley, oats and other foodstuffs which could not be easily obtained in large quantities in the Hebrides. Soon, a healthy export trade developed and for many years the black cattle were Skye's main source of income, apart from a few sheep and intermittent kelp sales. The western Highlands and islands became famous for their fine beasts which, it is said, gained a healthy bloom from the lush upland pastures, making them particularly attractive to dealers from England and southern Scotland. At the peak of the trade in 1813, it is estimated that between 5,000 and 8,000 black cattle were being exported annually.

The Isle of Skye was in a key central position for gathering cattle from the Outer Hebrides en route to the mainland drove routes and animals would be sent across from Lochmaddy, Lochboisdale, Rodel and Tarbert on the first stage of their journey. The beasts were landed in Uig Bay, on the shores of Loch Dunvegan and occasionally in Loch Pooltiel. From Uig, a drove road led south to Portree where a market was held. The cattle were then driven south to Sligachan either along the line of the present A850 through Glen Varragill, or more commonly along the coast via Braes. At Sligachan, another market was held and here the drove was joined by the cattle landed at Dunvegan and Loch Pooltiel which had taken a route through Bracadale. The next stop was Broadford, where there was yet another market for cattle from Sleat and Strathaird. From Broadford, the drove road led south along the line of the present A851, bending east at Kinloch to skirt round the southern flanks of Ben Aslak. The latter part of this route is still evident as a footpath on the 1:50,000 O.S. map. On reaching Kylerhea, the cattle were made to swim across the narrow channel at slack tide. To achieve this safely, the drovers cut 3ft lengths of rope and fashioned a noose at one end. This they secured around the jaw of each beast, leaving the animal's tongue free to prevent it from drowning. The cattle were then taken into the water and it is said that once afloat, all resistance stopped and each beast could then be tied to the tail of the animal in front. In this way, strings of 6 or 8 cows were led across the narrows, the rope of the foremost beast being held by a man in the stern of a boat. It is said that the ferrymen were very adept at this task and that few beasts were ever lost. Although this practice largely died out in the 19th century, there were isolated occurrences as late as 1906. By this time, cattle were commonly ferried across the narrows in boats.

From Glenelg, the cattle continued southwards, either by Spean Bridge or by the south end of Loch More. Until the mid 18th century, Crieff was the main tryst or gathering place on the mainland. After this time, Falkirk became the main destination and the Falkirk Tryst soon developed into the greatest Scottish cattle market of all time. Here, the Highland drovers would bargain with English dealers and the cattle would then be driven through the Southern Uplands to the meat markets of England.

SLEAT

The A851 to Armadale branches south between Breakish and Broadford. This road traverses the length of the Sleat Peninsula and ends at the Aird of Sleat from which there are spectacular views of the Small Isles. Sleat (pronounced "Slate") has long been known as the Garden of Skye because of its lush vegetation and it has a character all of its own, quite distinct from the rest of the island.

The Armadale road is single-track and can be quite busy immediately before and after ferry departures. Much distress is caused to locals and those used to driving on single-track roads by slow moving tourist traffic from the ferry. Please remember that it is an offence to hinder traffic which is travelling behind you - pull into the nearest passing place and permit following traffic to overtake.

On a lighter note, Sleat offers much to delight the visitor - stunning views, a sense of tranquility, excellent craft shops and a choice of several pleasant walks. If you are visiting during July, look out for the many events in the Feis an Eilein, a festival of traditional song and dance, exhibitions and workshops organised jointly by South Skye Community Arts Group SEALL (Gaelic for Look!) and the Gaelic College at Ostaig. Details of events can be obtained by contacting the Feis Director, Ostaig House, IV44 8RQ, tel (04714) 207 or the Feis Office at Sabhal Mor Ostaig between 0900 and 1700, tel (04714) 345.

On The Road To Isleornsay

The first stretch of road crosses an attractive area of heather moorland and then passes Lochain Dubha, the Black Lochs, so called because of their dark peaty water. These lochs are well known for their excellent trout fishing. Soon Loch Airigh na Saorach is seen to the right and here there is room to pull off by the left of the road - one of the few places where this is possible on the A851. If you are quiet, you may spot a heron fishing amidst the reeds and waterlilies in this pretty loch. As the road continues, the head of Loch Eishort comes into view on the right, while to the left an area of conifer plantation is passed. Also to the right can be seen the great horseshoe of Red Hills which surround the impressive corrie of Coire Gorm. The northern end of the horseshoe terminates in the rounded tip of Beinn na Caillich.

The road now begins to descend and traverses the narrow isthmus which separates Loch Eishort from Loch na Dal. Eishort is an Old Norse name whose meaning suggests that in the early days of Norse settlement it was common practice to drag boats across the neck of land between the two sea lochs to avoid the long journey around the Point of Sleat. Ahead at this point can also be seen Isle Ornsay which lies just off-shore from the settlement of the same name.   Ornsay is also an Old Norse word meaning "ebb-tide island" and this too is indicative of Viking settlement in the area.

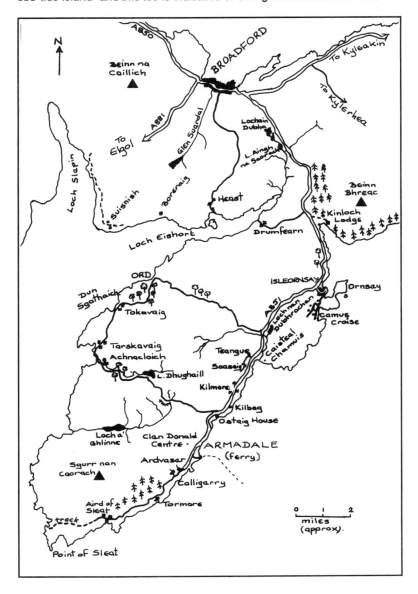

A minor road branches right to the scattered crofts of Drumfearn and just after this turn-off, a small road on the left leads to the starting point of a reasonably strenuous walk to Leitir Fura Clearance Village (see Walks for full details). As the A851 continues, the attractive white-walled Kinloch Lodge soon comes into view across the waters of Loch na Dal. Kinloch Lodge was originally built in the 1680's as a farmhouse and in Victorian days it was one of Lord MacDonald's shooting lodges. It has now been tastefully converted into a hotel and is the home of the present Clan Chief Lord MacDonald and his wife. Lady MacDonald is well known for her cookery books and, with the assistance of a chef, she personally cooks the meals for hotel guests. The splendid view across the loch to Beinn Bhreac is lost as the road enters an area of attractive natural forest.

DUISDALE

Eating Out: DUISDALE HOUSE HOTEL. Tel. (04713) 202/213. Situated by the right of the A851. Non-residents welcome for coffee, afternoon tea, bar snacks and evening meals. Open late March-December.

Exhibition: TALLA DUISDALE ART WORKSHOP. Located in the old church building by the left of the A851, between Duisdalemore and Duisdale Beag. Holds various exhibitions throughout the year. See local posters for details.

Shopping: HARLEQUIN KNITWEAR. Tel. (04713) 321. Situated down a small road to the right of the A851, shortly after the hotel. Knitwear in a variety of striking styles and colours. Shetland, Mohair, Supersoft wool and chenille. Open daily 0900-late.

You are now in the community of Duisdalemore. Much of the land here was once held by Clan Mackinnon in return for their services as standard bearers to the MacDonalds. As the road once again emerges from the trees, there is a good view left across the loch to the little island of Ornsay. By the left of the road can be seen an old church which was once dedicated to St Columba and now serves as an exhibition gallery.

The A852 branches left to the community of Isleornsay. Opposite the turn-off, on the main road, lies the old village schoolhouse which was constructed in 1876. This building is now the home of the Gaelic television company Abu-tele.

ISLEORNSAY

This picturesque little settlement overlooks a tranquil harbour created by the adjacent island of Ornsay. The village is also known by its Gaelic name of Eilean Iarmain. The serenity encountered here today belies the fact that this was once a major herring port with a large general merchant's shop and a salt store in the harbour buildings. It was at Isleornsay that the local crofters gathered last century to air their grievances to Lord Napier's Parliamentary Commissioners. The evidence collected by the Commissioners on their journey from Argyll to Easter Ross resulted in the passing of the Crofters Act in 1886 which greatly improved the lot of the crofters. Isleornsay is also famous for its public toilet which dates to 1820 - the first to be constructed on the island.

At the heart of Isleornsay lies the attractive white-walled Eilean Iarmain Hotel, a traditional Gaelic Inn which is part of the Estate of Fearann Eilean Iarmain owned by Sir Iain and Lady Noble. This private estate encompasses most of the northern part of the Sleat peninsula. The Eilean Iarmain Hotel and adjacent group of buildings date from 1800. One of the bedrooms contains a beautiful canopied bed which originally came from nearby Armadale Castle. The Hotel also manufactures its own whisky, a vatted malt known as Poit Dubh, and a blend, Te Bheag. This excellent dram is available to hotel guests.

From the pier there are breathtaking views to Isle Ornsay and the mainland hills of Knoydart beyond. The island can be reached at low tide by walking around the bay. Close to its southern shore lie the remains of an ancient nunnery chapel. Lying just off the south-eastern tip of Ornsay is the smaller island of Eilean Sionnach which contains an attractive lighthouse constructed by Robert Louis Stephenson's father in 1857. The lighthouse keeper's cottage was once home to the author Gavin Maxwell. Across the Sound at this point lies the remote area of Sandaig where Maxwell lived and wrote of life with his pet otters in "Ring of Bright Water". From Isleornsay, a small road branches south to Camus Croise. This attractive settlement was also once a busy fishing village but many of the pretty cottages are now holiday homes.

ISLEORNSAY

Eating Out: HOTEL EILEAN IARMAIN. Tel. (04713) 332/266. A traditional Gaelic inn with local Gaelic-speaking staff. Cruisgean Restaurant open to non-residents. Lunch is served from 1230-1400. The Dining Room offers a table d'hote menu every evening from 1930-2100 (last orders 2100) which features local fish, shellfish and game in season. Bar meals are served in the Am Praban Bar from 1230-1430 and 1830-2100 and include a variety of traditional Scottish dishes such as Brose. Accompanied children are allowed into the bar. Traditional afternoon teas are also served every day. Access and Visa accepted.

Exhibition: GALLERY AN TALLA DEARG. Tel. (04713) 266. A variety of art and sculpture exhibitions are held throughout the summer months, including Laurence Broderick's famous annual exhibition of otters and other animals in bronze and marble. Open July-October.

Petrol: TIGH OSDA EILEAN IARMAIN. Tel. (04713) 332. At the Eilean Iarmain Hotel. 4 star leaded only.

Shopping: AM BUTH. Tel. (04713) 266. Licensed general store. Groceries, drinks, books, cassettes and various videos. Open Monday-Saturday 0900-1800.

Toilets: Adjacent to the Hotel Eilean Iarmain.

Isleornsay To Kilmore

After the Isleornsay turn-off, the A851 begins to turn inland and the landscape becomes very lush, with patches of natural woodland hugging the base of the craggy hills. The striking crag on the left is known as Creag na Ba - the Crag of the Cattle. As the road begins to descend, Loch nan Dubhrachan is seen to the left. Legend has it that this stretch of water is haunted by an each uisge or water-horse. The each uisge is a supernatural being, usually of similar appearance to an ordinary horse but able to change its form at will. It is said that the Loch nan Dubhrachan water-horse resembles a cow with a very long mane. In the last century, this dreadful beast terrorised the neighbourhood for many years and attempted to waylay travellers who passed the loch at night. Eventually, in 1870, the terrified locals decided to get rid of the beast by systematically dragging the loch. The appointed day of the search was declared a holiday in the district and people came from far and wide to witness the event. A sturdy net was stretched across the water and pulled along by several men on each side of the loch. As they proceeded along the shore, the net suddenly became entangled with something under the water. The locals, believing they had indeed caught the dreaded water-horse, dropped the net in fright and the assembled crowd quickly dispersed amidst shrieks and screams of terror. As far as is known, the beast is there still!

On the right lies the minor road to Ord, Tokavaig and Tarskavaig (unsuitable for caravans). This road rejoins the A851 further south at Ostaig and makes an interesting detour on the return journey from the Aird (see below). The A851 continues to descend and the Toravaig House Hotel is passed on the left.

Eating Out: TORAVAIG HOUSE HOTEL. Tel. (04713) 231. Non-residents welcome. Bar lunches and suppers. Full dinner menu served from 1900-2000 in the dining room.

Caisteal Chamuis

As the road clears the trees, the gaunt ruin of Caisteal Chamuis or Knock Castle is seen on a knoll overlooking Knock Bay (for access details, see Walks section). The castle is thought to overlie the site of an earlier Iron Age fortification known as Dun Thorovaig, the Dun of the Bay of Thor, of which there is now no trace. The medieval castle first enters the history books in 1402 as the place where William, 4th Chief of the MacLeods, died. At that time, Sleat was part of the fiefdom of the Earl of Ross and it was as the Earl's vassals that the MacLeods held lands in the southern part of Skye. Following William's death, a regent was elected to look after the affairs of his ten year old son. Iain Mishealbhach or Ian the Ill-fated was well named for during his regency there arose many quarrels within the MacLeod clan and the castle was overrun by a group of MacDonalds. The MacLeods managed to regain the castle, but they were soon to have the MacDonalds as neighbours when the title of Earl of Ross was accorded to Donald MacDonald who had a legitimate claim through marriage. During this period it seems that the castle once again fell into MacDonald hands and in 1431 it was overrun by royal troops during the struggles between the MacDonalds and James I who perceived the Lordship of the Isles as a threat to his authority.

Caisteal Chamuis is next mentioned in 1513 when Sir Donald John MacDonald of Lochalsh attempted to resurrect the Lordship of the Isles following the death of James IV at Flodden Field. In the uprising, Alasdair Crotach MacLeod laid siege to the castle and a MacDonald heroine inspired the defenders to victory, forcing Alasdair to withdraw. This lady subsequently became known as Mary of the Castle.

James MacDonald, the 4th son of the 4th Chief, lived at Caisteal Chamuis during the second half of the 16th century. The castle was forfeited to the Crown in 1581 due to James's inability to fulfill a promise to pay the Bishop of the Isles the dues outstanding on the MacDonald lands. The Crown subsequently issued a new charter to Donald Gorm of Sleat in 1596 confirming him in lands at Sleat provided that the King and his successors be given free access to the castle of "Camys". The King never took advantage of this right and the last documentary evidence concerning Caisteal Chamuis dates to 31 August 1632 when MacConillreich signed a bond in the castle declaring Sir Donald MacDonald, the first Baronet of Sleat, to be his undoubted Chief. By 1689 the castle was abandoned and much of the stone was removed in 1825 to build nearby Knock Farm.

There are various traditions associated with Caisteal Chamuis, one of which concerns the arrival of two warships in 1690, dispatched by William of Orange to try to bring in Sir Donald MacDonald. It is said that the MacDonalds captured the naval landing party who had previously burned down the chief's house at Armadale, and hung them on gibbets made from their own oars on the beach below the castle. Tradition also holds that the castle was once defended single-handedly by one John Ban MacPherson against a group of MacLeods from Dunvegan around 1620. John Ban went on to found a line of famous clerics who served the church for over 200 years. Dr Martin MacPherson who entertained the well-known travellers Johnson and Boswell at Upper Ostaig was one of this clerical line.

Caisteal Chamuis was once said to be the haunt of a *glaistig* - a supernatural creature which took the form of a thin, grey woman with long hair reaching all the way to her heels, clad entirely in green. The glaistig was a solitary creature with a liking for cattle. She usually took up residence at a farm where there were cows and liked to arrange the utensils in the dairy. It was as well for humans to keep on the good side of this being, for she could yell loudly and be extremely mischievous. As a reward for her services, it was common to leave a small quantity of milk for her in the cavity of a stone and it was a rare sight to see the glaistig come at milking time to partake of her drink. It is said that in the days of the Lords of the Isles, the Chamuis glaistig was occasionally seen at nightfall, standing by her stone next to the castle.

At Knock Bay, the road passes the scattered houses of Teangue and Saasaig and begins to climb once more. Watch out for the picturesque Teangue Post Office to the right - one of the most photographed P.O.'s in the Highlands and Islands! Next come the communities of Ferrindonald and Kilmore. As you continue down the peninsula, scan the road sides for the many species of wild flowers which are to be found in the area. In spring, violets, primroses, wild garlic and great banks of bluebells are to be seen, while in summer there are wild irises and bright yellow broom.

Kilmore Church

At Kilmore, by the left of the road, can be seen the Parish Church of Scotland which was built in 1876. This site has been an important religious centre for many centuries, evidenced by the fact that the church gave rise to the name of the village - Kilmore or A' Chill Mhor in Gaelic - the Big Church. The first church on the site was established in the early 13th century by Crotach MacGille Gorm, a canon from Beauly. This building, which stood until the early 17th century, was set on fire by the MacLeods during a clan feud, killing a whole congregation of MacIntyres who had taken refuge there after losing a battle. A new church was built in 1681 by Lord MacDonald to replace the one destroyed by the MacLeods. This second building and associated mausoleum, now a picturesque ivy clad ruin, can be seen just to the left of the present church. It is said that such was the veneration for this new church that the devout congregation would kneel at first sight of the building. From this habit, the land between Ferrindonald and Kilmore came to be known as Bealach an t-Sleachd - the Pass of the Kneeling. It is worth taking the time to wander around the ancient burial ground which is filled with the countless grassy mounds of unmarked graves. Here you will find many interesting memorials, including the gravestones of prominent members of the Clan MacDonald. If you walk to the bottom of the graveyard a good view is obtained over the coastline at this point. Close by the church is the attractive castellated Manse which was built around 1811.

Kilmore To Armadale

After Kilmore Church, the road once again enters a stretch of woodland. At Kilbeg (the Little Church) can be seen Bun Sgoil Sleite, Sleat Primary School, one of the many new bi-lingual Gaelic schools which are emerging on Skye. The road to Tarskavaig and the Gaelic College branches right at Ostaig - this is the alternative return route mentioned above.

The visitor is now at the heart of Clan Donald country. The MacDonalds were once the most powerful of all the Highland clans and held extensive territories in the Western Isles. The clan takes its name from Donald, grandson of Somerled, King of the Isles. The MacDonalds of Sleat are descended from Hugh, the third brother of John, 10th Lord of the Isles, who died in 1498.

Just after the Tarskavaig turn-off, the trees to the left conceal the present Ostaig House. The old mansion house of Ostaig, once the home of the MacDonald chiefs, was burnt to the ground by King William's troops following the Battle of Killiecrankie in 1689. There is a pull-off on the left and then the road emerges from the trees giving stunning views across the Sound of Sleat to the mainland hills of the remote Knoydart peninsula opposite.

As the road clears the trees, it crosses the Allt a' Mhuilinn by the Mill Bridge. Prior to 1823, the old road which used to serve the southern tip of Sleat swung to the right away from the coast at Mill Bridge to climb the Drochaid a' Mhuilinn above Armadale Castle. The road then descended through the Castle gardens and continued southwards to Ardvasar. To increase the privacy of the Castle, the new coast road was constructed in 1823. This practice was fairly common in the last century, perhaps the most famous example being the diversion of the Deeside road in Grampian to ensure privacy for Queen Victoria and Prince Albert at Balmoral Castle.

Mill Bridge takes its name from the fact that a corn mill belonging to the MacDonald Estate once stood nearby. The mill, a smithy and two houses are depicted in a map dating from 1763. Unfortunately, all were destroyed during the contruction of the new coast road. The slopes adjacent to the Allt a' Mhuilinn were once home to a thriving population of small-holders, tenants of the MacDonald Estate. Cultivation was by means of lazy beds, a clever agricultural technique which enabled farmers to derive the most benefit from poor soil. First of all, manure and/or seaweed was laid out upon the ground in long parallel lines. Then the adjacent soil was dug up and piled on top of the fertilizer to create sizeable ridges. The intervening ditches ensured good drainage and in this way good crops of barley and potatoes were achieved. Today areas of lazy beds can still be distinguished on hill-sides throughout Skye when the light is right.

The Allt a' Mhuilinn lazy beds were last cultivated in 1811. The Clan MacDonald Estate then cleared the entire population to villages on the coast to make way for an extensive sheep farm. This pattern of coastal settlement still exists throughout the island today. The Armadale sheep farm is still in operation, caring for a vast flock of 1,200 black-faced sheep which roam free over the moorland hills to the coast on the west side of the Sleat peninsula. The lambs are sent south to be fattened for mutton and the wool is used in the manufacture of coarse cloths and carpets. Additionally the farm keeps a small herd of cows which produce beef calves.

ARMADALE

The road continues along the coast and soon Armadale Pier comes into view ahead. To the right and well signposted, lies the Clan Donald Centre. A short distance beyond this, a left turn will take you to Armadale Pier, the main shopping area. Armadale is part of the Clan Donald Estate, a vast property of 20,000 acres which stretches from the Point of Sleat in the south to Ord on the west coast. The land is owned and cared for by the Clan Donalds Lands Trust which was set up in 1972 to preserve the last remnants of the ancient clan domain. The lands are now held in trust for MacDonalds throughout the world and for all those with an interest in preserving Highland heritage. Being a considerable landowner (unlike other clan organistaions), the Trust must ensure the sustained economic growth of its properties and the estate is therefore actively engaged in crofting, farming and conservation work. The Clan Donald Lands Trust is a non-profit making charitable organisation with members throughout the world. For further details, contact The International Director, The Clan Donalds Lands Trust, Armadale Castle, Sleat, Isle of Skye, IV45 8RS. Tel. (04714) 227.

Heritage Centre: THE CLAN DONALD CENTRE. Tel. (04714) 305. Set within attractive landscaped grounds, the partially restored Armadale Castle houses a fascinating museum and there is a library and study centre in nearby Armadale House. A series of nature trails begin in the gardens and there is an adventure playground for children. The Stables building contains both a gift shop and restaurant. An all inclusive ticket provides access to the Castle ruins, museum and video show, study centre and exhibitions, the gardens and nature trails. Family tickets and group rates are available. Parking and entry to the Stables Restaurant, gift shop and Rangers' Hut are free. The Visitor Centre is open daily between April-October inclusive, 0930-1730 (last entry at 1700). The gardens are open throughout the year. The Centre and gardens are suitable for the disabled (wheelchairs are available). Dogs are permitted in the grounds but must be kept on a lead.

The Museum of the Isles This interesting museum is housed in part of the original mansion building. The "Headship of the Gael" exhibition recounts the history of Clan MacDonald from the early days to the dissolution of the clan system following the 1745 Jacobite Rebellion. There are also various historical artefacts connected with famous members of the clan. The exhibition also includes an audio-visual presentation "The Sea Kingdom" which tells the story of the Lordship of the Isles, the period during which the Gaelic nation flourished under the leadership of Clan

Donald. The museum contains a small shop which has a good range of Scottish antiquarian books and prints and also jewellery and other small gift items. There are toilet facilities at the museum (not suitable for the disabled).

Armadale House This attractive house and cottage garden was built in 1870 for the castle's gardener. It was converted to an excellent library and study centre in 1990 and only a year later this facility was awarded 1st prize in the Research Category of the Scottish Museums of the Year Awards. Here you can see various displays and items associated with the castle, including photographs of the beautiful staircase and facade of the Gillespie Graham castle extension before it was ravaged by fire. An exhibition gallery contains maps and photographs relating to Armadale. Here you can browse through an incredible collection of books, over 6,000 volumes, relating to all aspects of Scottish history and culture. There is also an archive of censuses, estate and parish records. The resident Archivist can assist in all matters of research.

The Gardens There are 40 acres of woodland gardens filled with exotic trees, shrubs and flowers to explore, as well as an attractive walled garden. Although Armadale lies further north than Moscow, rare plants flourish here thanks to the influence of the Gulf Stream which warms the Scottish west coast waters creating a mild, frost-free climate. 300 years ago a large orchard flourished here but after the castle was completed in 1841 many exotic trees were planted to provide shelter for the gardens. Today, the policies contain some of the oldest and largest trees on the island. The walled garden dates to the 1820's. The walls were once lined with fruit trees and the garden produced flowers, fruit and vegetables for the inhabitants of the castle. Enough surplus was produced to export to the mainland. When the MacDonalds moved away from the castle in 1925 the gardens became overgrown and remained in this sad state until the Clan Trust began renovations in 1972. After a massive clearance and replanting scheme, the whole area has regained its former glory and is now home to a variety of birds and animals which are rare elsewhere on the island. In particular, as you wander amongst the trees, look out for the Greater Spotted Woodpecker, the Tree-creeper and the Goldcrest. If you visit the gardens in early summer you will be rewarded with a colourful display of wild flowers which surround the castle in sweeping meadows. During wet weather umberellas can be hired from the gate-house.

Nature Trails A number of pleasant nature trails wind through the woodland and farmland surrounding the castle. The trails follow grass and sawdust paths and in wet weather suitable footwear is advisable.   There are three miles of trails to explore, with walks ranging from 1/2 hour to 3 hours in duration. An informative leaflet with historical narrative is available from the Countryside Ranger Base.

Countryside Ranger Service: Skye's only countryside ranger service. The two Rangers can provide information on the local and natural history of the area and the farming, crofting and conservation work being done on the estate. The Ranger Base located next to the gate house contains an information room with various wildlife displays. Several leaflets about the estate and its wildlife are also available. During the summer months, the Rangers organise a programme of guided walks for both adults and children.   There is also a summer environmental education programme for children. A leaflet containing full details of the current year's events is available from the Base. The Rangers can be contacted on (04714) 305 during office hours.

CLAN DONALD CENTRE, ARMADALE

Eating Out: THE STABLES RESTAURANT. Tel. (04714) 305/227. Located in the beautifully rebuilt Stables building. Licensed restaurant offering tea, coffee, snacks and full meals including a variety of home-baked items, soup, seafood and a selection of traditional dishes. Half portions are available for children. Open 1000-1800. Lunch served 1200-1430. During July and August evening meals are served from 1800 (last orders 2030).

Shopping: THE GIFT SHOP. Located in the Stables building. Gaelic/Celtic video tapes and cassettes, whisky, preserves, glasswear, jewellery and children's games. Bureau de Change facilities. Open daily 0930-1730.

Toilets: In the old stable block, next to the gift shop. Separate facilities for the disabled.

Armadale Castle

When the MacDonalds first arrived in Skye from the southern Hebrides in the 15th century, they took up residence in nearby Knock and Dunscaith Castles. The Clan's connection with Armadale can be traced back to around 1650 when it is known that they maintained two farmhouses there. After 1690 the Clan Chief and his family moved to Duntulm Castle in Trotternish, leaving the farms and gardens in the hands of various other MacDonalds. One notable event which occurred here on 6th November 1750 was the marriage of the famous Flora MacDonald, the romantic heroine who aided Bonnie Prince Charlie in his escape from the Redcoats. A new mansion house was built on the Armadale site around 1790 by the first Lord MacDonald. Part of this original structure now forms the present white Museum building. The mansion house was extended in 1815 to a design by the distinguished architect Gillespie Graham and was thereafter known as Armadale Castle. At this time, the MacDonald Estate was a thriving enterprise, self-sufficient in meat, poultry, grain and dairy produce from the adjacent farm and fruit and vegetables from the walled garden. The estate's horses were housed in a roomy stable block located at the castle entrance, also designed by Graham Gillespie in 1822. Tragically, much of the original mansion house was destroyed by fire in 1855. Today, part of the Gillespie Graham extension is retained as a sculptured ruin which contains a selection of plants from around the world. A section of the staircase remains intact. The damaged building was partly replaced by another, the present central block, designed by David Bryce. The MacDonalds remained in residence at Armadale Castle until 1925 when they moved to a smaller house nearby. Sadly, the castle was then left at the mercy of the elements and over the years the fabric of the building rotted and crumbled away and much damage was done by vandals. The buildings and gardens were finally restored by the Clan Donald Lands Trust which was formed in 1972 to preserve the remnants of the clan lands.

Johnson and Boswell At Armadale

The celebrated 18th century travellers Dr Samuel Johnson and James Boswell visited Skye during their tour of the Hebrides in 1773. They landed at Armadale on Thursday 2nd September after being ferried across the Sound of Sleat from Glenelg and were met on the sands by Sir Alexander and Lady MacDonald who were about to leave the island for Edinburgh. Boswell recorded in his journal, "Armidale is situated on a pretty bay of the narrow sea, which flows between the main land of Scotland and the Isle of Skye. In front there is a grand prospect of the rude mountains of Moidart and Knoidart. Behind are hills gently rising and covered with a finer verdure than I expected to see in this climate, and the scene is enlivened by a number of little clear brooks." Johnson and Boswell had expected to find the Chief and his Lady surrounded by members of the Clan and full of the generous hospitality for which the Highland chiefs were renowned. Instead, they were rather disappointed by Sir Alexander, who had been educated and married in England and had lost his fine Highland spirit and patriarchal courtesy. The pair were received at the house of one of Sir Alexander's tenants at Upper Ostaig, the Chief's residence having been burnt to the ground in 1690 by King William's troops. Boswell thought the building was a rather poor house for a Highland chief. Their reception was also rather dismal. That night they had "an ill-dressed dinner" and not even the fine wines were enough to lift Boswell's spirits. He later wrote in his journal, "I alone drank port wine. No claret appeared. We had indeed mountain and Frontignac and Scotch porter.

But except what I did myself, there was no hospitable convivial intercourse, no ringing of glasses." The whole episode led Dr Johnson to comment, "Sir, the Highland chiefs should not be allowed to go farther south than Aberdeen." Johnson and Boswell remained at Armadale until Monday 6th September when they left for Coirechatachan in Strathaird.

ARMADALE

Bicycle Hire: SKYE FERRY FILLING STATION. Tel. (04714) 249.

Cruises: CALEDONIAN MACBRAYNE offer day trips on board MV Iona from Armadale Pier to Tobermory on Mull. Departing Sundays only between June and August. Vehicular and passenger service. Cruising time approximately 2 1/2 hours each way with c. 7 hours to explore Mull. MV Iona has a licensed bar and self-service restaurant which offers full meals and snacks. Also sailings to the Small Isles (Eigg, Muck, Rum and Canna) via Mallaig. For tickets and further information, contact the Armadale Ferry Terminal Office on (04714) 248.

Eating Out: ARMADALE FERRY HOTEL. Tea, coffee, soup, filled rolls, sandwiches and all day grill. Fish & chips to takeaway.
BISTRO CAFE. Tel. (04714) 252. Fresh food, salads, tea and coffee. Outside dining area. Open 7 days a week throughout the summer season from 0830 until the last ferry.
THE SCALLOP BAR. Tel. (04714) 350/264. Seafood takeaway. Ice-cream.

Petrol: SKYE FERRY FILLING STATION. Tel. (04714) 249. Sells photographic film, cassettes, sweets, peat and coal. Access accepted. Open Monday-Saturday 0830-1830.

Shopping: RAGAMUFFIN, Armadale Pier, Sleat, IV45 8RS. Tel. (04714) 217. A stunning collection of Scottish knitwear including jumpers, cardigans, gloves, hats and scarves. Fair Isle, Shetland, hand-knitted and designer items together with a range of original clothes in silk, cotton and locally made tweed. Also a good selection of glasswear, jewellery, books, postcards and fudge. Open Monday-Saturday 0900-evening; Sunday 1200-1700.
SKYE BATIKS. Tel. (04714) 396. Quality poplin and hand-woven cotton batik wear including shirts, trousers, dressing gowns, jackets, smocks. scarves, cushion covers, table cloths and striking wall-hangings. A variety of ancient Celtic and Pictish designs. Also an exclusive range of Celtcraft pewter jewellery, hand-made in Armadale. Quality gifts and a free cup of coffee while you look round. Access and Visa accepted. Open Monday-Saturday 0900-evening; Sunday 1200-1700.
SLEAT TRADING. Tel. (04714) 265. Outdoor clothing, wellingtons, camping items, a great selection of new and secondhand Scottish books (fill the gaps in your collection!), jewellery, prints, maps, original watercolours, slate paintings, fishing tackle, O.S. maps and a wide variety of unusual gift items. Tax Free Shopping is available for overseas visitors. Open Monday-Saturday 0830-late; Sunday 1200-1700.

Armadale To Aird Of Sleat

After the pier at Armadale, the main road south becomes the A853 and this quickly deteriorates to a very narrow single-track road. The community of Ardvasar is the first settlement to be reached. To the right can be seen the attractive white-walled Ardvasar Hotel which was built in the early 18th century as a coaching inn, one of the oldest such establishments to be found in the west of Scotland.

ARDVASAR

Eating Out: ARDVASAR HOTEL.   Tel. (04714) 223.   Non-residents welcome.   Home cooked bar lunches and suppers are served in the Hideout and An Stabull Bars. The dining room serves a choice of dishes featuring the best of local produce including Scottish beef and lamb, prawns, scallops and crabs from the Minch, venison from the Clan Donald Estate.

Mountain Guiding: PINNACLE RIDGE MOUNTAIN GUIDING.   Tel. (04714) 239. Specialising in the Cuillin Ridge. Fully guided walking and climbing programme.   Day, weekend or week-long courses are available in the summer months. Contact Colin Threfall.

Shopping: VG STORES. Tel. (04714) 214. By right of road. Groceries, offsales, Calor Gas. COTTAGE CRAFTS. Tel. (04714) 382. Situated by the left of the main road. A selection of original knitwear, pottery, jewellery, needlecraft, leather work, paintings, unusual marquetry, all produced by local craftworkers. Closed Sunday. Access, Visa and Mastercard accepted.

Toilets: By right of road, just after V.G. Stores in Ardvasar.

Yacht Charter: SLEAT MARINE SERVICES. Contact John Mannall on (04714) 216/387. Seven yachts ranging from 34-40 feet (6-8 berths) are available for short and long term charter. All equipped to a high standard for long-range cruising. Cruising area: west coast of Scotland & islands of the Hebrides. Skippers available for less experienced sailors.

Beyond Ardvasar lie the houses of Calligarry and then a large expanse of forestry is passed on the right.   At this point there are stunning views across the Sound of Sleat to the mainland hills of Knoydart. Suddenly, as you round a bend in the road, the island of Eigg comes into view ahead. There are several places where it is possible to pull off but one spot in particular, on the left just before the road descends, gives an unimpeded view of the whole breathtaking scene. From here the beautiful sandy beaches of Morar can also be distinguished on the mainland opposite.

The road now continues to climb and descend, meandering through the scattered houses. The final descent gives another stunning view of Eigg and just to the right of it can be seen the southern tip of Rum. Ahead lie the picturesque white-washed crofts of the Aird of Sleat. The final stretch of road just beyond the telephone box was constructed in June 1968 by the Sheffield Squadron. A plaque commemorating the achievement is set into a rock by a minor road junction on the left, shortly after the telephone box. The road terminates just beyond the old church (now a private residence) where there is an unsealed parking area with room for several cars. From this point on a rough track leads all the way to the lighthouse on the Point of Sleat - the southernmost tip of Skye (see Walks for full details).

THE ROAD TO TARSKAVAIG AND ORD

This scenic road provides an alternative route for the return journey north. The narrow twisty road contains steep hills and tight bends and is unsuitable for caravans. As you travel north, the road (signposted to Achnacloich) branches left at Ostaig.

Sabhal Mor Ostaig

Immediately after the Tarskavaig junction, the Gaelic College, Sabhal Mor Ostaig, can be seen to your right. Sabhal Mor Ostaig translates as "The Big Barn of Ostaig". This attractive stone building was once the steading of a MacDonald farm, now beautifully restored to house the only further education college in Scotland where classes are taught in Gaelic. Renovation was carried out during the 1970's by Sir Iain Noble's Gaelic Estate, Fearann Eilean Iarmain and in the early days the college offered a variety of short courses in Gaelic and the traditional music and arts of the Highlands. Sabhal Mor gained official recognisation as a college of further education in 1983 and since then it has greatly expanded the range of subjects on offer. Today's full-time courses in business administration, computing, rural development and the media are designed to enable students to find meaningful employment in the Highlands and Islands while at the same time promoting the native language, traditional arts and music of the Gaidealtachd. During the summer the college runs a variety of short courses which may be of interest to the visitor. Plans for the future include an accommodation block which will enable students to live on-campus, additional classroom space and new facilities for the media course - an important resource considering the rapid growth in Gaelic broadcasting in recent years.

Summer Courses: SABHAL MOR OSTAIG. Tel. (04714) 373. The college offers week long courses in Gaelic, bagpipes, fiddle, clarsach, dance, singing and the environment. For full details contact the Short Courses Administrator.

Ostaig To Tokavaig

The road climbs up away from the coast across a fairly featureless moorland area. After a couple of miles it reaches its highest point, giving good views to the south-west across the Cuillin Sound to the islands of Rum and Eigg. Also to the south-west, lying close to the western shore of the peninsula at this point and hidden amongst the rolling moorland hills, lie the deserted villages of Dalavil and Caradal. Caradal village was cleared of its people around 1880. This remote area also has the distinction of having the only canal on Skye - a mile long stretch of water which connects the fresh-water Loch a' Ghlinne to the sea. To the north of this loch lies an extensive area of 19th century beechwoods. Loch a' Ghlinne and the deserted villages can only be reached by an arduous trek across the open moor.

The road now begins to descend to Loch Dhughaill, giving spectacular views to the Cuillin and Red Hills. The hill behind the loch is known as Sgurr na h-Iolaire - the Hill of the Eagle. From this point onwards, it is easy to see why Sleat is often referred to as the "Garden of Skye". The western side of the peninsula is underlain by limestone rocks which encourage a much lusher vegetation than is usually seen elsewhere on the island. This same limestone sequence is also to be found in Strath Suardal in Strathaird. The road now passes through an area of natural woodland and then follows the Gillean Burn down past the old farm of Gillean to a beautiful sandy beach which looks out over Tarskavaig Bay. There are a few places where it is possible to pull off onto the grassy verge. There is also a picnic table. From here there are views to the Cuillin Hills, Rum and the southern part of Soay.

The houses of the crofting township of Achnacloich are seen to the right as the road begins to ascend, giving good views across Tarskavaig Bay to Tarskavaig Point. The houses of Tarskavaig are dotted about the hillside on the left. Settlement here follows the same pattern as that already noted on the east coast of the Sleat peninsula. Farming communities in this area were cleared from the inland glens by Lord MacDonald's factors around 1811 to make way for a large sheep farm. People so evicted were forced to settle on the coast. Today, Tarskavaig exhibits a typical crofting pattern with each crofter having a house and 5-10 acres of land together with access to communal grazing lands. The next section of road between Tarskavaig and Tokavaig is very twisty with several blind summits and extra care should be taken. Before long, Loch Gauscavaig is seen to the left.

Dun Sgathaich

As the road once again descends towards the shore, the ruins of Dun Sgathaich or Dunscaith Castle can be seen across the bay of Ob Gauscavaig. This is a beautiful bay, with views to the Cuillin and a large flat grassy area by the left of the road where it is possible to park. The castle can be reached by walking around the eastern shore of the bay. Care should be taken as the ruin is in a dangerous state. Dun Sgathaich is of typical medieval construction, comprising a strong curtain wall which encloses the summit plateau of a small rock promontary, affording protection to interior buildings. The landward part of the wall contains a small tower at either end, each with its own privy, and seems to be of late construction. The interior courtyard contains a small well and there are the remains of a single-storey rectangular building, also of late construction, at the western extremity. Perhaps of most interest to the onlooker are the arches which span the cleft between the landward approach and the promontary. These originally carried a wooden drawbridge backed by a stout door which gave access to a flight of stairs, flanked on either side by thick walls. The stairs led up to the entrance passage of the castle.

Dun Sgathaich is the oldest castle on Skye and is one of the oldest fortified headlands in the Hebrides. In the Celtic oral tradition it is associated with the legendary 3rd century Ulster warrior Cu Chulainn who, it is said, visited the castle to learn the arts of war from the mighty Warrior Queen Sgathaich. Tradition also states that Black Donald, the founder of the MacAskills, was hereditary keeper of the castle in the days of the Norse Kings of Man. Whatever the truth of this claim, in the 14th century Dun Sgathaich was in the hands of the MacLeods who held lands in Sleat as vassals of the Earl of Ross. Like Caisteal Chamuis, control of Dunsgaith passed to and fro between the MacLeods and MacDonalds on several occassions. From 1389 until 1401 it seems likely that the castle was occupied by Godfrey, the half-brother of Donald, 2nd Lord of the Isles. It then passed back into the hands of the MacLeods only to be overrun once again by the MacDonalds during the mismanaged regency of Ian the Ill-fated. In 1431, the castle was siezed by James I in an attempt to crush the power of the Lords of the Isles.

In 1469, Hugh, brother of John, 10th Lord of the Isles, was granted land in Sleat. It is through Hugh that the MacDonalds of Sleat trace their descent. Hugh's possessions were confirmed by Royal Charter in 1495 and it seems that by this time Dun Sgathaich had become the main residence of the MacDonalds of Sleat. The castle is first mentioned by name in 1505 when Hugh's successor John, having no heirs of his own, granted Dun Sgathaich, to Ranaldo Alansoun. Despite this charter, the castle was next occupied by John's half-brother Donald Gallach who had succeeded to the title. Donald's incumbency was to be short lived however, for he was murdered by another half-brother, Gillespic Dubh, who was jealous of the chief's possessions. Gillespic spared the life of Donald's son, Donald Gruamach, and took him into his care. This was to be his undoing for Gruamach later avenged the death of his father by stabbing Gillespic while he slept.

Donald Gruamach had assumed the leadership by 1518 and it is during his time that one of the most bloody episodes in the castle's history occurred. While resident in Dun Sgathaich with his first wife Catherine, Donald received a visit from his cousin Ranald Herrach. It is said that Ranald took an immediate dislike to the relatives of the chief's wife, finding them haughty and lacking in respect for their host. Late that night, while everyone slept, Ranald crept by each bed and murdered twelve of Catherine's kinsfolk. He then threw their bodies out of a window onto the rocks below. Catherine was to have her revenge for this horrific deed for she later hired an assassin who eventually caught up with Ranald in Uist.

Donald Gruamach was succeeded by his son, Donald Gorm, in 1534. One of the last documentary references to the castle is dated 16 January 1572 when Donald Gorm, signed at "Dounsceiche" an obligation to the Bishop of the Isles. Dun Sgathaich was eventually abandoned in 1618 when Duntulm in Trotternish became the main residence of the MacDonalds.

On The Road To Ord

The road now climbs once again and beyond Tokavaig enters an area of natural woodland known as Coille Thogabhaig which is now designated as a National Nature Reserve by Scottish Natural Heritage. This beautiful ashwood grows upon the largest southerly outcrop of Durness limestone. Intermingled with the ashes are to be found bird cherry and hawthorn.

ORD

The road descends again to the tranquil settlement of Ord which looks out over the mouth of Loch Eishort. There is room to pull off the road just before and after the bridge over the Ord River. Keep an eye out for the little groups of seals which often frequent the sheltered coastal waters here. Seals are also common around the small islands which lie to the north of Ord. Take time to wander along the shore here and admire the spectacular view across the loch to the magnificent hill of Bla Bheinn in Strathaird. The outlook from Ord to the Cuillin Ridge is considered by many people to be one of the most beautiful in Scotland and if you are here in the evening you may be rewarded by an unforgettable sunset. This magnificent view was perfectly captured on canvas in "The Cuillins From Ord" c.1854 by Horatio McCulloch, Scotland's most popular Victorian landscape painter. McCulloch met his future wife, Marcella McLellan, while on a trip to Skye and he visited the island regularly after their marriage. Marcella was the niece of Charles MacDonald who owned nearby Ord House.

Ord House

By the shore lies Ord House, once the residence of a MacDonald Laird and now a private home. It is known that there was a house standing on this site as early as 1763 and various architectural details including the great thickness of the gable walls, the height of the first floor ceilings and the roof of thick Ballachulish slates verify a late 18th century date for the building. Ord House is believed to have been constructed by one Charles MacDonald, a staunch supporter of Bonnie Prince Charlie and the Jacobite cause. After the Jacobite defeat at the Battle of Culloden in 1746, Charles went into hiding in the wilds of Moidart for several years before returning to Ord to build his house.

It was at Ord House that the author Alexander Smith wrote most of his well-known book "A Summer In Skye", published in 1865. Smith, the son of an artist, and of Highland descent, wrote poems, dramas and essays and was a friend of the landscape painter Horatio McCulloch. At the age of 28 he married a Skye girl, Flora MacDonald, a descendant of the famous Flora who helped the Young Pretender in his daring escape. His father-in-law, a retired army officer who had taken a tack of land in Sleat, was the grandson of the builder of Ord House. "A Summer In Skye" is based on Smith's annual visits to his wife's home and is part fiction, his father-in-law appearing as "Mr M'Ian". This enjoyable book is recommended to those who wish to learn of the way of life on the island during the last century, as seen through privileged eyes. Although now out of print, copies are often to be found in libraries and second-hand book shops.

St Comgan

One of the early inhabitants of Ord was St Comgan (or Chaon), an itinerant missionary who founded a church here in the 8th century which was known as Teampuill Chaon. The scant remains of this church can still be traced today in the hills above the settlement. A well associated with the Saint, Tobar Chaon, is also to be found on the shoreline, just below Ord House. Comgan later became the Patron Saint of Lochalsh.

ORD

Garden: AN ARCARSAID. Garden open from 1200-1730 in aid of the Lifeboat Fund. Entrance is through the blue gate on the coast, at the pull off just after the bridge.

Shopping: THE STUDIO. Marquetry.

The road now turns east and follows the Ord River upstream through patches of birch, ash and oak woodland. As the glen begins to open up, the crags of Sgiath-bheinn an Uird can be seen to the left while to the right lies Sgiath-bheinn Chrossavaig. Another extensive area of birchwood known as Coill a' Ghasgain is passed. The road descends past Loch Meodal to rejoin the A851 at Loch nan Dubhrachan 2 1/4 miles south of Isleornsay.

STRATHAIRD

Strathaird has much to delight lovers of spectacular scenery. The views of the Cuillin from Elgol are thought by many to be the finest on the island while the east coast of the peninsula delights in the more serene aspect of the gentle hills of Sleat rising above the waters of Loch Slapin. Strathaird contains several sites of antiquarian interest and here too the visitor can follow in the footsteps of his Victorian predecessors by taking the famous boat trip to remote Loch Coruisk.

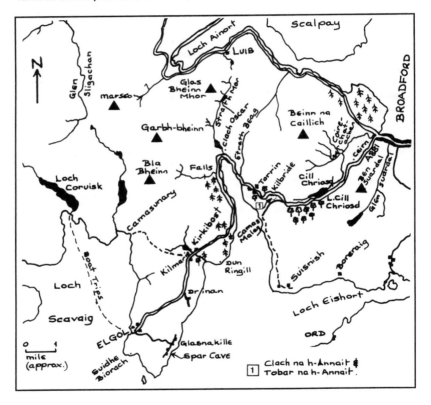

The single-track A881 to Elgol branches south from the A850 at Broadford. After the Broadford Hotel, the landscape opens up and the scene to the right is dominated by the great Beinn na Caillich horseshoe which surrounds Coire Gorm. The road passes through an attractive countryside of rolling hills and moorland, dotted here and there with patches of forestry.

Strictly speaking, this first low-lying section of ground centred on Broadford forms the district of Strath, which also includes the islands of Scalpay and Pabay. Strath was formerly the possession of Clan MacKinnon, who held the hereditary position of marshals to the MacDonalds of the Isles. The MacKinnons are one of the branches of the Siol Alpine and claim descent from Fingon, a great grandson of Kenneth MacAlpin, the 9th century King of Dalriada. The Clan obtained the lands of Strath in 1354 and also held extensive possessions in Mull. In 1409, Lachlan MacKinnon witnessed a charter to the Lord of the Isles and the history of the MacKinnons remained closely bound up with that of the MacDonalds until the forfeiture of the Lordship in 1493.

As the road reaches a sharp Z-bend, the remains of a chambered cairn can be seen on a little knoll to the right. It is possible to pull off onto the grassy verge nearby to examine the remains. Chambered cairns were the communal burial places of the first Neolithic settlers who farmed the fertile coastal areas of Skye. Originally, the burial passage would have been covered by a large mound of stones but much of this has been subsequently robbed and the site is now largely covered with turf. This cairn is known as An Sidhean or the Fairy Hill. The knoll on which it sits is a superb vantage point from which to view the surrounding countryside.

Coirechatachan

To the north-west of the chambered cairn, lying in the broad bottom of Strath Suardal close to the Broadford River, are the ruins of Coirechatachan. This was once the family home of the Chief of Clan MacKinnon. In 1772, the renowned Welsh traveller Thomas Pennant spent two nights there during his tour of Scotland. The following year, Dr Johnson and James Boswell were guests of the MacKinnon Chief from Monday 6th to Wednesday 8th September, and during their stay the two met with fine company and were lavishly entertained. In his *Journey To The Western Island Of Scotland* published in 1775, Johnson recorded, "From Armidel we came at night to Coriatachan, a house very pleasantly situated between two brooks, with one of the highest hills of the island behind it. It is the residence of Mr MacKinnon, by whom we were treated with very liberal hospitality, among a more numerous and elegant company than it could have been supposed easy to collect." Johnson was greatly impressed by the variety of fine books at Coirechatachan whereas Boswell was delighted by the excellent food: "We had for supper a large dish of minced beef collops, a large dish of fricassee of fowl, I believe a dish called fried chicken or something like it, a dish of ham or tongue, some excellent haddocks, some herrings, a large bowl of rich milk, frothed, as good a bread pudding as I ever tasted, full of raisins and lemon or orange peel, and sillabubs made with port wine and in sillabub glasses. There was a good table-cloth with napkins; china, silver spoons, porter if we chose it, and a large bowl of very good punch".

Johnson and Boswell later spent a further two days at Coirechatachan on their way back to Armadale. On this occassion Boswell drank cup after cup of punch and fell to calling the MacKinnon chief "Corri". He finally crawled into bed at 5am with little recollection of what had passed and awoke at noon the next day with a severe headache. The Chief and his friends later assembled in Boswell's bedroom and insisted that he partake of a little medicinal brandy. "Aye," said Dr Johnson, "Fill him drunk again. Do it in the morning, that we may laugh at him all day."

The Ben Suardal Marble Quarries

As the road emerges from the Z-bend, the keen-eyed traveller may be able to detect the faint line which runs horizontally across the hillside on the left. This is the line of the old narrow-guage railway which used to transport marble from quarries on Ben Suardal to the pier at Broadford. The Ben Suardal quarries were worked in the 19th century and extraction continued until 1912. The fine black, white and grey Strath marble was said to be more beautiful than Italian marble but harder to work. Marble from Strath was used for the Gothic fireplace and staircase in Gillespie Graham's Armadale Castle, the Duke of Hamilton paved the lobby of Hamilton Palace with it, the main altar at Iona is carved from it and the old manse of Strath was built entirely of the white and grey forms. It is also said to have been used in the Vatican and the Palace of Versailles.

The road now descends into Strath Suardal. To the right lies the Broadford River which winds its way along the broad bottom of the strath and flows into the sea at the west end of Broadford Bay.

Cill Chriosd

Before long, the ancient church of Cill Chriosd is seen to the right. There is a large parking space opposite. This church served as the Parish Church of Strath until 1840. The site first enters the history books in 1505 when it is recorded that Kenneth Adamson succeeded John MacGillivray as chaplain. Adamson was replaced firstly by Sir John Johneson and then in 1508 by John Ranaldson. In those days, the people of the glen were followers of the Catholic faith and it was not until 1627 that the first Protestant minister, Neil MacKinnon, was appointed. Many tales are told of MacKinnon's meanness. It is said that on Sundays the minister would only provide his workmen with one meal because it was a day of rest, whereas he was prepared to allow them two meals on other days. One Sunday, while MacKinnon was in the church preaching his usual sermon of charity and goodwill, some of his workmen seated on a nearby hill could stand their hunger no longer. Taking up their ploughs, they decided that it was better for them not to have a day of rest at all than to starve. This episode embarrassed the good Reverend MacKinnon who at that moment was leaving the church with his powerful and well-to-do friends and from that day on he saw to it that his workmen received two meals on Sundays.

The present church building is believed to date from the late 16th or early 17th century. It replaces an older stone building on the same site - fragments of a window from this earlier church were built into the apex of the west gable and can still be seen today. Further fragments of decorated architectural mouldings were discovered during recent renovations and these suggest that the original building was a finely decorated and imposing medieval church.

Legend also associates the site with St Maelrubha, an itinerant missionary who is believed to have set up a religious cell here in the 7th century. It is said that before the church was built, the saint and his followers preached and administered the mass on a small knoll between the present ruins and Loch Cill Chriosd known as Cnoc na-Aifhreann or The Hill of The Mass.

It is worth taking time to wander amongst the many interesting gravestones in the burial ground. Situated to the left as you enter the gate and lying flat on the ground is a medieval grave slab with beautifully carved foliate cross. Several accounts of the church made earlier this century record that there were a number of other decorated stones within the burial ground. Unfortunately, these have all since disappeared. The burial gound is also the last resting place of many of the Clan MacKinnon of Coirechatachan.

Loch Cill Chriosd

Shortly after the Cill Chriosd church, the road passes close to the shore of the pretty reed filled loch of the same name. In summer, this stretch of water is covered with attractive pink and white water lilies. Tradition holds that Loch Cill Chriosd was once the haunt of an evil spirit that was so malevolent anyone bathing in the waters or drinking from them would die. It is said that this spirit was chased away by St Columba when he visited Skye around 570, rendering the water safe and wholesome. The area must have proved highly attractive to supernatural beings however, for the loch later became the haunt of a black water horse or each uisge. This particular water horse appeared in the form of a handsome young man and in this guise, he seduced the young women of the area and galloped off into the loch with them. His reign of terror came to an end when he mistook a young priest in long flowing robes for a woman. The priest, under the protection of God, was able to convert the water horse to Christianity and the loch has been safe ever since.

There is a small pull-off opposite the eastern end of the loch which is the starting point of an easy walk to Cill Chriosd deserted village and the old marble quarries on Ben Suardal (see Walks for full details).

To the left of Loch Cill Chriosd is an area of attractive natural woodland known as Coille Gaireallach. The lush greenery here owes its existence to a band of limestone which runs through this part of Strathaird, giving rise to a very fertile soil. From this point there are good views to the Red Hills ahead.

Kilbride and Camas Malag

Shortly after Loch Cill Chriosd, a left fork leads to the houses of Kilbride. From this minor road there are excellent views to Torrin Marble Quarry (see below). Partially hidden by trees on the right is a large white house that was once the manse of Strath. When the old manse at Cill Chriosd fell into ruin early in the 19th century it was abandoned and the house and farm of Kilbride were rented out by John MacKinnon who became minister of Strath in 1825. One famous visitor to the Kilbride manse was the eminent 19th century geologist, Sir Archibald Geikie, whose studies took him on frequent expeditions to the Hebrides. There was once an early Christian chapel at Kilbride, dedicated to St Bridget, from which the place derives its name. Associated with this site is a standing stone known as Clach na h-Annait which can be seen in the field to the right, just before the old manse, and a spring, Tobar na h-Annait, now visible as a marshy area adjacent to the stone.

The left fork after "Ashbank" leads to the attractive bay of Camas Malag. This road is a little rutted but is easily navigable as far as the bay where there is plenty of room to park on the grassy verge. This pretty little bay with its pebble beach overlooking Loch Slapin is a lovely place for a picnic. There are excellent views across the loch to the lofty heights of Bla Bheinn and Garbh-bheinn. Camas Malag is the starting point of a popular walk to the Clearance villages of Suisnish and Boreraig (see Walks for full details).

The Torrin Marble Quarry

Retracing your route to the A881, the main road continues through an area of woodland which gives glimpses over the Torrin Marble Quarry on the left to Loch Slapin. The brilliant white marble found here is the result of ancient forces of heat and pressure acting on the band of limestone which runs through Strathaird at this point. The Torrin workings were begun in 1951 by William Thomson Forsyth, a Glasgow paint manufacturer. Forsyth took out a lease on the land, extracted the marble and ground it up for agricultural usage. By 1965, the works were producing up to 3,000 tons per year. Most of this output was sold locally in Skye, but a small amount was shipped to Lewis. In 1966, Messrs N. MacLeod & Co Ltd of Portree came to an arrangement with the quarry owners Kneeshaw Lupton & Co. to extract stone for building purposes. By 1969 they had built up a thriving business shipping marble all over Scotland and in 1970 they purchased the Torrin quarry. Today the marble is used in the manufacture of artificial stone panels and as decorative stone chips for pebble-dash. It has also been used locally in the manufacture of souvenirs.

Torrin To Kilmarie

Shortly after the entrance to the quarry is passed on the left, the road swings right into the settlement of Torrin and descends to the loch side. Here the scene is completely dominated by the huge mass of Bla Bheinn on the far shore of Loch Slapin. Just to the right of Bla Bheinn rises the slightly smaller Garbh-bheinn. These two gabbro mountains belong to the "Black" Cuillin group but are detached from the main ridge which rises above Glen Brittle. Another small marble quarry is passed on the right and then the road makes its way to the head of the loch.

It is possible to park by the side of the road, just before the bridge over the river at the head of Loch Slapin. If you walk up the distinct track on the right for c.200m you will see a large grey boulder just to the right of the river. This is known as Clach Oscar. Tradition holds that this great stone was thrown from an adjacent hilltop by Oscar, one of a mythical race of giants known as the Fienne. From this point, you can see the beginnings of Strath Mor, the broad strath which links Loch Slapin with Luib on the shores of Loch Ainort. This through route is very popular with walkers.

The road now crosses the Loch Slapin Bridge which was built with the aid of E.C. funding. Parking is also possible just after the bridge on a section of the old road on your right. The A881 now bends southwards and runs along the foot of Bla Bheinn. Here the difference between the Black and Red Cuillin can be seen clearly - the black gabbro of Bla Bheinn to the right, the red granite of Beinn na Caillich and Beinn na Cro behind Torrin. The road continues along the east coast of the Strathaird peninsula, a thin finger of land which juts down between Loch Slapin and Loch Scavaig. Before long, the Allt na Dunaiche is seen to the right. This small river flows into Loch Slapin immediately before a large conifer plantation. On this river lie the Falls of Slapin - they can be glimpsed from the road, just above the trees. If you would like a closer look, there is space for one car to park by the right of the road, just after the bridge. A distinct path follows the right bank of the river and passes the falls. This is the route commonly taken by walkers ascending Bla Bheinn.

The road now begins to climb, giving good views across the loch to the marble quarry opposite. In the loch can be seen the fish cages belonging to Strathaird Farms Ltd, one of the enterprises owned by rock star Iain Anderson, singer with Jethro Tull. The mountains are left behind as the road continues to climb high above Loch Slapin, passing through a lush area of conifers dotted with patches of natural woodland, bracken and foxgloves. Soon, the A881 begins to turn inland, passing the crag of An Carnach and at its highest point there is a view to the distant mainland hills.

Before long, the road enters the little settlement of Kirkibost which merges into the area known as Kilmarie, once home to the Chiefs of Clan MacKinnon. Just after the bridge, a small road branches left to Old Kilmarie Graveyard. This road follows the river bank through an area of attractive woodland to the old village graveyard. En route it passes Kilmarie House which was built for the chiefs of the MacKinnons after Castle Moil at Kyleakin had been abandoned - note the hunting kennels to the left of the road, just before the house. Kilmarie is the starting point of a pleasant coastal walk to Dun Ringill (see Walks for full details). The narrow road continues around the coast for a short distance, giving great views to the Sleat Peninsula opposite.

Kilmarie To Elgol

On returning to the main A881, note the large area of lazy beds on the hillside to the right, just after the Kilmarie turnoff, evidence of past agricultural activities in the area. Running across the same hillside is a track leading west to the secluded bay at Camasunary 2 1/2 miles away. From here, footpaths continue on to Loch Coruisk at the heart of the Cuillin and through to Glen Sligachan. The jeep track to the hunting lodge at Camasunary was cut by the Army back in 1968 amid great protests that it would destroy the feeling of wilderness in the remote Cuillin. The Army was also asked to build a footbridge across the Camasunary River, improve the track to Coruisk and bridge the River Scavaig. Happily, the "improvements" stopped short of the proposal to dynamite the Bad Step, a large rock outcrop which blocks the shore path to Coruisk making this a difficult approach for the casual tourist.

The road now climbs up away from the river, passing the modern village cemetery on the left. As height is gained there are good views to the Sleat Peninsula. An area of old peat cuttings is crossed at the foot of Ben Meabost - deer may sometimes be seen here. After the turnoff to Drinan, the road swings inland and begins to climb once again. Before long, the first houses of Elgol are reached, scattered along the foot of Ben Cleat. The road winds amongst the croft houses and begins a steep descent. This last section is unsuitable for caravans - there is a convenient parking spot at the top of the hill. As you pass through the village note the many remains of old black houses, evidence of the long period of settlement in this area.

The road descends to an excellent viewpoint which looks out across Loch Scavaig. Many people consider this to be the best roadside view of the Cuillin anywhere on the island. From right to left can be seen the jagged ridge of the Black Cuillin and the islands of Soay, Canna, Sanday and Rum. Brilliant sunsets can often be seen from this point, with the sun glinting off the water of the loch and back-lighting the jagged peaks of the Cuillin which sweep straight into the sea from a height of over 3,000 feet. On fair days Loch Slapin has an altogether serene appearance about it but in bad weather, with sudden gusts of wind rushing down from the mountains, it is a notoriously difficult stretch of water to navigate.

In Victorian days, Elgol was the departure point of a popular boat trip to remote Loch Coruisk, one of the most famous lochs in the Highlands, painted by J.M.W Turner and written about by Sir Walter Scott. This same boat trip can still be taken today and is highly recommended for those who do not wish to make the long trek in to the loch on foot. Elgol was also the departure point of Bonnie Prince Charlie in July 1746 during his lengthy flight from the Redcoat troops. It was here that the Prince, disguised as a servant,

met the elderly chief of the MacKinnons who helped him to escape to the wild Morar coastline. Legend has it that before leaving Skye, the Prince presented MacKinnon of Strathaird with the secret recipe of a whisky liqueur. Today this drink is known to us as Drambuie and is now manufactured in Edinburgh by a family owned company. The Drambuie motto - *Cuimhnich an tabhartas Prionnsa* (Remember the gift of the Prince) is proudly displayed on each bottle. Prior to his departure, the Young Pretender was hidden in a cave on the coast to the south of Elgol. Adjacent to this cave is the promontory known as Suidhe Biorach or the Sharp Seat. Tradition has it that childless women were supposed to become fertile after sitting there.

From the carpark, a right fork leads down to the little jetty. Parking is very tricky there and it is easier to take the time to walk down to the shore to explore the fascinating coastal cliffs. The Elgol cliffs are comprised of outcrops of Jurassic limestone, 150 million years old, which have weathered into an intricate honey-comb pattern. From the shore, the view to the Cuillin hills opens up to the right. This is the only road-side stop which allows a clear view to Sgurr na Stri (the Peak of Strife) at the heart of the Cuillin. The remote bay and buildings at Camasunary (Camas Fhionnairigh) can also be made out.

ELGOL

Cruises: Boat trips on board M.F.V. BELLA JANE depart from Elgol Pier, 7 days a week, April-October. Bookings are accepted for day trips - see Loch Coruisk the easy way! Climbers, anglers and diving parties are welcome. The Loch Coruisk trip is extremely popular so the earlier you arrive the better. All trips weather permitting. For full details, telephone the skipper/owner Donald S. MacKinnon on (04716) 244.

Eating Out: THE CUILLIN VIEW RESTAURANT. Opposite the parking area. Serves teas, coffees and takeaway foods. Crafts.

Mountain Guiding: BADGER'S GUIDED WALKS. Tel. (04716) 228.

Toilets: Situated on the A881, opposite the Elgol viewpoint.

The Island Of Soay

From Elgol, a good view is obtained of the adjacent island of Soay. Prior to 1823, only one family lived there, tending stock. Then, during the Highland Clearances, the island recieved an influx of land-hungry crofters who had been evicted from Skye to make way for sheep and by 1861 the population had risen to 129. In 1946, Soay was bought by the author Gavin Maxwell with the intention of setting up a basking shark fishery. He built a landing slip and a small factory, but due to a fall in the demand for shark oil, the enterprise ran into trouble soon afterwards and was abandoned in 1949. The failed project is described in his book "Harpoon At A Venture", published in 1952. In 1950, the idea was briefly revived by Maxwell's harpooner, Tex Geddes, operating on a reduced scale from Mallaig and Soay. Geddes wrote of his attempts in "Hebridean Sharker", published in 1960. Competition from a more sophisticated fleet of Norwegian shark boats brought this second venture to an end in 1951 and the Soay islanders were taken on board SS Hebrides amid much publicity and re-settled on Mull. By 1953, only Geddes and his family remained. Since then, Soay has received various settlers, most seeking an "alternative" way of life. In recent years the island has been home to lobster fishermen and a small artists' colony.

Elgol To Glasnakille

From the Elgol viewpoint, a left fork leads to the remote community of Glasnakille. This road is not for the faint-hearted - it must be one of the narrowest on the island and has few passing places. The road climbs from the viewpoint, following the Allt Port na Cullaidh for a short distance and passes close to a Trig Point on a small knoll to the left. It is possible to pull off by the left of the road here if you wish to climb up to the Trig Point to take in the view. The road continues to snake its way across open moorland and passes close to a Repeater Station on the right. The remains of old peat banks can be seen just to the right of the station. It is worth climbing up to this relay station for breathtaking views of the Cuillin and Small Isles. Also keep a look out for the deer which are often to be seen on this high moorland.

Then road now begins a long descent to the T-junction at Glasnakille. From the junction, the road to the left passes several houses, giving fine views to Sleat and ends in a turning circle. A track continues beyond the last cottage and cuts across the hillside to Drinan. Parking is extremely difficult here, the best option being a grassy cutting by the left of the road several hundred yards back. Do not block the turning circle. The right hand road at the junction also ends in a turning circle, with views to Canna, Rum, Muck, Eigg and Sleat. Again, parking is a problem, as there are few grassy areas on which to pull off. Do not block gateways.

Spar Cave

On the coast below the Glasnakille T-junction lies the fabled Spar Cave. Access is difficult, but it is possible to reach the cave at low tide by scrambling down a steep path which begins about 100m south of the junction, just beyond a stone byre. Remember to take a torch. Spar Cave was a favourite tourist destination in Victorian days and special excursions operated regularly from several points on Skye and from Mallaig. The main chamber has the lofty proportions of a cathedral and was once hung with hundreds of translucent stalactites. Beyond, a passageway leads to a great stone staircase which gives access to an inner water-filled chamber. Sir Walter Scott visited Spar Cave on 25 August 1814 and was moved to described it thus in his epic poem "Lord of the Isles":

"Mermaid's alabaster grot,
Who bathes her limbs in sunless well,
Deep in Strathaird's enchanted cell...
His foot is on the marble floor,
And o'er his head the dazzling spars,
Gleam like a firmament of stars."

Sadly, as fame of this natural wonder spread, the cave was pillaged by souvenir hunters. The owner, Mr M. Macallister, built a 9ft wall around the entrance with a stout door in an attempt to protect the stalactites. This did not meet with much success and people continued to climb in, including Scott and friends who scaled the wall with the aid of a rope. The black smoke from countless torches also began to dull the beautiful silver sheen which was originally one of the cave's chief attractions. By the time the cave was visited by Henry Thomas, Lord Cockburn in September 1841, this natural wonder was almost completely destroyed. Thomas later wrote, "At present the only reward for going in consists in getting out."

BROADFORD TO SLIGACHAN

BROADFORD

The little town of Broadford is the second largest on the island, after Portree. It is Skye's biggest crofting township, comprising several small settlements which have gradually merged to form one long, straggling village astride the A850. The wide bay which fronts the town has long been known as a safe anchorage and in the days of the steamships, Broadford was an important stopping off point for passenger and cargo boats en route to Portree. This part of the island is dominated by the huge outline of Beinn na Caillich which rises to the west of the town.

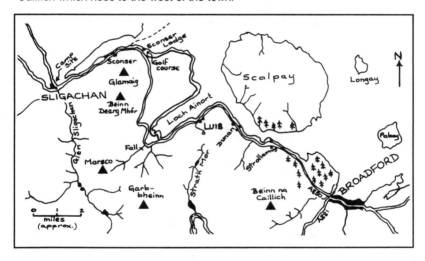

Broadford contains a well preserved lime kiln which is well worth seeing. In the 19th century, the limestone outcrops in the vicinity of the township were an important source of agricultural fertilizer. To find the kiln, park in the Tourist Office carpark and walk towards the petrol station. A blue sign points the way to the coast. A short 5 minute stroll will take you along the coast to the kiln and an attractive old stone pier (the route is only possible at low tide). The kiln would have been fuelled with coal or coke brought in by sea, although peat may also have been used. Fuel and limestone would have been unloaded straight into the shafts which can still be seen by climbing up behind the kiln. After burning, the quick-lime was removed through the draw-holes below. From the kiln, you can retrace your steps or head up past the Gallery and Borealis to the main Broadford road. Another pleasant walk can be had by taking the A854 to Corry at the west end of the town. From here, a short Forest Enterprise walk continues along the coast to Rubh' an Eireannaich or Irishman's Point.

BROADFORD

Bank: BANK OF SCOTLAND. Tel. (0471) 822 211.

Bike Hire: FAIRWINDS BICYCLE HIRE. Elgol Road (2nd bungalow on left past Broadford Hotel). Tel. (0471) 822 270. Bikes for daily and weekly hire. Also spares and repairs.

Car Hire: SUTHERLANDS GARAGE. Tel. (0471) 822 225. Free collection from Kyleakin. Collection and return to other places can be arranged. Credit cards accepted.

Early Closing: Wednesday.

Eating Out: BROADFORD HOTEL. Tel. (0471) 822 204. Non-residents welcome. Bar meals served throughout the day in the public and lounge bars. Table d'hote dinner available in the restaurant.
CLAYMORE RESTAURANT. Tel. (0471) 822 333. Teas, coffees, home baking, snacks, lunches and dinners using mainly local produce. Open April-October daily 1000-2200.
CREELERS. Tel. (0471) 822 281. Takeaway food and licensed delicatessen. Seafood, pizzas, baked potatoes, quiches, lasagnas, vegetarian dishes, cooked meats and cheeses. Open 1200 to 2330. Closed Wednesday.
DUNOLLIE HOTEL. Tel. (0471) 822 253. Non-residents welcome, bookings preferred. A la Carte and Table d'Hote menus are served in the Torridon View Restaurant and bar food is also available in the Crowlin Bar and Red Hills Lounge. The Crowlin Bar has regular live music.
HARBOUR GRILL. Full meals and snacks.
THE STRATHCORRIE. Tel. (0471) 822 616. Licensed restaurant. Open daily 1100-2100 or later. Take-away food situated round side of building - chips, pizzas etc.

Environmental Centre: SKYE ENVIRONMENTAL CENTRE. Tel. (0471) 822 487. The Centre acts as a base for the rescue of sick and injured wildlife and is also involved in geological and biological recording. An interesting museum contains displays on the geology and natural history of Skye. The Museum shop stocks a selection of postcards, posters and books on the natural history, geology and archaeology of the island. There is also a small wildlife garden and coastal trail and guided walks can be arranged. Open Monday-Saturday 0900-1700. Admission is free but donations are welcome.

Petrol: SUTHERLANDS GARAGE. Tel. (0471) 822 225. Also sells groceries, newspapers, crafts, ice-cream, coal and kindling.

Serpentarium: SKYE SERPENTARIUM, The Old Mill. Tel. (0471) 822 209/533. A fascinating reptile zoo containing a variety of beautiful snakes and lizards. Open daily Easter to October or by arrangement at all other times. Access is usually possible outwith normal hours by telephoning first.

Shopping: BOREALIS. Tel. (0471) 822 669. A herbal beauty shop which stocks a variety of skin care products including Beauty Without Cruelty make-up, moisturisers, shampoos, soaps, perfumes, essential oils and aromatherapy oils. Many products are made on the premises. Aromatherapy massage is available by appointment. The shop also stocks a range of wholefoods. Open Monday-Saturday 0930-1700.
BROADFORD BAY STORES & BAKERY. Tel. (0471) 822 224. Bread, scones, delicious Strath bread and sandwiches. Also groceries, hardware, 24-hour film developing. Here you can buy the amazing anti-midge hood - the only sure-fire protecting against these annoying little insects! Open Monday-Friday 0700-1700; Saturday 0730-1600.
BROADFORD BOOKS, The Old Post Office Building. Tel. (0471) 822 748. A wide selection of books including an excellent range of Scottish interest material. Also graphic and artists' materials, picture framing, book binding. Credit cards accepted.
BROADFORD GALLERY, Old Pier Road. Tel. (0471) 822 011. Prints, including a selection of Skye designs screenprinted by hand on to textiles by Rae of Solas Prints.
CO-OP SUPERMARKET. Tel. (0471) 822 203.

(Continued)

CRAFT ENCOUNTERS, Broadford Post Office. Tel. (0471) 822 201. A superb range of quality crafts hand-made in the Highlands and Islands including Aran, Fair Isle and Harris knitwear, Celtic jewellery, pottery, glassware, Pictish wall-hangings, Scottish books, cards and postcards. Open Monday-Saturday 0900-1730; Sunday 1100-1500.

LIVING LIGHT CANDLE WORKSHOP. Tel. (0471) 822 669. A wide range of unusual candles, including the Hanging Reed Candle made from a reed picked on Skye. Also hand painted and silk-screened T-shirts with Celtic designs, native birds and Skye scenery. It is occasionally possible to watch the candles and T-shirts being manufactured on the premises. Open Monday-Saturday 0930-1700.

STEWART OF SKYE. Tel. (0471) 822 535. A good selection of knitwear, tweeds and crafts.

SKYE JEWELLERY. Tel. (0471) 822 100. A range of jewellery, watches, clocks and dried flower arrangements. Also jewellery repairs, cleaning and watch batteries. Commissions accepted. You can watch the jeweller at work.

SUTHERLANDS GARAGE.   Tel. (0471) 822 225.   Crafts and gifts, drinks, snacks, photographic film and newspapers. Convenience store open 24 hours a day.

THE TOP SHOP. Licensed grocer and newsagent. Open until 2000.

Toilets: Situated by the A850, opposite the carpark at the Tourist Information Centre.

Tourist Information Centre: On the main street, next to Sutherland's Garage.

Broadford To Strollamus

Beyond Broadford, the view to the left is dominated by the rounded mass of Beinn na Caillich which rises above the flat expanse of Strath Suardal. At the summit of the mountain is a huge cairn which is clearly visible from the road. Tradition has it that this cairn covers the last resting place of the Norwegian Princess known as "Saucy Mary" who lived at Castle Moil in Kyleakin. Her dying wish was to be buried where the winds from her native land would pass over her grave.

The Island Of Scalpay

The road passes through an area of pine forestry and on emerging from the trees a fine view is to be had to the island of Scalpay which is separated from Skye by a narrow channel known as Caolas Scalpay. Scattered fish farm cages are often to be seen in the water at this point. The famous travellers Johnson and Boswell sailed past Scalpay on Wednesday 8 September 1773, en route from Coirechatachan in Strathaird to Raasay. In his journal, Boswell recorded that Dr Johnson was much taken with the island: "Dr Johnson proposed that he and I should buy it, and found a good school, and an episcopal church, and have a printing-press, where he would print all the Erse (Gaelic) that could be found." In the 19th century, Scalpay was bought and developed by Sir Donald Currie who spent a large amount of money on building roads and planting trees. Today, the island is mainly used for deer farming. To the west of Scalpay House lie the remains of a chapel which was built on an early Christian site dedicated to St Fillan.

Strollamus To Luib

The road continues around the coast, passing through the small communities of Strollamus, Dunan and Ard Dorch. The southern tip of the island of Raasay gradually comes into view behind Scalpay. After Ard Dorch, the road bends to the south-west to follow the shore of Loch Ainort. Ahead rises the dramatic hill of Glamaig, which appears as a striking round-topped pyramid from this angle. Before long, the settlement of Luib is reached, with its attractive reconstructed thatched and white-washed croft house by the shore.

LUIB

Museum: LUIB FOLK MUSEUM. Tel. (0471) 822 427. A fascinating museum opened in 1978 by local man Peter MacAskill, depicting living conditions in the early 20th century. The museum takes the form of a fully furnished and restored black-house, complete with thatched roof, which contains a wealth of genuine household and agricultural implements. During the restoration of the black-house, two guns dating from the 1745 Jacobite Rising were found hidden under the roof. Lots of interesting photographs and news cuttings tell of the restoration of the croft (all by local craftsmen), together with many articles concerning the island's recent history. A new display tells of the wanderings on Skye of the fugitive Bonnie Prince Charlie. An innovative museum which brings the island's past to life. Open daily 0900-1800. Admission fee applies.

Eating Out: THE PIPER'S MOON COFFEE HOUSE. Tel. (0471) 822 594. Located next to the Folk Museum. Tea, coffee, sandwiches and cream teas. Table licence. Also knitwear, gifts and cards. Open daily, including Sundays, 0900-1800.

Luib To Sconser

As you continue your journey up Loch Ainort, the Red Hills begin to close around, creating an almost claustraphobic atmosphere. Several of the main peaks can be seen from this point - Glas Bheinn Mhor, Bla Bheinn and Garbh-bheinn to the south, Marsco with its gushing burn to the south-west and the great mass of Glamaig to the north-west. In the late 19th century, this wild countryside began to attract artists to the island and as tales of the grand scenery spread, Skye became a mecca for landscape painters. One of the first to visit the island was the Victorian painter Sidney Cooper, who made the journey in the summer of 1882 accompanied by his son. In his autobiography published in 1890, Cooper wrote of his journey from Broadford to Sligachan,"...truly the road thither was full of wonders. The scenery was grand and sublime. The whole way to Sligachan was wonderfully beautiful; the glens through which we passed one after the other were all of the grand type, and I saw no scenery in Switzerland so suited for pictures as this part of Great Britain." Cooper was so impressed with the island that he urged other landscape painters to make the journey to Skye.

At the head of Loch Ainort, the motorist has a choice of two routes: the main A850 or the single track coastal road to Moll which rejoins the main road just before the Sconser Lodge Hotel. The latter is known as "The Scenic Route".

The Scenic Route To Sconser

The single track road to Moll branches right from the main road at the head Loch Ainort. This narrow road continues around the shore of the loch, crossing two rivers which descend from the Red Hills to the west. Before the building of the A850, this was the main route to the north of the island. This coastal road in turn replaced the original mid-19th century road which ascended the steep hillside on the left known as Druim nan Cleochd. Traces of this early route can still be seen by the white house a short distance beyond the second river. The original road followed the right bank of the burn just behind this house and climbed up and over the hillside before descending to Sconser. Today this road has been largely reclaimed by the moor but it can still be detected in places as a faint line in the vegetation. The Druim nan Cleochd was so steep that in the early days of motorized transport, bus passengers had to alight and walk behind their vehicles to enable them to ascend.

The road continues around the shore of Loch Ainort, past the jetty used by Cairidh Salmon Farm, whose fish farm cages are often to be seen at the head of the loch. This farm is owned by Marine Harvest. The road begins to climb and passes along the foot of the long slope of Leathad Chrithinn. From this point there are good views across the loch to the Red Hills opposite. At the mouth of Loch Ainort, the road bends north-westwards and dips to cross the Moll River. Here there are good views right across the narrow channel to the island of Scalpay. Ahead can be seen the southern tip of Raasay which is separated from Scalpay by the channel of Caol Mor. In summer, this section of road is very attractive, being lined by verges filled with foxgloves and pink and white rambling roses. There are a few places where it is possible to pull off by the roadside here and there is also a small parking space by a wooden seat surrounded by pink rambling roses from which there are good views to Raasay. At this point there are also footpaths to the shore. As the road bends westwards, there are views up the Narrows of Raasay to Trotternish beyond. The road now passes the Sconser quarry complex and crosses the Abhainn Torra-mhichaig before rejoining the A850 by Sconser golf course.

The Main Route (A850) To Sconser

At the head of Loch Ainort, the main A850 pulls away from the shore. Just before the road begins to ascend, an attractive waterfall is seen to the left as you cross a small bridge. This waterfall can be quite spectacular after heavy rain. As height is gained, fine views are to be had to the right over the loch - there are a couple of unmarked areas where it is possible to pull off to admire the scenery. The hills soon close in however, and the rest of the journey to Sconser is dominated by the brooding mass of Glamaig to the left. This part of the road can be quite gloomy, as the Red Hills often attract bad weather even while the northern part of the island is bathed in sunshine. During wet periods the scene can be dramatic, with myriad rivulets of water gushing down the sides of the hill. The slopes of the mountain are a striking mix of red and green streaks created by alternating strips of vegetation and rock scree. Glamaig has a long ridge with several tops and it seems to take an interminably long time to traverse the bleak moorland at its base. When the road eventually begins to descend and Gleann Torra-mhichaig opens up ahead, the view to the sea and the fantastically shaped Trotternish Ridge beyond comes as quite a relief. The distinctive flat topped mass of Dun Caan on the island of Raasay can also be seen to the right. Just before the road levels out, note the many small rounded hills on the lower slopes of Glamaig. These are glacial mounds, comprised of sand and gravel debris left here by a melting glacier at the end of the last Ice Age, some 10,000 years ago.

Sconser Lodge

At the foot of the glen, the road once again follows the coast, passing the Isle of Skye Golf Course and the Sconser Lodge Hotel. The present Sconser Lodge was built in 1881 by Lord MacDonald of Sleat as a hunting lodge. Prior to this, there was an old inn on the site which received many famous guests, including Dr Johnson and James Boswell who dined there on Saturday 25 September 1773 during their tour of the Hebrides. The old inn was also the clandestine meeting place of three Highland Chiefs during the time of the Jacobite Rebellion. Here, in August 1745, Clanranald, Chief of the MacDonalds of Uist was sent from Glenfinnan where the clans were gathering around the banner of Prince Charles, to meet with two Skye Chiefs, Sir Alexander MacDonald of Sleat and MacLeod of MacLeod, to debate whether to ride out with Bonnie Prince Charlie. It is said that at first support was forthcoming, but after the receipt of several letters from Inverness a few hours later the two Skye Chiefs decided against rising with the Prince. They went on instead to summon their clans to support King George, but this met with poor response because Skye was largely sympathetic to the Young Pretender and indeed many clansmen disobeyed their chiefs and went to fight for the Prince as private individuals.

SCONSER

Eating Out: SCONSER LODGE HOTEL. Tel. (0478) 650 333. Non-residents welcome. Restaurant open 1900-2100. 3-course bar meals and snacks are also available: bar lunches are served from 1200-1400 and bar suppers from 1800 onwards.

Golf: THE ISLE OF SKYE GOLF COURSE. Visitors welcome. 9-hole course. Clubhouse with extended facilities.

The Raasay Ferry: Skye's neighbouring island of Raasay is reached by a 15 minute trip on board a small vehicular ferry which departs from Sconser Pier. The ferry operates from April-October on Mondays-Saturdays only. Several trips are made each day. There is no petrol on Raasay so if you take your car be sure to fill up on Skye before you go. For further details, see the current timetable at Sconser Pier.

Toilets: Public toilets are located at the Raasay Ferry pier.

The Island of Raasay

The island of Raasay was once the possession of the Siol Torquil branch of Clan MacLeod who also held lands in Lewis, Waternish and Assynt. At the turn of the 16th century Calum, the 9th Chief of Lewis, granted the lands of Raasay and Rona to his younger son, Calum Garbh, who was thereafter known as MacGillichaluim. MacGillichaluim became the first Chief of the Raasay MacLeods. When the main lines of the Lewis MacLeods became extinct in the early 17th century, the chiefship of Siol Torquil passed to the MacLeods of Raasay.

The island suffered greatly at the hands of Government troops following the 1745 Jacobite Rebellion. The Raasay MacLeods were staunch supporters of the Young Pretender and gave shelter to the fugitive Prince during his long flight from Government forces after the Battle of Culloden. In retribution, the Redcoats burned down every dwelling on the island, destroyed all the boats and killed or removed the sheep and cattle, leaving the inhabitants to starve.

Miraculously, the people of Raasay managed to survive this tragic episode and gradually the island's population began to increase once again.

In the early 19th century, in common with other areas of the Highlands, the crofting tenants were faced with poverty and in 1843, John MacLeod was forced by heavy debts to sell the island to George Rainy of Edinburgh for £36,750. The last descendant of the MacLeods of Raasay then emigrated to Australia in 1846.

When Rainy took possession of Raasay, he initially tried to improve conditions for the islanders, but after initial attempts failed, he turned to sheep farming and had no qualms about evicting 120 families and shipping them off to Australia to make way for his flocks. After his death in 1863, the island passed to his son who used it as a holiday retreat until his death in 1872 at the early age of 27. There followed a succession of owners who had little or no sympathy for the indigenous crofting population. During this time the island became the centre of a breakaway section of the Free Church, formed in 1893 by Mr MacFarlane. This sect was even more rigorous than the original Free Kirk and demanded strict observation of the Sabbath and a ban on all music, poetry and dancing.

In 1907, Raasay was put up for auction with a reserve price of £45,000 and in 1912 it was bought by Baird & Co who intended to extract the island's iron ore deposits which had been discovered in 1893 by a Fellow of the Geographical Society. Mining operations began in 1913 and the outbreak of the First World War increased the ecenomic importance of the deposits. The ore was worked mainly by German P.O.W.'s, many of whom died in the great 'flu epidemic of 1918 and lie buried on the island. After the war, the operation was no longer economically viable and the enterprise soon ground to a halt. Most of the machinery was removed during the Second World War when the price of scrap metal was high. The island was subsequently sold to the Department of Agriculture.

Access to Raasay today is by the vehicular ferry service which was started by Caledonian MacBrayne in July 1976 after a long campaign by the islanders. The ferry docks at East Suisnish pier, opposite which lies an abandoned processing plant connected with the iron-ore mine. The ore was extracted in the hills above Inverarish 1 1/2 miles away and transported to the pier by narrow guage railway for shipment. East of Suisnish, the road continues around the coast for a couple of miles and terminates at the lighthouse on Eyre Point.

Raasay's main village, Inverarish, lies about a mile to the north of East Suisnish. Here can be seen the neat terraced houses which were built by Baird & Co. for the iron-ore mineworkers. At Inverarish, the visitor has a choice of two routes. The road east of the village passes through Raasay Forest, close to the disused iron mine and then continues across the moor to

North and South Fearns. Here can be seen the restored cottages which were once the homes of the Rona Raiders, a group of crofters who had been cleared from their land on the neighbouring island of Rona. In 1919, these destitute families crossed to Raasay and in desperation seized land from Bairds. For this they were put on trial, but such was the public outcry at their treatment, the crofters were soon released and were piped home to Raasay in triumph. Beyond North Fearns, a path continues north along the coast for two miles to the waterfall at Hallaig.

The road north from Inverarish skirts alongside Churchton Bay and soon passes close to Raasay House. Writing in 1549, Dean Monro makes mention of a three storey tower house on this site which later became known as Clachan. Following the abandonment of Brochel Castle in the late 17th century, it appears that the Clachan tower house became the main residence of the MacLeod Chiefs for a time. The old tower was finally demolished following the construction of a new clan seat, Raasay House, in the mid-18th century. When Johnson and Boswell visited the island during their tour of the Hebrides in 1773, they were received by MacLeod and his Lady at Raasay House. Here the pair stayed from Wednesday 8th to Sunday 12th September and were so lavishly entertained that Johnson commented, "I know not how we shall get away".

In the early 19th century, the Estate was improved by James MacLeod and a Regency frontage was added to Raasay House. Also dating from this time is the Battery, a small defensive structure built in 1807 in front of the house, armed with cannon and two mermaids. Between the years of 1937 and 1960, the mansion was run as a hotel. Then followed another distressing episode in the island's history when a doctor from Sussex bought Raasay House together with the Home Farm and various other buildings. Displaying an attitude sadly reminiscent of the absentee landlords of the 19th century, he allowed the house, its contents and garden to fall into decay and also refused to sell the more suitable pier at Clachan to the islanders for use as a ferry terminal. Happily, Raasay House was subsequently sold and turned into an adventure school and is now known as Raasay Outdoor Centre.

Standing in the grounds of Raasay House is a Pictish symbol stone of early type which is thought to date to the 8th century. This roughly hewn stone bears a crescent and tuning fork symbol, together with a Christian cross set within a square which contains a simple *rho* symbol (the second letter of Christ's name in the Greek alphabet). It has been suggested that stones such as this one which bear only one or two symbols might represent territorial markers. The Christian cross is an unusual inclusion on a stone of early type and probably represents the conversion of a Pictish ruler to Christianity. A similar cross is also incised on a sloping rock just to the south of the pier in Churchton Bay. Behind Raasay House lies an ancient burial ground which contains the ruins of a 13th century chapel dedicated to St Molnag and an adjacent smaller building which may date to the 11th century.

Beyond Raasay House, the road winds north along the coast to Oskaig and continues round Holoman Bay to Balmeanach. Here, a path leaves the road and heads south-east across the moor to Dun Caan, the highest point on the island. James Boswell ascended this distinctive flat-topped mountain during his stay on the island in 1773. Dr Johnson commented, "Boswell climbed to the top of Duncaan, and danced a reel in sheer exuberance." The road continues north across the moor for three miles, passing Brae and Glame, and then bends right to begin the descent to the east coast of the island. Just before the coast is reached, a track branches right and heads into Raasay Forest. This soon becomes a footpath which leads to the ruins of Screapadal village, 1 1/4 miles to the south.

The main road continues towards the east coast and passes above Brochel Castle, ancient clan seat of the MacLeods of Raasay. Sadly, this castle is now in a very poor state of preservation but an accurate reconstruction of its original appearance can be had by examining antiquarian descriptions and paintings of the building. The castle occupies a position of strength atop a stack of Torridonian sandstone and was originally approached via a long flight of stairs which led to a deep gatehouse passage on the eastern coastal side. This passage gave access to a small and rather claustraphobic courtyard which once contained a well. The castle itself was comprised of four towers, each a separate apartment, linked by short stretches of curtain wall or rockface. During their visit to the castle in 1773, Johnson and Boswell noted a projection above the entrance with an opening through which boiling water or stones could be thrown at hostile visitors. Additionally, there was a sentry box at the top of the stairs, formed from a recess in the bedrock. Boswell also wrote of "...a certain accommodation rarely to be found at the modern houses of Scotland, and which Dr Johnson and I sought for in vain at the Laird of Rasay's new-built mansion where nothing else was wanting." It seems that the famous travellers were very much taken with the small privy in the north-west tower!

Although there is a lack of documentary evidence concerning the early history of Brochel Castle, the style of building suggests a construction date sometime in the 15th century. It may have been built for Calum MacGillichaluim, the first Chief of Raasay, at the turn of the 16th century. Tradition says that the last chief to live there was Iain Garbh who succeeded his father Alexander in 1648. Iain was known as Mighty John because of his great strength and he met with an untimely death in 1671 when he fell into the sea in a drunken stupor. Following this tragic event, there appears to be a

gap in the succession until 1692 when the title of 8th Chief was taken by
Iain's cousin Alexander. It was around this time that Brochel Castle was
abandoned and Clachan became the main residence of the Raasay
MacLeods.

Beyond Brochel Castle, the road continues on to Arnish. Until fairly
recent times, this remote northern tip of the island contained a bustling
indigenous crofting population. Even the tiny island of Eilean Fladday lying
just off the north-west coast of Raasay at one time contained four families
with their own school. For many years, the people canvassed the authorities
to extend the road north beyond Brochel Castle but their pleas were met with
refusal. Gradually, due to the hardships created by inaccessibility, the
indigenous population began to drift away from the north end of the island. In
1960, the little township of Torran lost its post office and school. Then, in an
attempt to stem the tide of rural depopulation, a local crofter, the late Calum
MacLeod, decided to build the much-needed road by himself. Calum set to
work with pick, shovel and wheelbarrow and singlehandedly constructed the
3,000 yards of tarred roadway between Brochel Castle and his home at
Arnish. When he began this arduous task in 1966 there were still seven
families living in this area. Sadly, by the time he had finished more than 10
years later, only he and his wife were left. Today, the road that weaves
across the moor from Brochel to Arnish stands as a monument to Calum's
vision.

Sconser To Sligachan

From Sconser, the A850 continues to bend south-westwards and
travels along the shore of Loch Sligachan. Across the water lie the white
crofts of Peinchorran with Ben Lee rising just to the left. As the marshy head
of the loch is approached, an attractive waterfall can be seen opposite,
tumbling down Cnoc an t-Sithean - the Hill of the Fairies. At the head of the
loch lies the Sligachan Hotel and campsite - a welcome sight for the weary
traveller. Sligachan is the starting point of a popular walk to the Loch Coruisk
viewpoint (see Walks for full details).

The Sligachan Hotel

The Sligachan Hotel was originally a coaching inn, a convenient
stopping place for travellers heading to Portree or Dunvegan. In Victorian
days it was the haunt of artists who had travelled north to capture the wild
scenery of Skye on canvas. Many of the early Cuillin climbers also based
themselves here and, as mountaineering grew in popularity during the 19th
century, the hotel became an important European centre for climbing. The
first ever scramble amongst the Cuillin was made by the Reverend Charles
Lesingham Smith of Gloucestershire. Smith stayed at the Sligachan Inn on 4
September 1835 and despite finding the surroundings rather gloomy, he was

pleased with the accommodation. In an account of his travels published in 1837 Smith wrote of the hotel, "It is a recent building, infinitely superior to the old one. Its situation is the dreariest spot that could have been selected for the abode of man: it stands at the base of the mountains, just in front of a torrent which, for a hundred yards on each side of its channel, has strewn the ground with fragments of rock, hurried down from the crags. Such is the view from my bed-room, which serves me for parlour also. The interior however is more cheerful, and I am enjoying extremely the humble luxury of a peat fire, while the clean napkin on the table and the fine coloured tea-things, invite me to a sober meal."

Things were rather different when Charles Richard Weld, member of the Alpine Club and writer of guide-books, visited the island in the summer of 1859. While there, he made the first recorded ascent of Sgurr na Stri. Weld stayed at the Sligachan Inn for four days, two of which were so stormy that he could not venture out. He described the accommodation as "...extremely uncomfortable" and went on to say, "How soon you can detect the influence of a clever and clean hostess, and that of the reverse. It was very easy to see that the domesticities of Sligachan were out of joint, for the landlady neglected her duty, and the landlord went about the house with a heavy heart. And no wonder, for when you hear that his wife was not allowed access to the liquor closet, you will understand that she was not fit for the office of landlady." The luxurious accommodation to be found today is a far cry from that encountered by Weld in 1859 and the Sligachan Hotel continues to attract climbers and walkers from all over the world.

Eating Out: THE SLIGACHAN HOTEL. Tel. (0478) 650 204. Bar meals are served in Seumas's Bar from 0800-2400. The Bar has an extensive selection of malts. A special fixed price Camper's Breakfast is available from 0800-1100. The dining room is open to non-residents and offers a Table d'Hote menu between 1830 and 2100 with a selection of local seafood, game dishes & vegetarian options. Children's menu available. Children's play area.

The Sligachan Cattle Market

Sligachan was once the site of a great cattle market where drovers from the south met with local farmers to purchase stock for England and the Lowlands. Similar markets were also held regularly at Broadford and Portree. Such events were not only of economic importance to the islanders, but were also seen as major social events which always attracted a large number of people. Shopkeepers and innkeepers were always in attendance to cater to the needs of the busy market goers. Here, farmers and cottars came together to sell their animals and locals met to exchange news, eat, drink and settle outstanding debts. The first major Sligachan fair was opened by Colonel MacLeod of MacLeod on Wednesday 22 October 1794.

A fascinating desription of one of the great Sligachan markets comes down to us from the renowned 19th century engineer Joseph Mitchell, who spent a large part of his life travelling all over the Highlands building roads, bridges and railways. In mid September 1837 he was in Skye. In his *Reminiscences* published in 1883-4, Mitchell described the Sligachan market: "At Sligachan the road was lined with tents. It was about eleven o'clock of the second day, and the tent-keepers were engaged in cooking broth, mutton, and potatoes for the country people inside, with the only drink, mountain dew. The tents, if they could be called such, were temporary, formed of blankets, and were miserable. The whole aspect of the place - a bare and barren mountain-side - was wild and savage. It had been raining all night, and as most of the people had been either up drinking or sleeping on the bare ground during the night, they had a dirty and dishevelled appearance. The gentlemen had a blowsy un-shaven aspect, the horses were ungroomed, and there being no stables, little gillies with kilts, bare heads, and bare legs, were mounted, and with much glee were riding backwards and forwards along the road. The cattle and sheep extending over an immense space were standing quietly looking at each other, while the gillies, their drovers, were leaning on their sticks or lying on the damp ground, their faithful collies at their feet, panting for employment. Such was the fair at Sligachan, which I viewed with no very favourable impression of the civilization of the people."

The Glamaig Hill Race

From the Sligacan Hotel there is a good view back to Glamaig. If you are visiting the island during July, watch out for the incredible Glamaig Hill Race, a spectacular race up and down the tortuously steep slopes which now attracts around 100 runners each year. In 1899 the 775m (2,537 ft) Glamaig was ascended from the old Sligachan Bridge in 37 minutes and descended in 18 minutes with no stop in between - an incredible total time of only 55 minutes for the round trip. This amazing feat was achieved barefoot by a soldier of the 1/5th Gurkhas, Havildar Harkabir Tharpa or Herkia. Tharpa had been brought to the island by a Major Bruce who later became well-known for his exploits in the Himalayas.

Gurkha Tharpa's climb was witnessed by MacLeod of MacLeod and timed by a Percy Caldecott. Caldecott later described the event in a letter to the writer Alasdair Alpin MacGregor which is reproduced in MacGregor's book *Skye and the Inner Hebrides*, published in 1953: "To this day I can see in my mind the spray thrown high up by Herkia as he ran along, regardless of any pools or any other obstruction. The speed with which he climbed Glamaig was incredible, more like a spider than anything else. On reaching the top he waved his arms to us, and then immediately started the descent, which he made at the run. As you probably know, on that side of Glamaig there is much fine loose scree. He came down this in what one might call a series of jumps, and each time his foot landed, he slid for some distance as the scree moved with him. The most wonderful thing about it was that he arrived at the bridge barely out of breath."

The record remained intact for nearly 90 years, although in 1955 one George Rhodes (wearing basketball shoes) came close at 56 1/2 minutes. In 1988 the Glamaig Hill Race was declared an official event in the Scottish Hill Running Association's annual calendar and this status attracted a wider field of runners to the hill. In 1989 Gurkha Tharpa's record was finally broken when a runner from Lochaber, Billy Rodgers, completed the race in 51 1/2 minutes.

MINGINISH AND THE CUILLIN

The B8009 to Carbost and Portnalong branches westwards from the A863 at Drynoch. This route makes a pleasant drive on a fine evening as spectacular sunsets are often to be seen over Loch Harport and Fiskavaig Bay. The road is mainly single track, although the initial section has recently undergone many improvements.

From the junction, the B8009 descends to cross the River Drynoch and the Vikisgill Burn which flow into Loch Harport. When the tide is out, the mud flats at the head of the loch can be a good area for birdwatching. The scattered houses of Merkadale are soon reached and here a small unclassified road branches left for Glen Brittle and the Cuillin.

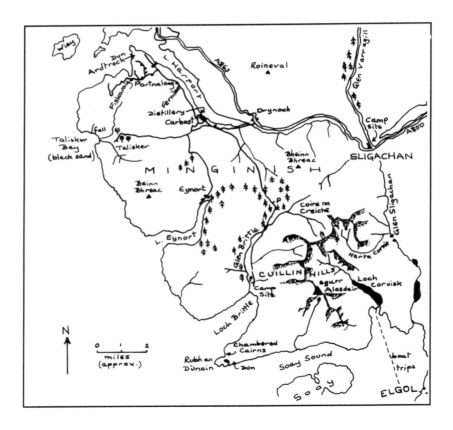

THE GLEN BRITTLE ROAD

This newly improved single-track road branches left at Merkadale and heads south towards the Cuillin mountains. This route gives superb ever-changing views of the Cuillin and is the closest you can come to this great mountain range by road. The first stretch crosses a peat moor which is still cut today to provide fuel for local crofters. After 3 miles, the road enters a conifer plantation. A small track on the left towards the end of the plantation leads into the trees where there is a picnic area with a wooden table and room for several cars to park. This is one of the few areas where parking is possible on this narrow road.

Coire Na Creiche

Beyond the plantation the road begins to descend and a magnificent view opens up left of the spectacular Coire na Creiche. The corrie is backed by a great horseshoe of hills which jut out like fingers. On the left is Bruach na Frithe, then Sgurr an Fheadain in the middle with its great Waterpipe Gully clearly visible and finally Sgurr Thuilm to the right. Behind these fingers rises the jagged ridge formed by Sgurr na Bhairnich, Bidein Druim nan Ramh and Sgurr a' Mhadaidh. The Waterpipe Gully is caused by the differential weathering of a fine-grained volcanic rock which has been intruded into the coarser grained gabbro. Such near-vertical dykes occur throughout the Cuillin and provide fine sport for experienced climbers. Other well-known examples of this phenomenon are the Bhasteir Tooth, the Inaccessible Pinnacle of Sgurr Dearg and the Pinnacle Ridge of Sgurr nan Gillean.

Coire na Creiche was the site of the last great battle to be fought between the MacLeods and the MacDonalds in 1601. This battle was the culmination of a long conflict known as the War of the One-Eyed Woman which had its origins in the ancient island custom of handfasting. Handfasting permitted a man to choose a mate and to keep her as his wife for a trial period of a year. After this time, if the woman met with his approval, the man would marry her and legitimize her children; if not, she would be returned to her parents. In the late 16th century, Donald Gorm Mor entered into a handfasting agreement with Margaret MacLeod, the sister of the great MacLeod Chief Rory Mor. Donald took Margaret to live with him in Duntulm Castle and while there it seems that the unfortunate woman injured one of her eyes. At the end of the trial period, Donald Gorm decided that he did not wish to marry a deformed woman and he sent Margaret back to her brother at Dunvegan. To add insult to injury, Donald sent the poor woman home mounted on a one-eyed nag, accompanied by a one-eyed groom and followed by a mangy one-eyed dog. This unkind act precipitated the most savage fued ever fought between the MacLeods and MacDonalds. The conflict lasted for two years during which time there were countless raids and counter-raids, burnings and bloody massacres. The MacLeods were eventually routed by the MacDonalds at Coire na Creiche in 1601, the last clan battle ever fought on Skye.

The Cuillin Conquerors

On reaching the broad flat bottom of the glen, the road crosses over the meandering River Brittle and proceeds around the foot of the main Cuillin massif. Here you begin to get some idea of the scale of this huge mountain range and can appreciate why famous poets such as Alfred Lord Tennyson and C. Day Lewis were inspired to verse after walking in these hills.

The complex ridge of grey gabbro with its many pinnacles, crevasses and stunning cliffs has long attracted climbers and walkers from all over the world. The first recorded scramble amongst the Cuillin was made by the Rev. Charles Lesingham Smith of Gloucestershire on 5 September 1835. Accompanied by Lord MacDonald's forester, Duncan MacIntyre, he set off from Sligachan and reached Loch Coruisk in 2 1/2 hours. On the way back, MacIntyre suggested that they take a short cut and so the pair scrambled up and over a steep ridge and descended into Lota Corrie. Smith thus became the first gentleman to traverse a pass known previously only to local shepherds. Of his adventure he later wrote,: "I here found my umbrella a sad nuisance; but the forester's two dogs were much worse, for they were constantly in my way. Sometimes we climbed up a cleft in the bare rock, just like a chimney; and sometimes the one was obliged to push the other up; and he in return pulled up the first."

The earliest recorded ascent of a Cuillin peak was made on 7 July 1836 by James David Forbes, the pioneer of Swiss mountaineering. Forbes became Professor of Natural Philosophy at Glasgow University at the young age of 23 and was highly acclaimed for his work on glaciers and the polarisation of heat and light. With Duncan MacIntyre as guide, he climbed to the top of Sgurr nan Gillean, the Peak of the Young Men. He returned to the island in 1845 to climb Bruach na Frithe and also compiled the first accurate map of the range for climbers. Prior to this time, the only map of the area was that produced by Arrowsmith in 1807 which gave only an approximate position for each peak and completely omitted Loch Coruisk.

In the next few decades, as tales of the magnificent Cuillin range spread, many climbers headed to Skye to tackle the unconquered peaks. In 1857, Professor Nicol and the poet Swinburne ascended Blabheinn. Sgurr na Stri, the Peak of Strife, was conquered in 1859 by C.R. Weld, a member of the Alpine Club. In 1870, Sgurr a'Ghreadaidh fell to W. Tribe and John MacKenzie. Then, in 1873, Sgurr na Banachdich was climbed by local man Sheriff Alexander Nicolson who went on to become the most famous of the Skye mountaineers. Born at Husabost near Dunvegan in 1827, Nicolson was a journalist and brilliant Gaelic scholar. He later took up law and was called to the Scottish Bar at the age of 23. In 1873 he ascended Sgurr Sgumain (the Stack Peak), the highest in the range, which was subsequently renamed Sgurr Alasdair in his honour. On 6 September 1874 he climbed Sgurr Dubh na Da-Bheinn and one of the two peaks of Sgurr a Mhadaidh-Ruaidh. Sgurr Dubh Mor also fell to the Sheriff that same year.

The next peak to be conquered was the north top of Bidein Druim nan Ramh (the Pinnacle of the Ridge of Oars) which was ascended by W.W. Smith in 1880. In the same year, the treacherous Inaccessible Pinnacle of Sgurr Dearg was mastered by the well known climbing partnership of Charles and Laurence Pilkington. Charles later became President of the Alpine Club and between them, the brothers went on to conquer many of the remaining peaks. Laurence and party ascended the main top of Bidein Druim nan Ramh in 1883. In 1887, Charles and his party climbed Sgurr Mhic Coinnich (MacKenzie's Mountain), named after the famous Cuillin guide John MacKenzie; Sgurr Thearlaich (Charles's Peak), named after Pilkington himself; Sgurr na h-Uamha (the Peak of the Cave); and Clach Glas (the Grey Stone).

In 1889, Professor Norman Collie made the first ascent of Am Bhasteir (the Executioner) and in 1896 he returned with a party to climb Sgurr Coir' an Lochain. Collie was a renowned scientist, accredited with producing the first X-Ray photograph and with helping to identify the rare gasses. He is often described as the greatest of the Skye climbers and Sgurr Thormaid (Norman's Peak) is named after him. Much of the later exploration in the Cuillin was carried out by Collie in partnership with John MacKenzie, the first professional Skye guide. MacKenzie, born at Sconser in 1856, made the ascent of Sgurr nan Gillean when he was only ten. It was MacKenzie and Collie who discovered and climbed in 1906 the dangerous rock projection now known as Cioch which juts out of the cliff face of Sron na Ciche above Glen Brittle. This event was to become a great mile-stone in the history of rock climbing. MacKenzie died in 1933 at the age of 76 and was laid to rest in the graveyard of the Free Presbyterian Church at Struan. Collie spent his final years at the Sligachan Hotel close to his beloved Cuillin and at his request now lies buried close to his friend.

Today, one of the most sought-after mountaineering achievements is a continuous traverse of the 10 1/2 km (6 1/2 mile) ridge which stretches from Sgurr nan Gillean near Sligachan in the north to Gars-bheinn above Loch Slapin in the south. This incredible feat involves over 13,000 feet of ascent and takes in nearly forty summits and tops, including the highest peak, Sgurr Alasdair (993m, 3,251 ft). The unbroken traverse of the main ridge was first accomplished in 1911 by Shadbolt and Maclaren in a time of 16 hours and 45 minutes. In more recent times, the ridge has been run in a time of around 4 hours and it is estimated that most fit and appropriately equipped parties can complete the traverse in two days with one overnight bivouac stop.

Glen Brittle To Loch Brittle

As the road continues south through Glen Brittle, it passes a large expanse of conifers on the lower slopes of Beinn a' Bhraghad and Beinn Staic. Since 1932 the Forestry Commission has been establishing thousands of acres of trees on Skye and those in Glen Brittle were the first to be planted. Sitka spruce is the most commonly used species but there are also areas of lodgepole pine, Japanese larch, Hybrid larch and a small amount of noble fir. Trees from these forests are felled and transported to the pulp and paper mill at Fort William.

Glenbrittle used to be the site of the island's landing strip and was served by De Havilland Rapide planes operated by Scottish Airways. The Skye stopover on the Glasgow-Hebrides air service was discontinued after the Second World War largely because the road from Glen Brittle was so bad that it negated any time advantage gained by flying to the island.

Before long, Glen Brittle Youth Hostel is passed on the right and the waters of Loch Brittle come into view ahead. The road terminates in a large carpark overlooking Loch Brittle, just before the Glen Brittle campsite. This carpark gives access to the little beach at the head of the loch and is a convenient starting point for the popular walk to Rubh' an Dunain (see Walks for full details).

GLENBRITTLE CAMPSITE The ideal base for climbing the Cuillins or for exploring this fascinating area of Skye. Spectacular lochside setting; safe sandy beach; on-site shop for all your needs; caravan available for rent; experienced and knowledgeable staff. For further details, telephone (0478) 640 404. *Display Advert*

Mountain Guiding: CUILLIN GUIDES. Tel. (047 842) 289. J. Akroyd.

MERKADALE TO CARBOST

From Merkadale, the B8009 continues to follow the line of Loch Harport and descends to the little village of Carbost (the left fork at the top of the hill leads to Glen Eynort and Gleann Oraid - see below).

The Talisker Whisky Distillery

The Talisker Distillery was originally founded by Hugh and Kenneth MacAskill, the sons of a doctor from the Isle of Eigg. The brothers were sheep farmers and Kenneth resided at nearby Talisker. After false starts at Snizort and Fiskavaig, the operation was moved to Carbost in 1830 and the MacAskills were given a 60 year lease by MacLeod of MacLeod. The Uisge Beatha or "water of life" which the distillery produced soon gained a fine reputation and Talisker was praised by Robert Louis Stevenson in his poem "The Scotsman's Return From Abroad", which was published in 1880:

> *The King o' drinks, as I conceive it,*
> *Talisker, Isla, or Glenlivet.*

In the early days, the distillery workers were paid by the owner in specially struck coins which detailed the number of days worked. The workers could then exchange these coins for staple foodstuffs such as oatmeal, flour and herring. After various changes, the business was taken over by Roderick Kemp & Co. and in 1895 the company merged with Dailuaine Distillery on Speyside to form Dailuaine-Talisker Distilleries Ltd. In 1900 permission was granted to build a pier in nearby Carbostbeg to allow small steamers or "puffers" to bring in barley from the mainland to the distillery. On the return journey the puffers carried wooden casks filled with whisky. This practice continued until the 1960's. The pier still exists but is now used only by pleasure craft. A small tramway was also constructed in 1900 to carry goods between the distillery and the pier. In 1914 a feu charter was granted which permitted the company to take water from the Carbost Burn and peats from Bracadale.

The business was acquired by the Distillers Company in 1916. At that time, the distillery used a triple distillation process, that is the malt was run through three linked pot-stills. This was changed to double distillation in 1928. Sadly, the original still-house was completely destroyed by fire in 1960, but the company immediately commissioned exact replicas of the lost stills to ensure that the distinctive peaty character of the malt would be retained and the distillery opened again two years later. Today, Talisker is produced by United Distillers, using barley brought in by road from Muir of Ord. Local peat is still used for drying the malted barley and this gives the malt its distinctive peaty character. The distillery manager and locals also believe that the flavour owes much to the design of the worm loops which have a distinctly bulbous shape. Water is still taken from the Carbost Burn but this is now used only in the cooling process; that used in production comes from springs in the hills behind the distillery. The finished product is matured in Spanish sherry casks. Although most of the output is used in blending, a small portion is turned into the well-known 10 year old Talisker single-malt, which has a pungent, smoky, sweet taste.

CARBOST

Distillery Tour: Guided tours of the TALISKER DISTILLERY leave from the Visitor's Reception Area approximately every 25 minutes. These fascinating tours explain the entire process of whisky making and include visits to the attractive copper stills, the spirit safe and the bonded warehouse. As you await the tour in the Visitor Centre, a complementary dram of generous size is provided. The Centre also has a display area which tells of the origins of the distillery, the distillery today and the process of distilling. The walls are hung with a variety of old implements which were once used in the distilling process. Other displays deal with Flora MacDonald, early travellers to Skye and myths and legends. Tours operate from Easter to October, Monday-Friday between 0930 and 1630 (the last tour is at 1600); November to March, Monday-Friday between 1400 and 1630. Admission fee applies. Large parties must arrange their visit in advance by telephoning (0478) 640 203.

Eating Out: THE OLD INN. Tel. (0478) 640 205. Meals available. Credit cards accepted.

Shopping: CARBOST STORES. Tel. (0478) 201. General groceries.
CARBOSTCRAFT. Tel. (0478) 640 259. Handcrafted gift items including pottery, soft furnishings, hobby horses and pot pourri. Items can be mailed home and commissions are accepted. Also courses in hobby ceramics, ceramic and wood painting, glass engraving and small softgoods. Open Monday-Saturday 1000-1900 (until 2100 on Tuesdays and Fridays). Closed Sundays and the 1st Monday of every month.
TALISKER DISTILLERY. Tel. (0478) 640 203. The Visitor Centre shop stocks Talisker and other single malt whiskys, both miniatures and full bottles, postcards of the distillery, quaichs (a nice gift set including a miniature), sporran flasks, cups and Talisker Distillery umberellas.

Toilets: Portaloo facilities, by the right of the B8009, just before the Talisker Distillery.

Glen Eynort

From Carbost, two minor roads branch left to Glen Eynort from the B8009, one just before and one just after the village. The one after the village gives a good view of the waterfalls on the Carbost Burn. Both of these single track roads follow the lower reaches of the burn and then merge into one after about a mile. A short distance on from this point, a left fork leads to Glen Eynort. This road passes high above the Eynort River and then descends into Eynort village, giving pleasant views across the head of the sea loch. The road ends in a large turning circle. Lying a short distance along the coast from this point, at an area known as Borline, is a large 18th century church and a small church of earlier date. A 16th century baptismal font was discovered in the churchyard of the latter and is now in the Royal Museums of Scotland in Edinburgh.

Gleann Oraid

Gleann Oraid is reached by taking either of the two roads described above for Glen Eynort. After these roads merge a mile beyond the village, keep straight on. The small unclassified road heads west, passing between the hills of Arnaval to the right and Stockval to the left. The headwaters of the River Talisker are soon seen on the left. The road begins to descend towards the coast and ends in a turning circle just before Talisker House.

Talisker was traditionally in the possession of the son of the MacLeod Chief. Visitors must park here and continue on foot if they wish to visit the black sand beach at Talisker Bay (see Walks for full details).

Carbost To Fiskavaig

From Carbost, the B8009 climbs steeply and rounds a hairpin bend. Here, the unclassified road which leads to Glen Eynort and Gleann Oraid may be joined (see above). The B road continues high above Loch Harport and passes through the scattered settlements of Carbostbeg and Fernilea, giving good views to the hills opposite.

PORTNALONG

From Fernilea, the road continues to Portnalong and here you may choose to drive straight on to visit the Taigh Ailean Hotel and the Little Gallery, or turn left to visit the other village shops and continue your journey to Fiskavaig. The road straight ahead ends in a small pier. The bay here is used by Marine Harvest Ltd.

After the First World War, the Department of Agriculture removed a number of families from the overcrowded islands of Lewis, Harris and Scalpay and re-settled them on more fertile crofting land in Portnalong. The people came in two waves and each family was given 15-20 acres of land, 3 cows and a share in 4,000 acres of common sheep pasture. By combining crofting and fishing with the manufacture of quality tweeds, the families were able to attain a better standard of living than had been possible on their native islands. Prior to 1939, the year's tweed was sold at a special annual gathering or *feill*. After the war, the industry was revived by Ballantynes Ltd of Peebles who supplied the local crofters with looms and sent yarn to be woven to specific instructions. The resulting homespun products were sold mainly to the U.S.A. and Japan. Sadly, as a result of price increases, sales fell and the business became uneconomic, causing Ballantynes to cease dealing with the Portnalong weavers in 1968.

PORTNALONG

Bike Hire: TAIGH AILEAN HOTEL. Tel. (0478) 640 271. On the road to Portnalong Pier. Mountain bikes are available for hire throughout the year.

Eating Out: TAIGH AILEAN HOTEL. Tel. (0478) 640 271. Bar lunches served daily from 1200-1400. Also morning coffee and afternoon tea. Fishing tackle hire available. Calor gas available. Open January-December.

Shopping: GARDEN PLANTS AND CRAFTS. Tel. (0478) 640 383. On the Fiskavaig road. Craftwork gifts for home and garden. A good selection of bird boxes and bird tables. Also exchange paperbacks. Organically grown fruit and vegetables in season. Also garden plants, shrubs, trees, heathers and house plants. Open daily.
THE LITTLE GALLERY. Tel. (0478) 640 254. On the road to Portnalong Pier. Beautifully detailed etchings (both framed and unframed), watercolours and cards by artist Jean Thomas, depicting wildlife and Skye scenery. All etched and printed at the gallery - a quality memento of your stay on the island. Major credit cards accepted. Open daily, 0930-1800.
PORTNALONG STORES. At the junction of the Fiskavaig & pier roads. General groceries.
WOODCRAFT AND WOOLCABIN. Tel. (0478) 640 408. Located to the right of the Fiskavaig road, further down the same lane as Garden Plants and Crafts. Selection of hand-knitted and hand-woven items by Heather Williams including jumpers, rugs, wall-hangings and peg bags. Also wood turned items including lamps, bowls and solitaire games by Fred Williams. All handcrafted on the premises. Day and weekend courses available in hand spinning and woodturning. Telephone for full details.

Portnalong To Fiskavaig

If you travel the next section of road in early summer before the verge cutters have set to work, you will be rewarded with one of the best displays of wild flowers on the island. Chamomiles, foxgloves and a variety of other native flowers crowd the roadside in a medley of bright colours. Here and there you may even spot a few native orchids.

Eating Out: HOPSCOTCH CAFE. Tel. (0478) 640 388. Adjacent to Hopscotch Knitwear, the tearoom serves coffee, home baking, soups and snacks. Open Monday-Saturday 0900-1800; Sunday 1200-1700. Open from Easter to October.

Shopping: HOPSCOTCH KNITWEAR. Tel. (0478) 640 388. Signposted, 1/4 mile up track on left, shortly after Portnalong village. Scottish designer originals and craft knitwear in natural fibres including beautiful Harris wool sweaters, Fair Isles, Aran knitwear and Harris Tweed. Credit cards accepted. If you visit on a Monday between 1300-1700 you can see traditional spinning and try it for yourself. Open January-December.

A small road branches right to the houses at Ardtreck and then the B8009 descends to cross the Allt Ribhein. Shortly after the bridge, another minor road branches right and leads to the starting point of an easy coastal walk to Dun Ardtreck and the Ardtreck Lighthouse (see Walks for full details). The B8009 now ascends to give fine views across Fiskavaig Bay to

MacLeod's Tables on the Duirinish Peninsula. In the foreground can be seen the islands of Wiay and Oronsay, the latter perfectly mimicking the shape of the much larger Tables behind.

Shopping: CURLEW CRAFTS STUDIO, Fiskavaig. Tel. (0478) 640 269. Situated in modern bungalow by left of road. A wide range of hand-decorated china and porcelain items, all fired on the premises. Also hand-crafted domestic and decorative wooden items. Commissions accepted. Commemorative gold inscriptions can be arranged. Open daily 1000 to dusk.

The road passes Fiskavaig Bay and continues to twist up and down amongst the scattered crofts until it reaches a hairpin bend. This is the starting point of an attractive walk to Talisker Bay which can be extended to take in the rugged and beautiful coastline of Rubha nan Clach (see Walks for full details). From the hairpin bend, the road descends to a turning circle. It is not possible to park here for any length of time, but you can stop briefly to take in the view across the bay to Isle Oronsay and the lighthouse on Ardtreck Point.

SLIGACHAN TO PORTREE

At the Sligachan Hotel, the A850 bends northwards and heads away from the Cuillin and Red Hills, crossing a flat boggy land with patches of forest on either side. A few hundred yards beyond the hotel there is a parking area to the right of the road. It is well worth pulling in here for the spectacular view back towards the mountains. The entire length of Glen Sligachan is visible, flanked on the left by the Red Hills and on the right by the Black Cuillin. Sgurr na Stri, the Peak of Strife, with its distinctive pointed top, can be made out some eight miles distant, beyond the head of the glen. The scene is particularly striking on fine evenings when the sun's rays light up the red flanks of Marsco in the middle distance.

The road continues through Glen Varragill, following the course of the River Varragill which can be seen just to the left. As you proceed through the glen, the keen-eyed may notice a series of small hillocks lying close to the river and on the lower slopes of the adjacent hills. These are glacial mounds comprised of sand and gravel, left here towards the end of the last Ice Age 10,000 years ago by the melting ice of retreating glaciers. Suddenly, the striking profile of the Old Man of Storr on the Trotternish Ridge comes into view ahead. This isolated basalt pinnacle has provided inspiration for many artists over the years and is the subject of countless prints and paintings.

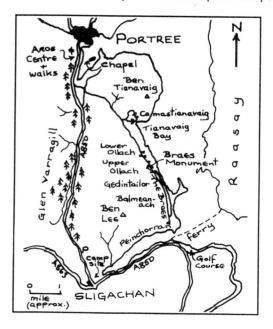

The surrounding landscape now becomes more undulating and wooded, giving fleeting glimpses of the houses of Portree which nestle at the foot of the hills ahead. The single-track B883 branches right to the scattered settlements of the Braes.

THE BRAES ROAD

If you are in no hurry to reach Portree, a pleasant detour may be had by taking the B883 to Braes. This single-track road heads south-east towards the coast, giving fine views to Ben Tianavaig which stands guard over the southern approach to Portree Harbour. The houses of Camastianavaig can be seen to the left above Tianavaig Bay and then the road passes the settlements of Conordan, Achnahannait and Lower and Upper Ollach.

The Battle of the Braes

Just before the signpost for Gedintailor is reached, a small cairn is located by the right of the road (Grid Ref. 523357). The cairn is difficult to spot as you drive past - look out for a black and white sign on the grass by the right of the road, just as you come over a small hill. The Braes cairn was erected to commemorate the 100th anniversary of the Battle of the Braes, an event which was of great importance not only to Skye crofters but to the Scottish crofting community as a whole.

The Battle of the Braes took place at the time of the Clearances, the tragic period in Scottish history when thousands of crofters were cleared from their land by landlords keen to reap a greater profit from sheep. The Braes incident began as a dispute between local crofters and their landlord over grazing rights on nearby Ben Lee. Most of the fertile hill-land on Ben Lee was taken from the people in 1865 by Lord MacDonald and his factor without any corresponding

reduction in rent and was subsequently let to one sheep farmer. This caused great hardship to the crofters who had to allow a large portion of their arable land to run to grass to provide fodder for their livestock. The Braes area at this time was already heavily

overcrowded, having been settled by families evicted previously from Sgoirebreac, Torra-Micheig, Kilmuir and Staffin. The Braes crofters gradually found themselves being pushed down towards the less fertile coastal lands and year by year they became poorer and poorer. It is said that prior to 1865, each man in the township had at least one horse. Due to lack of grazing land, this number subsequently dwindled until there was barely one horse for every three men. The number of sheep and cattle likewise fell until eventually the people were facing starvation.

The sheep farmer's lease on Ben Lee was due to come to an end in 1882 and the Braes people were determined to regain their hill-land at this time. The crofters had been told previously by Lord MacDonald's factor that the grazings would be returned to them but this promise was broken and the factor re-let the hill on a new lease and then resigned. In desperation, the Braes people put their stock back on Ben Lee and refused to pay any additional rent. The landlord's reaction to this course of events was immediate: on 7 April 1882 sheriff officer Angus Martin was sent from Portree to serve eviction orders on a dozen of Lord MacDonald's tenants. Instead of quitting their homes and land quietly, as so many had done before, the Braes crofters decided to stand up to their oppressors. An angry crowd went out to meet Martin on the road and he was forced to make a pile of the summonses which were then set alight with a burning peat.

The landlord next arranged for Sheriff Ivory to send a large force to surprise and arrest the ring-leaders of this defiant act. On 17 April, 2 sheriffs, 2 fiscals, a police captain, 47 Glasgow policemen, 12 constables from the mainland County of Inverness and the Skye section of the police force were sent out from Portree to the Braes. This event came to be known as The March of The Dismal Brigade. As they arrived at the boundary of Balmeanach, the officers were met by a crowd of women, children and old folk. Most of the young men of the township were away from home at this time, engaged in fishing and other seasonal occupations. Within twenty minutes, the police had arrested the five suspects: Alexander Finlayson, his son Malcolm, Peter MacDonald, Donald Nicolson and James Nicolson. It was at this point that the women declared an attack. Amid a hail of stones and clods of earth, the police drew their batons and charged, but such was the fury of the women that they were soon forced back along the road. Professor J.S. Blackie, the great champion of the crofters' cause, described how the outraged women continued their assault until, "...like the great Napoleon at Waterloo, the police were forced to forget their dignity and seek safety in inglorious flight." The police continued their retreat until they reached a narrow defile where around 100 angry Braes folk were waiting for them. The crofters rushed towards the constables and a pitched battle ensued. This is often said to have been the last battle fought on British soil.

The presence of journalists at the Braes ensured nationwide coverage of the atrocious events which subsequently resulted in widespread sympathy for the crofters' cause. Mr Alexander Gow, special correspondent with the Dundee Advertiser, wrote of the terrible injuries sustained by the Braes women: "Scores of bloody faces could be seen on the slope of the hill. One woman, named Mary Nicolson, was fearfully cut in the head, and fainted on the road. When she was found, blood was pouring down her neck and ears. Another woman, Mrs Finlayson, was badly gashed on the cheek with some missile. Mrs Nicolson, whose husband, James Nicolson, was one of the prisoners, had her head badly laid open, but whether with a truncheon or stone is not known."

The police were eventually able to make their way back to Portree without further trouble. As they passed through Somerled Square to place the suspected ringleaders in prison, they were loudly hissed and booed. They were also jeered as they subsequently made their way from the Court House to the Royal Hotel. It is said that a group of crofters marched to Portree that same day to storm the jail, but they turned back just before reaching the town on the advice of local ministers.

The five Braes men were imprisoned for a week without seeing an adviser. After this time, they could no longer be legally held without being charged and so they were committed for trial and then released on bail. The bail bond was paid from donations given by members of the public, for by this time there was a great deal of sympathy for the crofters, not only in the Highlands but in the large cities of the south. The Crown Agent denied the Braes men trial by jury and instead ordered them to be summarily tried before the Sheriff of Inverness on 11 May for the crimes of deforcement and assault. In the eyes of many, such a trial was grossly unfair for it incurred all the inconvenience and expense of a jury trial without having any of the advantages. Mr Kenneth Macdonald, solicitor and Town Clerk of Inverness, appeared for the prisoners. Largely due to lack of evidence and a general feeling that the authorities were resorting to unworthy means to obtain a conviction, the charge against the Braes men was reduced to one of assault. For this lesser crime they were found guilty and fined. This was immediately paid for by well-wishers, together with the bill for the crofters' lodgings at the Glenalbyn Hotel and the train and steamer back to Portree the following day. As they walked free from Inverness Castle, the triumphant Braes crofters were cheered by a large crowd.

The matter did not end there however, for the question of the Ben Lee grazings was still unresolved. Several months later, the people of Braes once again let their sheep out onto the hill-lands. Lord MacDonald's Edinburgh agents sent letters to the crofters demanding that the animals be withdrawn from Ben Lee. When these were ignored, the Court of Session immediately issued notes of suspension and interdict against the Braes folk and on Saturday 2 September, Mr Alexander MacDonald, Messanger-at-arms, accompanied by Lord MacDonald's ground-officer, set out from Portree to serve the writs. They were able to accomplish their task at Gedintailor, but as they proceeded towards Balmeanach, they were met by a large crowd of women and children. Once again there was a hail of stones and clods which caused the officers to make a hasty retreat. Following this latest event, Sheriff Ivory pressed the Lord Advocate to send a gunboat and marines to quell the crofters, but this request was refused. A second attempt was made to serve the writs on Tuesday 24 October, but again the officers and accompanying force of nine policemen were stopped at Balmeanach by a large crowd of men, women and children.

This latest sequence of events was extensively reported by the special correspondent of the Inverness Courier and some landlords began to wonder whether there might be something in the complaints of the crofters after all. Many people believed it ridiculous that a military force should have been called on to solve a dispute which could have been settled by any sensible landlord in a matter of minutes. Certain Highland lairds thus began to pressure Lord MacDonald to reach a settlement with his tenants. Eventually, after much correspondence in certain influential circles, Lord MacDonald's new factor, Alexander MacDonald, visited the Braes on 27 November. This meeting resulted in an agreement whereby the Ben Lee grazings were let to the crofters at a yearly rent of just over half that paid by the old tenant. The case against the crofters was withdrawn in December.

The sequence of events at Braes inspired crofters throughout the island to stand up to their landlords and to re-occupy land which had been taken from their ancestors. Soon agitation was widespread and in October 1884 Sheriff Ivory once again wrote to the Lord Advocate asking that a gunboat and marines be immediately sent to Skye, "...to protect the police and assist them in protecting the property and persons of the lieges of that island." This time the Sheriff's request was granted. The steamship Lochiel was commissioned from David MacBrayne but the Police Authority had to find new men to replace the Highland skipper and crew who refused to be party to this distasteful act. At Portree, the Lochiel was joined by the gunboat Assistance with 350 marines and 100 bluejackets and the Bantever with 65 marines. This impressive military force then set out to quell the troubled townships but the crofters had decided upon a course of passive resistance and as the fleet proceeded around the coast they were everywhere met with the sight of the villagers out in the fields digging potatoes. This demonstration of might was to backfire on the authorities, for there was subsequently an increase in the number of rent strikes and soon some landlords were reciving no rents at all.

The troubles on Skye and elsewhere received widespread publicity in the national newspapers and caused outrage throughout the country. The general populace were regularly confronted with images of Highland poverty and the cruelty of the landlords and there was a great deal of public sympathy for the plight of the crofters. Largely due to the Braes incident, great pressure was put on the Government to better the lot of the crofter and eventually Prime Minister Gladstone set up a Royal Commission to look into the problems of crofting tenure. As a direct result of the Commission's findings, the Crofters Act was passed in 1886. This Act went a long way to providing security of tenure for crofters and helped amend the law which was being used by landlords to prevent the people recovering the land taken from their ancestors.

Gedintailor To Peinchorran

After Gedintailor, the B883 passes the Balmeanach junction and continues down through the Braes. Braes is the home of the famous Gaelic poet, Somhairle MacGill-Eain (Sorley MacLean), who was born on the adjacent island of Raasay in 1911. MacGill-Eain's work has inspired many Gaels to write in their native language and he is largely responsible for the recent flowering of creative writing in Gaelic. Of his early work, perhaps the most important is the sequence of love poems, Dain do Eimhir, published in 1943. MacGill-Eain is also a champion of the crofters' cause and has written about the indigenous societies that maintain a precarious existence in the depopulated north-west Highlands. Anti-landlord and anti-clerical views are a recurrent theme in his work.

The B883 now passes the second Balmeanach junction, at the corner of which lies Glamaig Garden and The Workshop.

Garden and Crafts: GLAMAIG GARDEN AND THE WORKSHOP. Tel. (047 852) 226. A beautiful garden containing many unusual and tender species which flourish on Skye due to the mild climate. The garden features a miniature gorge with waterfalls, attractive herbaceous borders and a rockery. Plants are often offered for sale. (The garden is not suitable for wheelchairs). Open daily from Easter to mid September. Admission is by donation to the Scottish Society for the Prevention of Cruelty to Animals. While visiting the garden, call in to see the many fine woodturned items in The Workshop. Cabinet maker Richard Townsend manufactures a range of furniture and other turned goods in a variety of woods, including solid native hardwoods. Commissions are undertaken and Richard specialises in the repair and restoration of antique and modern furniture. The showroom is open on weekdays from Easter to mid September.

The B883 continues to Peinchorran and ends at a parking space with two picnic tables. From here you can watch the Raasay ferry come and go from Sconser. There is also a good view south to the great rounded mass of

Glamaig. A pleasant detour is to be had on the return journey by taking the minor road to Balmeanach which branches right at Glamaig Garden. This route gives fine views to Raasay and the Trotternish coast to the north.

BRAES TO PORTREE

Returning to the main A850 road, Loch Portree is soon seen to the right. Lying close to the far shore of the loch is a tiny tidal island which contains the scant remains of a chapel dedicated to Saint Columba. Tradition has it that the chapel was actually founded by the saint during his wanderings across Scotland. Just before you enter Portree proper, the attractive new Aros Centre can be seen to the left of the road.

AROS: Skye's Heritage Centre

All the ingredients for a perfect day out.....

- The **Skye: The Island** exhibition
- Commentary available in six languages.
- The highly acclaimed "**Skye-Lights**" audio-visual show.
- Forest walks and the Gaelic Alphabet Trail.
- 80-seat **An Darach** restaurant overlooking Portree bay and Ben Tianavaig.
- Aros's well-stocked and original shop.

Open every day 9am - 6pm (until 9pm high season)

Aros, Viewfield Road, Portree.
Phone 0478 613649 Fax 0478 613100

Heritage Centre: THE AROS CENTRE. Tel. (0478) 613 649. A newly opened heritage centre, not to be missed. *Aros* is an old Gaelic word meaning "home" or "homestead". An atmospheric and emotionally moving exhibition of Skye's history, Gaelic language and culture. Headphones provide a personal commentary to guide you around displays on Bonnie Prince Charlie, the Highland Clearances, the Napier Commission, the journey of the slave-ship William and Johnson and Boswell's visit to the island. At the end of the tour there is a stunning audio-visual display on Skye today with music by Skye musician Blair Douglas. Admission fee applies, reduced rates for Children, Senior Citizens, Students and the Disabled. Under 5's admitted free. Special family tickets are also available. When you have finished looking round, call into the attractive 80 seat fully licensed Darach Restaurant for refreshments - hot and cold drinks, meals, snacks and a mouthwatering selection of cakes. The Centre also contains an excellent shop which sells a wide selection of Scottish and walking books, ceramics, jewellery, postcards, Scottish interest videos, C.D.'s and cassettes and a range of shortbread and cakes. Credit cards/Switch are accepted. The complex also includes toilets. Access for the disabled. The Centre is open throughout the year, from 0900-2100 in the high season and from 1000-1800 in the off season.

Forest Walks: The Aros Centre carpark is the starting point for several signposted Forest Enterprise walks through Coille Phortrigh (Portree Forest) which have recently been upgraded to co-incide with the opening of the Centre. From here you can ascend Suidh Fhinn, Fingal's Seat, a small hill above the forest which gives excellent views of the surrounding countryside. There is also an innovative and educational nature trail based on the letters of the classical Gaelic alphabet which has been specially created for disabled visitors.

PORTREE

The town of Portree is the largest settlement on the island. This busy fishing port is the administrative centre for local government in Skye & Lochalsh and much of the trade and commerce on the island is focussed on the Portree area. Here the visitor will find many fine craft shops, a good variety of places to eat out and the only banks on the island which have cash-line machines. There is also ample opportunity for the self-catering holiday-maker to stock up on provisions from the wide range of food shops. If you are visiting in the summer, look out for the many events associated with the "Skye Week" Festival (usually late June), the Skye Folk Festival (July) and the annual Highland Games (early August).

Many people believe that the name Portree is an anglicisation of the Gaelic *Port-an-Righ*, which means "The King's Harbour". It is said to have taken this name following a visit to the town in 1540 by King James V during his "pageant and progress" through the Isles which was designed to impress the unruly clan chiefs and gain their submission to the Scottish Crown. The King set sail from Leith with a fleet of 12 ships and was accompanied on his journey by several important men, including Cardinal Beaton and the Earls of Arran and Huntly. This was intended to demonstrate the power of the Crown. After visiting Duntulm, the fleet sailed around the north of the island and anchored in Loch Portree, which was then known as Loch Chaluim Chille. King James came ashore and held court, receiving the various chiefs and lairds who had travelled from far and wide to pay duty to their sovereign. Prior to the King's visit, the small township of scattered houses was known as Kiltaraglen, the Cell of Talorgan, an early Christian missionary. Modern-day Gaelic scholars say that the name "Portree" is more properly *Port Ruighe*, the Port of the Slopes, a less romantic but nevertheless accurate description of the town's location at the foot of the surrounding hills.

The town as we know it today began to evolve in the latter part of the 18th century. The present lay-out owes much to Sir James MacDonald (1741-1766), the 8th Baronet of the MacDonalds, whose dream it was to enlarge Portree and establish the town as a major centre for trade and industry. Sir James was the son of Lady Margaret of Monkstadt who assisted Prince Charles in his escape from the island. He was an enlightened man, educated at Eton and Oxford and with a great aptitude for languages, speaking seven fluently. Sir James made the Grand Tour of Europe with the great Scottish economist Adam Smith and on his return to Skye he set about improving his lands and bettering conditions for his tenants. One important innovation carried out by the baronet was the establishment of the first Portree High School. Sir James's work was cut short by a shooting accident in Uist which led to a decline in his already frail health. He went to the Mediterranean to recuperate, but died in Rome in July 1766 at the early age of 25. The family commissioned a monument to be carved in Rome and this was brought to the island and erected in Kilmore Church, Sleat in 1768. Several of the later chiefs carried on Sir James's work and many of the place names in the town derive from famous MacDonalds, for example Wentworth Street which is named after George Wentworth, the son of the 17th Chief and Bosville Terrace, a family name of the MacDonalds of Sleat.

In the early 19th century Portree was an important centre for the herring industry. During the months of July and August, the Sound of Raasay would be fished by up to 70 boats from Portree Parish and the adjacent parishes of Glenelg, Lochalsh, Lochcarron, Applecross, Gairloch and Loch Broom. The catch was landed in Portree Harbour. With the decline of the herring industry, attention turned to other fish resources and in 1842, a southern gentleman leased all the fishing rights on Lord MacDonald's property and set up a company to process the catch. The fish, including salmon, was cured and sent from Portree by steamer to Glasgow and then on to London.

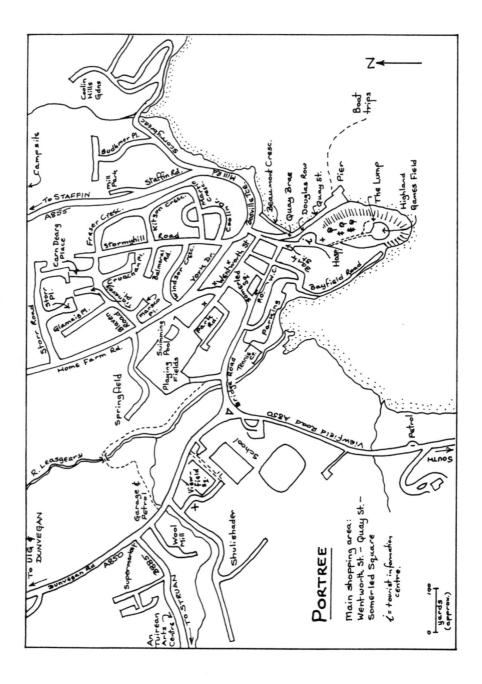

PORTREE

Main shopping area:
Wentworth St. – Quay St. –
Somerled Square

i = tourist information centre.

0 _____ 100
yards
(approx.)

Although there are no public ferry services operating from Portree today, the town was once well-served by a network of passenger ships. The island was visited by large sailing packets as early as 1756 at which date there was a regular service between Loch Carron and Portree. When the Dingwall & Skye Railway reached Strome Ferry in 1870, the railway company started a daily ferry service to Portree, with reduced sailings in the winter months. This service was taken over by David MacBrayne in 1880 and when the railway pushed through to Kyle of Lochalsh in 1897, the steamers were transferred there from Strome Ferry. By the end of the 19th century, it was possible to sail from Portree on various days of the week to Kyleakin, Broadford, Isleornsay, Armadale, Staffin, Kilmaluag, Stein, Dunvegan, Kyle of Lochalsh, Raasay, Eigg, Glenelg, Arisaig, Balmacara, Lochaline, Oban, Tarbert and Rodel on Harris, Lochmaddy on North Uist and Tobermory, Salen and Craignure on Mull. The steamships continued to serve the island until the outbreak of the First World War.

The first port of call for most visitors to the town will probably be the Tourist Information Centre. This was formerly the sheriff's court and jail-house for the whole island and it dates to 1810 which makes it the oldest building in Portree. The former jail still retains the original death cell and the exterior of the building has changed little since it was depicted in an early 19th century print by the artist and aquatinter William Daniell. Daniell executed his sketch of the town while engaged in an attempt to circumnavigate the coastline of Britain, a grand tour which he had begun at Land's End in the summer of 1813. His engravings of Skye appeared in 1819. The old court-house continued in use until a new facility, the present court-house, was built in 1867 in Somerled Square.

Lying behind the Tourist Information Centre is a little hill known as The Lump or Sron a'' Mhill (the Point of the Hill). This was formerly used for public hangings. The last execution to take place here occurred on 18 June 1742 when Angus Buchanan was put to death for the murder of a travelling chapman. Around 5,000 islanders turned out to watch the proceedings. The Lump also contains a natural arena which has been used as the setting of the annual Skye Highland Games since 1877. Today, the Games are usually held in early August and if you are on the island at this time it is well worth-while trying to catch this exciting spectacle. The highest point of The Lump gives a good view out over Portree Harbour and here you can see the remains of a round look-out tower which was built by Alexander MacLeod (also known as Dr Ban), a visionary whose dream it was to transform Portree into a second Oban. It is said that the tower was once used by an apothecary. MacLeod is also responsible for planting the trees and shrubs on the Lump.

Also lying behind the Tourist Information Centre is the Skye Gathering Hall which was built in the 1870's to host the famous annual Skye Ball, an event which still takes place each year in August. The idea of the Skye Ball was started by a group of local landowners who, with the encouragement of Lady MacDonald, formed a society to organize an annual Gathering for those resident on Skye and the adjacent mainland. Membership of the society was strictly limited to fifty. £1,200 was raised to build a hall and the first Gathering took place in 1878. For many years the event consisted of two formal balls held at the end of summer with a day of games in between (the Skye Games are now an independent event). The balls were exclusive affairs, with only 60 dancers being admitted - full Highland dress essential. Tickets were extremely scarce, and could be obtained only at the request of a society member. The Gathering Hall was purpose built and originally contained all the facilities deemed necessary for a successful ball. In addition to the dance floor, there was a public gallery, a supper room, a sitting-out room, a kitchen and a cloakroom. After a gap during the First World War, the Skye Ball was started up once again, with members' wives donating refreshments and maids for the occasion. Much of the interior detail of the hall was lost in the 1930's when the building was altered to make room for more dancers.

The present Royal Hotel in Bank Street is built on the site of the old thatched MacNabs Inn where, in July 1746, Prince Charles said farewell to brave Flora MacDonald who had aided his escape from Benbecula. Here the Young Pretender lay hidden in an upstairs room waiting for a boat to take him to the adjacent island of Raasay. Dr Johnson and James Boswell also called at MacNab's on Sunday 12 September 1773 en route from Raasay to Kingsburgh. The renowned travellers had "...a very good dinner, porter and punch," with the innkeeper, James MacDonald, who was about to emigrate to North America. At that time Portree was a small township of scattered cottages and MacNab's Inn was the only hotel in the area. The accommodation to be found at the inn was not to the liking of the geologist Robert Jameson who visited Skye in the last years of the 18th century. Writing in 1800 Jameson says, "There are in the Highlands, as in other countries, places where strangers find bad accommodation; but certainly the inn of Portree has seldom been equalled for dirtiness: a traveller from among the Hottentots might well recognize the kraal, although so far removed from its customary situation."

At the heart of the town centre lies Somerled Square which is named after the 12th century founder of Clan Donald, the first Lord of the Isles. Somerled married Ragnihildis, the daughter of Olav the Black, King of Man and the Isles and eventually became king himself in 1156. The Square contains the attractive town war memorial which is fashioned in the style of an old Scottish Mercat Cross.

The buildings which line the way to the pier date from the early 19th century and were designed by Thomas Telford. Also of note on the waterfront is the attractive Rosedale Hotel. This large building was created by knocking through a row of fishermen's houses which date from the early 19th century.

Another building of interest is the Skye Woollen Mill in Dunvegan Road which started life over a hundred years ago as Hogg's Woollen Manufactory. Hogg's was built with the remains of a special "Destitution Fund" which had been collected to alleviate the terrible poverty caused by the Clearances and the failure of the potato harvest in 1846. The mill opened in the mid-1800's and was originally powered by a water-wheel driven by the nearby burn. Although Hogg's did employ a large number of the local populace, conditions were rather akin to those of a sweatshop and in the eyes of some it was just another means of exploiting the poor. There was also a certain irony that many of the destitute were now processing wool from the backs of the very sheep that had displaced them. In October 1851, Hogg's Woollen Manufactory was visited by the philanthropist Lady MacCaskill who was greatly disturbed by what she saw. In her book, *Twelve Days In Skye*, she described her visit: "By the side of the school stands Hogg's Woollen Manufactory - a water-mill sets the machinery in motion - towards the end of one endless room lie the skins of sheep in a heap, dirty and daubed with tar; on a bench beside them sat two strong-looking girls (they were fed!) who with their shears cut off the tarred points of the wool which was used up for coarse purposes; at the extreme end of this long room lay in heaps, the progress of human industry, *ingenuity and* INIQUITY! - stockings, socks, gloves, shirts, comforters, and drawers - all from the sheep's back! The articles were all arranged, paired, tied and bound together, as if for the London market!" In order to make anything approaching a living wage, the women who produced articles for the mill had to knit in every spare minute, even while weighed down with huge baskets of peats: "Slightly bending beneath their load, blow high or blow low, through wind and rain, and mud and mire, bare headed and bare legged they wend their way *and they knit as they go!!*" When Queen Victoria read Lady MacCaskill's account of conditions on the island, she sent a donation of £100. Hogg's later became the Skye Wool Mill and in 1945 it was taken over by James Pringle. His two sons, William and Hamish, ran the mills at Portree and Inverness until 1970 when a new company "Skye Woollen Mills Ltd" was formed. During its long and varied history, the mill has been employed in the manufacture of fishing ropes and blankets and in later years spun carpet yarn for the Glasgow carpet mills. King Edward VII was appreciative of the fine cloth produced at the mill and is said to have boasted that on eight successive visits to Scotland he wore a sporting suit made of Portree tweed.

Those interested in the story of Bonnie Prince Charlie may wish to visit St Columba's Church which contains a three-pane window commemorating Flora MacDonald.

PORTREE

Arts Centre: AN TUIREAN ARTS CENTRE, Struan Road. Tel. (0478) 613 306. *An Tuirean* is Gaelic for a spark struck from an anvil. A variety of exhibitions, performances and workshops are held throughout the year - watch local posters for information. Access for the disabled. Open Tuesday-Sunday 1000-1700 throughout the year. The Centre also incorporates the Anvil Cafe. A range of soups, cakes, homemade breads, snacks and full meals are available Tuesday-Sunday from 1000-1700. Additionally, evening meals are served between 1830-2100 on Tuesdays, Wednesdays, Fridays and Saturdays. Bookings are advisable. The imaginative menu includes traditional dishes which use unusual ingredients such as seaweeds and rowanberries. A range of vegetarian and vegan dishes are also offered, as well as game and seafood, a variety of puddings and Highland cheeses. The restaurant is licensed.

Banks: CLYDESDALE BANK, Somerled Square. Tel. (0478) 612 050. Autobank machine. Facilities: TSB (Scotland only), Northern Bank, Midland, Yorkshire, Link, Access.
BANK OF SCOTLAND, Somerled Square. Tel. (0478) 612 338. Facilities: Lloyds, Barclays, Visa, Link, Access, American Express, Mastercard.
ROYAL BANK OF SCOTLAND, Bank Street (next to Tourist Information Centre). Tel. (0478) 612 822. Autobank machine. Facilities: Lloyds, American Express, Eurocheque, Telebanco and Multibanco.

Bike Hire: ISLAND CYCLES, The Green. Tel. (0478) 613 121. Mountain bikes, touring and sports cycles available for daily and half daily hire and for longer periods at reduced prices. Children's sizes available. Lock, tools and pump supplied. Helmets, saddle bags and panniers are also available. I.D. and deposit required when booking. Also touring repairs while you wait. The workshop carries a range of tyres and tools for sale. Open Monday-Saturday 1030-1700.

Bus Tours: HIGHLAND BUS & COACH. Boards at Somerled Square. A choice of two tours. Dunvegan Castle: Departs 1030 and returns at 1515; Monday, Wednesday and Friday. North End and Skye Museum of Island Life: Departs 1030 and returns 1515; Tuesday and Thursday. Tel. (0478) 612 622 for bookings.
SUTHERLANDS BUS SERVICE. Boards at Somerled Square. All day tour to Talisker Distillery, Glenbrittle Beach and the Cuillin. Departs 1000 and returns to Portree by 1328 or 1730. Bus waits at Glenbrittle Beach from 1103 to 1225. Lunch at Old Inn, Carbost. Also to Fiskavaig Bay, Portnalong. Tel. (047 842) 286/280 for details. In addition, timetables are posted at each stand.

Car Hire: MACRAES GARAGE, Dunvegan Road. Tel. (0478) 612 554.

Cruises: SKYE CRUISES. Two hour cruises with descriptive commentary down the scenic Sound of Raasay on board the 75 passenger M.V. Tristar. The boat has an all-weather saloon, refreshments bar and toilet. Sailings depart from Portree Pier afternoons and evenings from April to October with additional morning sailings from June to August. Book at The Tackle Shop on Portree Pier or telephone (047 842) 272 for full details.
SKYES'L CHARTERS. Day cruises from 1000-1600 with lunch provided; evening sails from 1800 with Cordon Bleu cooking and wine; activity days at Raasay; two or three day wildlife cruises. Can be tailored to suit individual requirements. All sailings start and finish from Portree Harbour. Skyes'l Charters also offer week long holidays through spring and summer on board the Britannia, a 6 berth 60' Gaff cutter. Cruises give passengers the opportunity to explore the remote lochs and sounds of the Western Highlands and Islands. Sailing experience is not necessary and beginners are welcome. For full details of all cruises, telephone Vicki Samuels on (047 032) 413.   *(Continued)*

Early Closing: Wednesday.

Eating Out: BAYVIEW FISH & CHIPS. Tel. (0478) 612 846. Open Monday-Saturday 1200-1400 and 1630-2200. Closed Sunday.

BEN TIANAVAIG BISTRO, Bosville Terrace. Tel. (0478) 612 152. Excellent selection of vegetarian meals. Separate menu for fish and meat. Mains include vegetable pilau, curry, pasta Milanaise, moussaka and lasagna. There are a couple of outside tables (picnic benches) which overlook the harbour. Bring your own wine. Open Tuesday-Sunday 1200-1600 and 1800-2100 (last orders 2100, 2000 out of season).

BOSVILLE HOTEL, Bosville Terrace. Tel. (0478) 612 846. Licensed restaurant open 0800-2000 to non-residents. Popular with visitors and locals alike. Lunch is served from 1200-1700. Options include soup, fried haddock, poached salmon and a range of traditional puddings - all excellent value for money. Dinner is served from 1700-2000 and includes fried haddock, poached wild Skye salmon, scampi, rump steak and Skye strawberries & cream. A snack menu including a vegetarian option, sandwiches, scones, tea and coffee is also available throughout the day.

THE CAFE, Wentworth Street. Cafe, restaurant, ice-cream. Open Monday-Saturday from 0900 onwards.

CALEDONIAN HOTEL, Wentworth Street. Tel. (0478) 612 641. A fixed price high tea is served from 1800-2000. Choices include roast chicken, fried haddock, ham salad, gammon and pineapple, all with vegetables and chips. Bread and butter, scones & jam, tea or coffee. Or choose from the menu which includes soup, vegetable lasagne served with vegetables, chips or potatoes, beefburgers, bacon rolls and various sweets.

CUILLIN HILLS HOTEL, on outskirts of Portree. Tel. (0478) 612 003. Non-residents welcome. Bar lunches served daily 1200-1430 and bar suppers 1830-2100. Afternoon teas served 1430-1730. Morning coffee is also available. Dinner is served daily in the restaurant from 1830-2100. Scottish music is played every Tuesday from 2000 onwards.

FISH & CHIP SHOP, Pier Brae. Tel. (0478) 612 033. Open daily, including Sunday 0900-2300. Extensive takeaway menu including fresh seafood sandwiches.

GANDHI, Bayfield Road. Tel. (0478) 612 681. Indian Tandoori restaurant and takeaway. A full range of starters, main dishes and accompaniments, together with a selection of European dishes. Specialities include lamb pasanda, chicken tikka masala and tandoori mixed grill. Open daily 1200-1430 and 1730-2400 (until 2330 Sunday-Wednesday).

THE GRANARY COFFEE SHOP, Somerled Square. Tel. (0478) 612 873. A variety of snacks and meals including soup, fish, salads, baked potatoes and Vienna rolls with a selection of fillings. Vegetarian dish of the day. Gateaux, cheesecakes and other homemade sweets from the trolley.. Tea, coffee, wines, spirits, beers, soft drinks. Non Smoking section. A pleasant place for coffee or lunch. Dinner served Monday-Saturday 1800-2100.

THE ISLES HOTEL, Somerled Square. Tel. (0478) 612 129. Restaurant open to non-residents.

THE KING'S HAVEN HOTEL, Bosville Terrace. Tel. (0478) 612 290. Open to non-residents. Coffee shop open Monday-Saturday 1000-1700. Dinner served at 2000 daily, including Sunday.

PIER HOTEL. Tel. (0478) 612 094. Bar meals served from 1800-2100. Choices include soup, seafood, baked potatoes, various sweets, tea and coffee.

PORTREE HOTEL, Somerled Square. Tel. (0478) 612 511. A variety of options to choose from. The Carvery serves a special fixed price "Feast" from 1800-2130. Choices include Skye salmon, venison, baked snapper, salads and sweets. The Cocktail Bar serves a variety of food including starters, quiche, curry, Aberdeen Angus steak, fish and seafood, vegetarian meals, sweets, tea and coffee. Food is served from 1730, last orders are at 2200. The Somerled Suite offers an extensive a la carte menu from 1800-2130. Bar meals are also available in the Camanachd Bar from 1200-2200.

PORTREE HOUSE, Home Farm Road. Tel. (0478) 612 796. Bar lunches served 1200-1630 (1230-1545 on Sundays); evening meals served 1730-2200 (1800-2200 on Sundays). Children's play area.   *(Continued)*

ROYAL HOTEL, Bank Street. Tel. (0478) 612 525. Non-residents welcome. A La Carte and Table d'hote menus are available in the hotel restaurant and bistro. Cold buffet table, morning coffee and afternoon tea. Bar meals are also served throughout the day. Access, Visa, Mastercard and Eurocheque accepted.

THE SQUARE MEAL, Somerled Square. Open 0900-2100. Hot meals served from 1200 onwards. A variety of food including, soup, hot and cold meals, baked potatoes with a variety of fillings, filled rolls, sweets, scones, tea, coffee and cold drinks.

STEVIE'S KITCHEN, Bayfield Road. Tel. (0478) 613 210. Chinese takeaway. A variety of main meals, special set dinners and all the usual accompaniments. Open Monday-Saturday 1200-1400 and 1700-2300; Sunday 1700-2300.

TONGADALE HOTEL, Wentworth Street. Tel. (0478) 612 115. Meals served from 1200-2000 (children are allowed into the bar for meals until 2000). Starters, mains, sweets, tea, coffee, sandwiches, selection of Highland cheeses. Children's portions and vegetarian options are available by request. Every evening, except Wednesday, a special seafood menu is served in the licensed restaurant from 2000-2200 (until 2100 on Sundays). This includes lobster thermidore, moules mariniere, scallops genevieve, king prawn Provencale, a selection of sweets and Scottish cheeses.

Hairdressers: MARGARET ANN, Wentworth Street. Hair stylist. Tel. (0478) 612 276.
ROSEBANK SALON, Rosebank. Hair stylist. Sun bed also available. Tel. (0478) 612 788.

Library: PORTREE LIBRARY, Bayfield Road. Tel. (0478) 612 697. Open Monday and Wednesday 1400-2000; Thursday and Friday 1000-1700; Saturday 1000-1200; closed Tuesday and Sunday. The library holds parish registers on micro-fiche for tracing your family tree.

Market: PORTREE MARKET. A local market is held at various times of the year in the Skye Gathering Hall behind the Tourist Information Office. Items on sale include local crafts, knitwear, plants, ceramics, stamps and postcards. Watch local notices for information or telephone the Secretary on (0478) 640 383.

Open Air Games: Giant chess and petanque (the French game of aerial bowls) can be played in the Camanachd Square recreation area. Fee applies, reduced rate for children. There is also a picnic area and a children's playground. Tel. (0478) 613 755 for full details.

Petrol: EWEN MACRAE, Dunvegan Road. Tel. (0478) 612 554/002. Open 0800-2100. Sells Calor and Camping Gas. Hot car wash. Credit cards accepted.
PORTREE FILLING STATION, Viewfield Road. Tel. (0478) 612 251. Sells confectionery, coal. Open Monday-Saturday throughout the year 0800-2100; Sunday (April-November only) 0930-1730. Credit cards accepted.

Shopping: A' BHUTH BHEAG, Wentworth Street. Tel. (0478) 612 443. A wide range of unusual curios including antique jewellery, fishing gear, china and brass ware, old tools, books, paintings and prints. The shop also stocks the famous Isle of Skye Tartan cloth. Open Monday-Saturday, 0900-1730.
CALDER & LILEY, (Claigan Plants), Hedgefield Road. Tel. (0478) 612 969. Garden centre. Open Monday-Friday 1000-1230 and 1330-1730; Saturday all day. Access, Visa, Mastercard and Eurocard accepted.
CO-OP SUPERMARKET, Dunvegan Road. Tel. (0478) 612 845.
THE CORNER SHOP, Wentworth Street. Tel. (0478) 612 572. Bookshop and newsagent. A good range of Scottish guides and novels. A selection of crafts and photographic accessories. 1, 4 and 24 hour film processing. Open Monday-Saturday 0900-2100.
EISD MUSIC SHOP, Quay Brae. Tel. (0478) 612 990. Musical instruments and books, Gaelic and Scottish folk music.
JACKSON'S WHOLEFOODS, Park Lane. Tel. (0478) 613 326.
JANSPORT, Wentworth Street. Tel. (0478) 612 559. Camping equipment, waterproof clothing, jackets, insect repellant, tents, bedrolls, walking boots, waterproofing, O.S. maps and a good selection of Scottish walking, climbing and fishing books.

(Continued)

THE FISH SHOP, Pier Brae. Tel. (0478) 612 033. Fresh fish and shellfish arriving daily. Oak smoked fish products including Isle of Skye Smoked Salmon. Fish can be packed in a special box which keeps it fresh for up to 72 hours. Also fruit, vegetables and groceries. Open daily, including Sunday, 0900-2300.

FRASER MACINTYRE, Wentworth Street. Tel. (0478) 612 918. Newsagent. Selection of O.S. maps, Scottish books and postcards.

ALISTAIR MACKENZIE, The Pier. Tel. (0478) 612 181. Fishing tackle and gifts including Scottish and Gaelic cassettes, souvenirs and postcards. Cameras and film.

MACKENZIE'S BAKERY, Somerled Square. Tel. (0478) 612 028. Good selection of fresh breads and pastries.

D.A. MACLEOD, Wentworth Street. Tel. (0478) 612 100. Pharmacy, toiletries and photographic materials. Also a selection of gifts including Caithness Glass and Edinburgh Crystal. Credit cards accepted.

N. & D. MACLEOD, Industrial Estate. Tel. (0478) 612 222. Wholefoods, fruit and vegetables.

M. MATHESON, Wentworth Street. Tel. (0478) 612 551. Butcher.

A.M. MILLER, Wentworth Street. Tel. (0478) 612 585. Butcher, delicatessen and off-licence. Meat, poultry, fish, cheeses, Highland wines and a wide range of malt whiskies including Skye's own Talisker. Open Monday-Saturday 0830-2130.

MORAYFISH. On Portree Pier. Fresh fish and shellfish sold on landing.

NORTH SKYE FISHERMEN LTD, the Harbour, Quay Street. Tel. (0478) 612 245. Chandlers. Oilskins, wellington boots, socks and shirts.

OVER THE RAINBOW, Quay Brae. Tel. (0478) 612 555. Unusual designer knitwear manufactured on Skye. Also jewellery, accessories, lingerie, and hosiery. Open daily 0900-late.

PORTREE FREEZER CENTRE, Dunvegan Road. Tel. (0478) 612 720. Frozen food and groceries. Open 0830-1900.

PORTREE KNITWEAR COMPANY, Wentworth Street. Tel. (0478) 612 496. Designer knitwear including Arans. Also tartans, tweeds, kilts, skirts and a selection of gift items.

PRESTOS, Bank Street. Tel. (0478) 612 855. Open Monday-Wednesday & Saturday 0830-1730; Thursday 0830-1930; Friday 0830-1800; closed Sunday.

SKYE ORIGINAL PRINTS, Wentworth Street. Tel. (0478) 612 388. Beautiful colour etchings, both large and small, of the Skye landscape by artist Tom Mackenzie. A striking memento of the island. Open Monday-Friday 1000-1300 and 1400-1700. The studio also offers 1, 4 and 24 hour photographic development (0900-2100 Monday-Saturday). Credit cards accepted.

SKYE WOOLLEN MILL, Dunvegan Road. Tel. (0478) 612 889. A wide range of Shetland, lambswool and cashmere knitwear, tartans and tweeds at direct-from-the-mill prices. Also coats, skirts, trousers and jackets and accessories such as tammies, socks, ties, shawls and Heraldic Crests. Goods can be mailed to any part of the world and tax free shopping is available to overseas visitors. The mill has a cafeteria which serves light meals and snacks. During May open Monday-Saturday 0900-1730; June-September Monday-Saturday 0900-1800 and Sunday 1100-1600. Visa, Access, American Express, Diners Club and JCB cards are accepted. Most major currencies and travellers cheques also accepted.

D. STUART & CO, Wentworth Street. Tel. (0478) 612 181. Hardware. Closed Sunday.

TIPPECANOE, Wentworth Street. Tel. (0478) 612 970. A variety of attractive quality gifts including Celtic design mugs, coasters, placemats and teapot stands, pottery, jewellery, T-shirts, O.S. maps and a selection of Scottish books.

UP COUNTRY SHOP (North Eastern Farmers), Struan Road. Tel. (0478) 612 212. Wax jackets, wellies, boots, jeans, body warmers, Household and D.I.Y. products and a variety of equestrian and pet care products.

Slide Shows: The Skye and Lochalsh District Council Building in Park Lane, Tigh na Sgire, holds daily slide shows throughout the summer months. The building is also the venue for various evening concerts and films. For information, watch out for local posters.

(Continued)

Swimming Pool: SKYE SWIMMING POOL, Park Road. Tel. (0478) 613 755. 20m x 7.1m heated indoor pool. Access for the disabled. Costumes, towels and armbands are available for hire. Admission fee applies, reduced rates for Children, Senior Citizens and the Unemployed. Disabled and under 5's are admitted free. The pool is open Monday-Saturday throughout school term time and the local summer school holidays. Opening hours vary - please telephone for full details.

Tennis & Squash: Tel. (0478) 613 755. Equipment hire available. Two tennis courts and one squash court.

Tourist Information Centre: Tel. (0478) 2137. Located upstairs in Meall House, Bank Street in the town centre. Open all year, Monday-Saturday 0930-1900 (0900-2000 High Season). When the office is closed, an electronic window display provides information on accommodation and visitor attractions in the area.

Toilets: Opposite Post Office, Bridge Street; Playing Fields, Park Road.

SLIGACHAN TO DUNVEGAN

The A863 to Dunvegan branches westwards at the Sligachan Hotel and begins to climb steadily amidst a landscape of rounded grassy hills. To the left is a breathtaking view down the full extent of Glen Sligachan, flanked on the left by the Red Hills and on the right by the Black Cuillin. These magnificent mountains are actually the root of a great volcano which was active some 60 million years ago. The Red Hills are comprised of granite which formed deep underground when the heat from the upwelling molten basalt altered the surrounding rocks. The gabbro of the Black Cuillin represents the solidified reservoir from which the lava erupted to the surface. These great masses of rock were subsequently laid bare over a long period of time by the forces of ice, sea and rain to produce the spectacular mountains seen today. The junction of the two rock types is roughly denoted by the course of the River Sligachan.

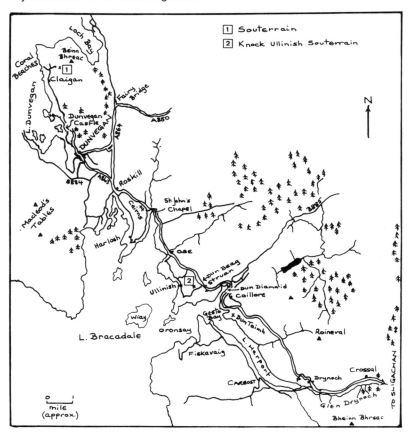

Glen Sligachan is a fine example of a vast "U"-shaped valley, carved by ice as great glaciers pushed their way across this land during the last Ice Age 10,000 years ago. At the far end of the glen, the buff coloured scar which marks the footpath to the Coruisk viewpoint can be seen with the naked eye as it makes its way over the Druim Hain ridge some five miles distant. It is very difficult to gain a true appreciation of the scale of this grand landscape, a feature which leads to numerous emergency call-outs each year to rescue walkers who have overestimated their abilities.

The A863 continues through Glen Drynoch, following the meandering course of the River Drynoch. To the left lies Beinn Bhreac and on the flat ground before can be seen numerous rounded hillocks. Once you begin to look, you will see that there are many such mounds on either side of the road. These are glacial in origin and are comprised of coarse sands and gravels which were deposited here when the ice melted at the end of the last Ice Age.

About 3 miles from the Sligachan junction, the road passes an area known as Crossal. In the 19th century this was home to a vast encampment of gypsies who were attracted to the area by the great cattle markets which used to be held regularly at nearby Sligachan.

Glen Drynoch

Although deserted today, Glen Drynoch was once home to a thriving population of crofters. 1500 people were cleared from the glen in the early 1820's and the land was converted into two sheep farms. The renowned engineer Joseph Mitchell was engaged on the building of the Drynoch road in 1825-26 shortly after the evictions took place and he later described the scene in his *Reminiscences*: "The ruined cottages and green spots of the once cultivated crofts were to be seen scattered on the hill sides, indicating the sites of the abodes of the expatriated families; but all was then a solitude, and nothing was heard by the passing traveller but the bleating of sheep." All traces of the croft buildings have long since vanished, but here and there may be seen traces of lazy beds and drainage ditches. Most of those evicted subsequently emigrated to Australia and it is believed that these families founded the district of Skye on the Hunter River in New South Wales.

Glen Drynoch was also the site of one of the earliest battles to be fought between the MacDonalds and the MacLeods. The outcome of this encounter, which occurred in 1375, was the rout of the MacDonalds.

Drynoch To Struan

After passing the B8009 junction to Carbost, the A863 begins to climb high above Loch Harport. Towards the top of the ascent, there is a large carpark on the left from which there are spectacular views back to the Cuillin. The scene is particularly striking on clear evenings when the sunlight brings out the fine detail on the long ridge. The road continues across a peat moor, still in use today, and crosses the Meadale Burn. Here, the green fertile glen down to the left still bears traces of drainage ditches and ridge-and-furrow cultivation - remnants of the old agricultural system of the pre-Clearance crofters.

Glen Vidigill now opens up on the right and the Sumardale River is crossed. Sections of the old road can be seen to the right - note the attractive stone embankment just before the Coillore turnoff. At this point, on a hill to the left lie the tumbled remains of Dun Taimh. Within the walls of this Iron Age fort there is a small cairn which was erected in 1887 to commemorate the Jubilee of Queen Victoria. The road now bends left, giving views over Loch Harport to the tidal island of Oronsay and the lighthouse on Ardtreck Point. There are several parking spots on the left where you can stop to admire this scene.

A small road branches left and descends to Gesto House. The old mansion house, now in ruins, was once owned by MacLeod of Gesto and is said to have had the first slate roof in Skye. Gesto was also home for centuries to a famous herd of cattle which tradition says were descended from Fairy stock. Whatever the truth of this statement, the cattle were of striking appearance - large, with a pure white long coat and black-tipped horns. Sadly, there are none of these fine beasts left today. The present Gesto Farm is of an unusual type known as a courtyard farm. This architectural form is common in Ulster but rare in the Western Isles.

The A863 continues round to the head of Loch Beag. Just before the causeway over the loch is reached, the tumbled remains of Dun Diarmaid can be seen on a prominent knoll by the left of the road. This is a good vantage point from which to scan the loch for the herons which are often to be seen feeding here. If you are lucky you may also spot an otter playing in the shallows. Before the new causeway was built, travellers had to follow the old road all the way to the head of the loch to cross the Allt Mor by means of a small stone bridge. This single-track road is still in use today and provides access to several houses. The causeway crossing gives good views down the loch and then the road begins to ascend to the settlements of Bracadale and Struan. There is a large parking area to the right of the road by the Struan Grill.

STRUAN

Cruises: SKYECREWS CHARTERS. Tel. (0470) 521 492/373. Cruises on board Banrigh nan Tonn, a 32' Aquastar, depart daily throughout the year from Struan Jetty. There are two routes to choose from. Sail to Ardtreck Lighthouse and explore the spectacular Rhu na Clach cliffs before sailing amidst the islands in Loch Bracadale; the highlight of this cruise is a close encounter with MacLeod's Maidens, the fantastic rock pinnacles which lie just to the south of Idrigill Point. A shorter cruise operates down Loch Harport passing the Talisker Distillery and one of the largest fish farms in Scotland. Approximate cruise times (according to the tide): 1000-1230; 1400-1630; 1830-2000; 2030-dusk. Telephone for full details.

Eating Out: THE STRUAN GRILL. Tel. (0470) 572 293. Licensed restaurant, set in an elevated position with spectacular views across Loch Harport to the Cuillin Hills. Open Monday-Saturday 1100-2300; Sunday 1200-1400 and 1800-2300. Coffees, teas and snacks are served from 1100-1700, lunch from 1200-1400 and dinner from 1800-2300 (last orders 2130). Specialising in char grilled Aberdeen Angus steaks. Also venison, turkey, ham, prawns, salmon and trout. Popular with the locals, so booking is advisable.

Petrol: R.J. MACKINNON & SON, The Garage. Tel. (0470) 572 204.

Shopping: BRACADALE STORES. General groceries. Open Mon-Sat, 0900-1800.
STRUAN CRAFT WORKSHOP. Tel. (0470) 572 284. Specialist knitting shop. Designer knitwear by Di Gilpin available as handknits and as knitting kits. Mail order facilities are available. Also a variety of beautiful yarns for hand knitting including hand dyed Colinette yarns and Shilasdair yarns spun from locally produced fleeces. Beautiful wood engravings by Kathleen Lindsley - bird, animal and landscape limited edition prints on hand-made papers - superbly detailed. Open Monday-Saturday 1000-1700, April-October.

After Struan, there are several parking spots along this stretch of road which have good views out over the loch. A minor road branches left to Ullinish.

The Ullinish Road

About 1/3 mile down this single track road, by a farm gate on the right can be seen a small metal sign with red-brown lettering. This sign marks the way to Cnoc Ullinish Souterrain, an ancient stone-built underground storage facility. It is possible to park near the gate but take care not to block access. To locate the souterrain, go through the gate and walk to the grassy knoll directly ahead. Now walk to the right around the base of the knoll. The souterrain is reached after about 5 minutes and can be identified as a depression in the ground at the base of the knoll. A small entrance hole leads down into the structure. It is a good idea to bring a torch if you wish to examine the interior. Dating evidence from several sites suggests that souterrains belong largely to the first three centuries A.D. Apart from examples in eastern Scotland, these stone-built structures were entirely subterranean and were reached by a sloping passage whose entrance could be easily camouflaged. The inner chamber provided storage facilities for food and other items. The Cnoc Ullinish souterrain was visited by Dr Samuel Johnson and James Boswell during their tour of the Hebrides in 1773. In those days it was generally believed that such structures were the dwelling places of the first pygmy-like inhabitants of the island, although Dr Johnson thought it more likely that they served as hiding places in times of trouble. He later wrote in his *Journey To The Western Isles of Scotland*, "This cave we entered, but could not proceed the whole length, and went away without knowing how far it was carried. For this omission we shall be blamed, as we perhaps have blamed other travellers; but the day was rainy, and the ground was damp. We had with us neither spades nor pickaxes, and if love of ease surmounted our desire of knowledge, the offence has not the invidiousness of singularity." From the souterrain, continue down the Ullinish road and take the first left. Cioch Direct mountain sports equipment is located in the first house on the left.

Shopping: CIOCH DIRECT. Tel. (0470) 572 307. Mountain sports and leisure wear including fleece tops, waterproof jackets, salopettes, over trousers, bivi bags and paragliding suits. Mail order available.

Continue on past Cioch Direct for excellent views across the loch to the spectacular cliffs of Fiskavaig. At the end of this minor road there is a large quarry cutting on the left just before the last house. This is a convenient starting point for the popular walk to the tidal island of Oronsay (see Walks for full details).

Retrace your route past Cioch Direct and turn left back onto the Ullinish road. Before long you will reach the Ullinish Lodge Hotel, an attractive building which dates from the 18th century. Dr Johnson and James Boswell stayed here as guests of Sheriff MacLeod from Tuesday 21 to Thursday 23 September during their visit to Skye in 1773. Boswell recorded in his *Journal*, "We got to Ulinish about six o'clock, and found a very good farmhouse, of two stories. There is a plentiful garden (a great rarity in Sky,) and several trees; and near the house is a hill, which has an Erse name, signifying *'the hill of strife'* where justice was of old administered. It is singular that this spot should happen now to be the sheriff's residence."

Eating Out: ULLINISH LODGE HOTEL. Tel. (0470) 572 214. Open from Easter to October. Non-residents welcome for dinner from 1900. Booking essential. The hotel offers a variety of fine Scottish dishes with the emphasis on fresh local produce including Bracadale Scallops in Talisker sauce, dressed crab, venison in red wine and pheasant with redcurrants and walnuts. The house speciality is a seafood dish for two comprising lobster, local prawns and a selection of local shellfish.

At the Ullinish Lodge Hotel, the road takes a sharp right turn and shortly afterwards several stones can be seen on a little hill to the left. These are the remains of a Neolithic chambered cairn. Such funerary monuments are the communal burial places of the first farmers who began to settle the fertile coastal areas of Scotland in the fourth millennium B.C. The Ullinish cairn is of the passage-grave type, a broad class of monuments which occur throughout Cromarty, Orkney and the Hebrides. Passage-graves generally consist of a burial chamber reached by a short passage, the whole structure being covered with a circular cairn of stones. At Ullinish much of the cairn has been disturbed but the chamber, measuring c.17 feet by 10ft 3in, is still discernable. After the cairn, the road passes the houses of Ullinish and draws close to the shore, giving good views out across Loch Bracadale to Tarner Island. The road then takes a sharp right and continues around the base of Ben Toirlean to rejoin the A863.

Dun Beag

If you remain on the A863 after Struan instead of turning left to Ullinish, you will see a carpark and picnic area on the left, immediately after the junction. This viewpoint contains information boards about the area and is an ideal vantage point from which to view Dun Beag on the hillside opposite. Dun Beag is one of the best preserved brochs on the island and it is well worth while climbing up to have a closer look. To reach the monument entails an easy 5 minute walk each way.

The defensive towers known as brochs are unique to Scotland and appear to have evolved by about 100 B.C. Their distribution is almost exclusively confined to the far north of the Scottish mainland, western coastal areas, the Northern Isles and the Hebrides. Dun Beag is a classic example of this type of monument, consisting of an impressive circular dry-stone wall, some 4m thick at the base, pierced by an entrance passage which gives access to an inner courtyard. The passageway would once have been barred with a stout wooden door. As you enter the interior, a well preserved guard cell can be seen just to the right. Set within the wall to the left of the passage are the remains of a stone staircase which would once have given access to the wall top and perhaps to several upper floors. Although no evidence exists of roofing methods, it is likely that the tower was covered by timber and thatch. Brochs were primarily defensive structures and in times of danger would have provided refuge for the Iron Age communities which farmed the surrounding area.

Dun Beag was excavated between 1914 and 1920 by the Countess Vincent Baillet de Latour. The finds uncovered are typical of an Iron Age community: an iron knife and fish spear for hunting; a stone mould and clay crucibles for bronze working; a stone lamp; a pick fashioned from deer antler and coarse decorated pottery for everyday use. Also discovered were several beautifully made personal ornaments: a gold ring, bronze belt buckle, bronze pins, a segment of a glass arm band, glass beads, stone pendant and a possible stone pin head. A variety of other finds, including coins ranging in date from the 12th to 18th centuries, suggest that the site continued to be occupied, perhaps intermittently, for almost 2,000 years.

The renowned Welsh traveller Thomas Pennant visited Dun Beag in 1772, at which time the walls were standing to a height of 18 feet. Much of the stone was subsequently robbed for local building purposes. Dr Samuel Johnson and James Boswell also made the trek up to the broch in 1773 during their stay on the island and Johnson noted some flimsy buildings associated with the structure. These were later removed during the excavation of the interior.

Struan To Dunvegan

The A863 continues past Dun Beag and shortly after the northern Ullinish junction, a minor road branches right to Aurora Crafts.

Shopping: AURORA CRAFTS, Ose. Tel. (047 072) 208. Beautiful hand-made lace, mainly from original designs, manufactured on the premises. Also lace bobbins, corn dollies, candles and other hand-made craft items. Lace-making lessons can be arranged.

The A863 now crosses the river Ose and Loch Caroy soon comes into view on the left. Towards the head of the loch amidst a clump of trees lies the old Church of St John the Baptist. Although signposted, it is easily missed. There is a small parking area by the left of the road. The Episcopal church of St John the Baptist was built at the behest of several local Episcopalian families with the encouragement of MacLeod of Gesto. It is said that MacLeod changed his faith after he was preached against in the old Church of Scotland at Struan (now a ruin) for shooting a seal on a Sunday. The church and graveyard were consecrated in 1838. The graveyard wall was rebuilt in 1959 partly by the congregation of St Columba's Church in Portree and partly by Roger and Otta Swire (authoress of *Skye: The Island and Its Legends*) in memory of their parents. Tradition holds that the church is built on fairy ground and that here the little people "waulk" or shrink their cloth. It is said that if you put your ear to the ground, the sound of their waulking songs can still be heard faintly at certain times of the year.

After the church, the A863 crosses the Caroy River at the head of the loch and begins to climb. A minor road branches left to Feorlig and then another branches right to the crofts of Upper Feorlig which lie strung out along Glen Heysdal. Directly opposite this second turnoff, to the left of the A863, can be seen two impressive chambered cairns which occupy a conspicuous position on the hillside. These Neolithic tombs are still largely intact and the large mounds of white stone which cover the burial chambers are easily seen from the road.

Eating Out: HARLOSH HOUSE HOTEL. Tel. (0470) 521 367. Located on the minor road to Harlosh. Licensed restaurant open to non-residents. Booking is essential. Meals are served from 1830-2100. The restaurant uses fresh Scottish produce and specialises in locally caught fish and shellfish. The mouthwatering menu also features homemade breads, soups, deserts and chocolates. Open from Easter until mid October only.

Giant Angus MacAskill
MUSEUM

The tallest Scotsman, and the tallest recorded 'true' (non-pathological) giant, was
Angus MacAskill (1825-63), born on the island of Berneray, in the Sound of Harris,
in the Western Isles. He stood 7ft 9in (236cm) and died in St Anns', on Cape Breton
Island, Nova Scotia, Canada. — *Guinness Book of Records*

ANGUS MACASKILL (1825-63)
Height 7ft 9in · Weight 425lbs
The Museum contains a life-size model of Angus MacAskill

SITUATED IN THE CENTRE OF DUNVEGAN
NEAR THE PUBLIC CAR PARK

Telephone Dunvegan 296

OPEN DAILY
Monday-Saturday 9.30am-6.00pm
Sunday 12.30-5.00pm

● COACHES WELCOME ●

The A863 now crosses open moorland, giving good views left over Loch
Bracadale to MacLeod's Tables. A road branches left for Roag and Orbost
and then there are two junctions on the right for Portree. The B884 branches
left for Glendale just as the main road reaches the outskirts of Dunvegan.

DUNVEGAN

The little town of Dunvegan stands at the head of a long sea loch,
once known as Loch Follart, with splendid views across the water to the
Duirinish peninsula. The settlement lies at the heart of the crofting
communities of north-west Skye and here the visitor will find fine crafts,
grocery shops and of course the famous fairytale castle.

While in Dunvegan, those interested in clan history may wish to visit
the ruined church of Kilmuir which is situated about 1/2 mile along the A850
Dunvegan-Portree road. There is room for one car to park by the gate. The
church contains tablets commemorating many of the MacLeod Chiefs,
including the 28th Chief Dame Flora MacLeod, a tireless emissary for the
Clan who spent much of her life establishing contact with Clan members
across the world. Dame Flora died in 1976 aged 98. Here too can be seen
the grave of Roderick MacLeod, the MacLeod family historian. The outside
wall of the church contains a memorial to the famous MacCrimmons,

hereditary pipers to the MacLeods for 300 years. Ten generations of MacCrimmon pipers are buried at Kilmuir. Among the grand memorials of prominent families erected in the graveyard may be found commemorative stones to those who were forced to emigrate to Canada, Australia and New Zealand at the time of the Clearanaces. Kilmuir is also the last resting place of the great Bardess and Seannachie Frances Tolmie (1840-1926) who dedicated most of her life to preserving the ancient songs and traditions of Skye.

DUNVEGAN

Bike Hire: CROFT BIKES. Tel. (0470) 521 383. Mountain bikes are available for hire from Croft Bikes at the Croft Studio, on A850 just east of Dunvegan. Open throughout the year.

Cruises: LOCH DUNVEGAN BOAT TRIPS. Tel. (0470) 521 206. Located north of the village on the A850. Before the castle, a small road branches left to the jetty. There are two boats trips to choose from. Cruises operate from March to October.
1. Dunvegan Castle Seal Colony. Sail on board a traditional seal boat to see the famous Dunvegan Castle seal colony on Gairbh Eilean and the other small islands in the shallow waters near the Castle. The boatmen are trained to approach the seals quietly, enabling you to get some wonderful close-up shots. The trip takes approximately 25 minutes. Boats depart from the jetty at regular intervals throughout the day.
2. Loch Dunvegan. A 1 1/2 hour loch cruise on board the personal motor vessel of Clan Chief John MacLeod of MacLeod. A chance to explore the many islands in Loch Dunvegan and to see the multitude of sea birds and marine life which dwell there. If you are lucky, you may spot the dolphins and whales which enter the loch at certain times of the year. The boat sails as far as the island of Isay at the mouth of the loch. Cruises depart at 1100, 1400 and 1600 depending on weather and sea conditions.

Eating Out: ATHOLL HOUSE HOTEL. Tel. (0470) 521 219. Licensed restaurant open to non-residents. Morning coffee served 1000-1130; lunch 1230-1400; afternoon tea 1500-1630; dinner 1930-2130. Visa and Mastercard accepted. Open January-December.
DUNVEGAN BAKERY. Tel. (0470) 521 326. Takeaway service including rolls, soup, cakes, fish & chips and hot pies.
DUNVEGAN HOTEL. Tel. (0470) 521 497. Non-residents welcome. Bar meals served 1200-1400 and 1700-2100. An A La Carte dinner menu is available each evening in the dining room. Live entertainment. Open all year.
MISTY ISLE HOTEL. Tel. (0470) 521 208. Bar meals available. Also tea, coffee, breakfast, lunch and dinner. The hotel stages a ceilidh most weekends. Open January-December.
THE OLD SCHOOL RESTAURANT. Tel. (0470) 521 421. Serves morning coffee, lunch, afternoon tea with home baking and a la carte dinner, including seafood. Vegetarian and children's menu. Open daily, March to December. Licensed. Visa & Mastercard accepted.
THE TABLES HOTEL & RESTAURANT. Tel. (0470) 521 404. Non-residents welcome. Licensed. Open daily throughout the year. Teas, coffees and snacks served from 1000-1700, lunch 1230-1430 and dinner 1900-2200. Vegetarian meals available.

Museum: GIANT ANGUS MACASKILL MUSEUM. Tel. (0470) 521 296. A unique museum which tells of the life and times of Angus MacAskill, at 7ft 9in the tallest true giant on record. MacAskill was born on the island of Berneray in 1825 and was brought up in Cape Breton, Nova Scotia. He died at the age of 38 from fever. The fascinating displays include tales of his tours of New York with General Tom Thumb, a life size model and family history. Open Monday-Saturday 0930-1800; Sunday 1230-1700. Admission fee applies, reduced rates for Senior Citizens.

Petrol: ATHOLL FILLING STATION. Tel. (0470) 521 487. Open Sunday.
DUNVEGAN GARAGE. Tel. (0470) 521 234. Sells Calor Gas. Shell credit cards accepted. Closed Sundays. *(Continued)*

Shopping: THE CROFT STUDIO. Tel. (0470) 521 383. Situated just to the east of the village, on the A850 Portree road. Adjacent parking space. A quality selection of arts and crafts bearing original designs inspired by ancient Celtic manuscripts. Beautiful Celtic prints and watercolours, silk screened blouses, scarves, wall hangings and table linen, silver and pewter jewellery and Skye flora lampshades - all original and produced on the premises by the Budge family. Other locally produced crafts include handmade knives, illuminated calligraphy and wooden boxes. Credit cards accepted. Coffee available. Open Monday-Saturday 0930-1730; Sunday 1000-1630. Open throughout the year (closed Sundays November-February).
DUNVEGAN BAKERY. Tel. (0470) 521 326. Bakery and takeaway foods.
DUNVEGAN CRAFTS. Tel. (0470) 521 375. A selection of gift items including knitwear, pottery, wooden and leather goods, heather pot pourri, honey and postcards. Also sells postage stamps. Open January-December.
DUNVEGAN SPORTS. Fishing tackle.
FASGADH STORES. Tel. (0470) 521 432. General grocers and off licence.
THE FRUIT AND NUT PLACE. A fine selection of vegetables and wholefoods. Lots of varieties of potatoes in season.
AL. MACLEAN. Tel. (0470) 521 297. Newsagent & general merchant; photographic film.
PAUL ROSHER LEATHERWORKER. Tel. (0470) 521 458. Located at "Grianac" on the the A863 at the south end of the village. Hand forged leather goods, repairs and commissions. Open April-October, Mon-Friday 0930-1800, also some Saturdays - please telephone first.
THE ST KILDA CONNECTION. Situated by the left of the A850 en route to the castle, just after the large church. A wide selection of traditional woollens and designer knitwear. Beautiful handloomed sweaters in natural wools. Also a selection of other quality gift items including coats, waistcoats, scarves, gloves, hats, rugs, handpainted glass and handmade leather goods.

Toilets: Situated in carpark by left of A863, as you enter Dunvegan from the south. Separate facilities for the disabled. Drinking water tap on outside wall.

North To The Castle

The A850 heads out of Dunvegan village in a north-westerly direction and passes through an attractive area of forest. A small road branches left to Dunvegan Castle jetty (see above for cruise details). The jetty carpark gives fine views of the castle perched atop its rock. This fortification was described by Sir Donald Monro, High Dean of the Isles in 1549 as "...the castle of Dunbeggan pertaining to McCloyd of Herray, ane starke strengthe, biggit upon ane craig." There are several picnic tables adjacent to the carpark and also a board with a map of the castle and grounds. Continuing north on the main road, Dunvegan Castle itself is soon reached. There is a large carpark to the right of the road.

Dunvegan Castle

There can be few people who have not heard of the famous fairytale Castle of Dunvegan. A visit to this fascinating place should be high on the list of things to do when on Skye. The castle has been continuously occupied by the Chiefs of Clan MacLeod for more than 700 years, a fact which makes it the oldest continuously inhabited residence in Scotland. It has served as the seat of MacLeod of MacLeod for 30 generations and today is the home of the present Chief, John MacLeod of MacLeod, the 29th of the line, and his family.

Romantic and Historic
DUNVEGAN CASTLE

WELCOME
TO THE ISLE OF SKYE

Any visit to this enchanted Isle must be deemed incomplete without savouring the wealth of history offered by Dunvegan Castle.

- Licensed restaurant.
- Two craft and souvenir shops.
- Castle water gardens.
- Audio-visual theatre.
- Clan exhibition.
- Items belonging to Bonnie Prince Charlie.
- Loch boat trips.
- Famous seal colony.
- Pedigree highland cattle herd.
- Loch cruises.

OPENING TIMES
21st MARCH - 29th OCTOBER

Romantic and Historic

DUNVEGAN
C A S T L E

THE HOME OF THE CHIEFS OF MACLEOD FOR NEARLY 800 YEARS

Before you leave DUNVEGAN you'll have to call in at

The St. Kilda Connection

WE OFFER TRADITIONAL WOOLLENS AND HAND CRAFTED GIFTS AT AFFORDABLE PRICES.

The St. Kilda Connection offers a selection of handloomed sweaters produced from natural wool and finest quality yarns. Subtle soft dyes reflecting the mood of the landscape are contrasted with the vibrant colours and intricate patterns of other styles.

A celebration and collection which echoes the skills of craftsmen and women passed from generation to generation.

ALSO AVAILABLE ARE: CAPES, WRAPS, COATS, SCARVES, TIES, WAISTCOATS, GLOVES, HATS, SOCKS, RUGS, HANDPAINTED GLASS, HANDMADE LEATHER GOODS WITH CELTIC DESIGNS, DESIGNER WOOLLENS, COTTONS, TEE-SHIRTS, PLUS MANY OTHER GIFTS.

We welcome browsers.

We are confident that this exciting selection of woollens and gifts will tempt you.

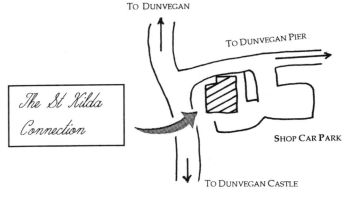

The St. Kilda Connection

Exceptional quality at affordable prices.

So why not call in, we're on the corner of the road leading to Dunvegan Pier.

The MacLeods are descended from Leod, grandson of Godred the Black, the 12th century King of Man and the Isles. Leod acquired Dunvegan, together with various lands on Skye, partly through his marriage to the daughter of the MacRaild chief whose seat was at Dunvegan and partly as foster son and heir to Pal Balkeson, the sheriff who administered the island on behalf of the King of Man and the Isles (Skye at that time was a possession of the Norwegian Crown). Leod's sons, Tormod and Torquil, were the founders of the two main branches of the clan; from Tormod come the MacLeods of Glenelg, Harris and Dunvegan and from Torquil the MacLeods of Lewis, Waternish and Assynt.

Dunvegan Castle originally took the form of a traditional Highland keep with surrounding ramparts which may have replaced an earlier Iron Age fortification on the same site. The oldest part of the castle is the 13th century curtain wall which once completely encircled the summit of the rocky outcrop. This was pierced by a sea gate which remained the only entrance to the castle until the landward gate was constructed in 1748. The interior timber or stone buildings belonging to this early castle have been largely obliterated by later additions. In the 14th century, a sturdy four storey tower containing a kitchen and feasting hall was erected at the north-east end of the platform. This was later substantially modified in the 1790's by Norman, the 25th chief. In the mid-16th century, the feasting hall witnessed the bloody slaughter of eleven Campbells as they sat at dinner, a gruesome deed which was ordered by the notorious Iain Dubh in an attempt to maintain his position as chief. The famous Fairy Tower dates to the early 16th century and is said to have been built by the 8th Chief, Alasdair Crotach or Hunchback (1500-1547), so called because of a deformity resulting from an axe blow. A spacious residential hall was erected adjoining the north wall of the Fairy Tower in 1623 by the distinguished chief Sir Roderick MacLeod, the great Rory Mor. Roderick was knighted by King James VI in 1603 and was held in high esteem by the clan. Upon his death in 1626 Patrick Mor MacCrimmon composed the famous piobaireachd "Rory Mor's Lament" in his honour. The last major building phase at the castle involved the addition of a three storey wing adjoining the west wall of the Fairy Tower. This was undertaken by the 16th chief, Iain Breac, in 1684-86. The Fairy Tower was also restored at this time. It is said that Iain Breac was the last Scottish Chief to employ a full retinue of bard, harper, piper and jester in his household. The exterior appearance of the castle today is largely the result of 19th century renovations.

In days of old, the generosity of the MacLeod chiefs was renowned throughout the country and in the 18th and 19th centuries many distinguished visitors to the Western Isles made their way to the castle to partake of the famous hospitality. Johnson and Boswell stayed there from Monday 15 to Tuesday 21 September 1773 and here the pair were so lavishly entertained with "admirable venison and generous wine" that Johnson commented, "Boswell, we came in at the wrong end of this island." Great care was taken of Dr Johnson who was suffering from a bad cold, and one of the young ladies of the household made a large flannel nightcap for him to wear in bed. Johnson celebrated his 64th birthday while at the castle.

Dunvegan was also visited by Sir Walter Scott during his cruise around the north of Scotland on board the yacht of the Lighthouse Commissioners in the autumn of 1814. His stay inspired him to write his famous work "Lord of The Isles". Scott arrived at Dunvegan on the 23rd of August and was taken to the castle by the MacLeod chief. He later recorded, "We were most kindly and hospitably received by the Chieftain, his lady, and his sister; the two last are pretty and accomplished young women, a sort of person whom we have not seen for some time;" Scott spent a night in the Fairy Tower, in the same bedroom as that previously occupied by Samuel Johnson, which by this time was supposed to be haunted by the ghost of the great chief Rory Mor: "I took possession about the witching hour. Except, perhaps, some tapestry hangings, and the extreme thickness of the walls, which argued great antiquity, nothing could have been more comfortable than the interior of the apartment; but if you looked from the windows the view was such as to correspond with the highest tone of superstition." The ghost of Rory Mor did not put in an appearance however and Sir Walter slept soundly until he was roused by his servant next morning.

Visitors to the castle today can see the three great treasures of the Clan MacLeod: the Fairy Flag, the Dunvegan Horn and the Dunvegan Cup. Of these, the Fairy Flag or Bratach Sith MhicLeoid is undoubtedly the most famous. Tradition relates that this flag first came into the possession of the MacLeods through William, the 4th chief, around the year 1380. It is said that William fell in love with a woman from the fairy world and took her as his wife. All went well until the birth of their son, whereupon the fairy woman was commanded by her kin to return to her own people. With heavy hearts, the couple took leave of one another on the Fairy Bridge at Waternish and the Chief returned to Dunvegan Castle. One evening, as the baby son lay asleep in his crib neglected by his nurse, he kicked off his covers and awoke cold and shivering. His cries were heard by his mother and she returned to comfort him and covered him with a fine cloth. This ancient cloth is now known as the Fairy Flag. The flag is said to have three magical properties: when waved in battle, it ensures victory for the MacLeods; when spread on the marriage bed it grants children, and when hoisted at Dunvegan Castle, it charms herring into the loch. Other traditions say that the flag may only be unfurled when the clan is facing defeat on the battlefield, when the life of the heir is in danger or when the clan is facing extinction. The flag may only be waved three times and it is believed that the MacLeods have already sought its aid on two occassions. It brought victory to the clan at the Battle of the Spoiling of the Dyke c.1540 (see Waternish section) and is also variously said to have been used at the Battle of Glendale, the Battle of Loch Sligachan, the Battle of Bloody Bay and to end a terrible cattle plague which was wiping out the island's main source of income. Whatever the truth of these claims, it is likely that the cased flag was often carried into battle to provide a rallying point and to give courage to the MacLeod forces. This tradition continued right up until the Second World War when many young clansmen in the armed forces carried a photograph of the flag as a lucky charm. Whenever the Fairy Flag was carried into battle, it was defended by a specially chosen guard of twelve champion swordsmen. The honoured position of standard-bearer was a hereditary one which carried with it the gift of free lands in Bracadale. The Fairy Flag has been examined by textile experts at the Victoria and Albert Museum who are of the opinion that it was woven in Syria or Rhodes. The flag is of strong yellow-brown silk, now faded, with patches of red embroidery which have come to be known as "elf-spots". It was probably a holy relic, perhaps a saint's shirt, which served as the consecrated banner of an order of the Knights Templar. It may have been brought back to Dunvegan from the Holy Land by a MacLeod chief at the time of the Crusades.

The Dunvegan Horn dates to the time of the 3rd MacLeod Chief, Malcolm (1296-1370). One day, as Malcolm was returning home to the castle following a secret meeting with the wife of Fraser of Glenelg, he was attacked by a wild bull. Armed only with a small dagger, he managed to kill the bull and cut off one of its horns as a token of his manhood. This incident is said to have given rise to the MacLeod crest of a bull's head and the motto "Hold Fast". The large ox horn, now rimmed with a deep silver band on which is engraved a Celtic lacing pattern, holds 5 pints of liquid. Today this item is of great importance to the Clan and each male heir to the line must drink a great draught of claret from the horn to prove his worth. Nowadays a false bottom is inserted to make this feat possible. The third clan treasure, the Dunvegan Cup, dates from the Middle Ages and was presented to the great MacLeod chief, Rory Mor, by the O'Neils of Ulster to thank him for his support against the English in 1596. The cup stands on four little silver feet and bears the date 1493.

Other prized articles on display include a lock of Bonnie Prince Charlie's hair cut by Flora MacDonald as a memento and placed in a locket, the glasses worn by Prince Charlie's boatman, Donald MacLeod of Galtrigill, one of Flora MacDonald's pin cushions which contains the names of various people connected with the 1745 Rebellion, letters from Dr Samuel Johnson and Sir Walter Scott and the great two-handed sword of Rory Mor. The Castle also contains many antiques and oil paintings, including family portraits by Raeburn and Ramsay, and the Library is well stocked with a variety of rare books. Visitors can also see the gruesome bottle-dungeon.

The Castle is surrounded by beautiful gardens which were originally laid out in the 18th Century. A variety of paths lead through the shady woodland glades to a formal round garden. The woods of beech, oak, cherry, chestnut, pine and cypress were planted in 1780. Over 40,000 of the trees were blown down in the great hurricane of March 1921 and much restoration work has been carried out since to return them to their former glory. Additionally, much replanting and landscaping work has been undertaken in recent years and the gardens now feature a wide variety of herbaceous plants and rhododendrons. The grounds contain a pretty cascade which is known as Rory Mor's Nurse. It is said that the great chief never enjoyed a night's rest when removed from the soothing murmur of this fall.

DUNVEGAN CASTLE, DUNVEGAN

Castle Visits: DUNVEGAN CASTLE is open from March to October, Monday-Saturday 0900-1730 (last entry 1700), Sunday 1300-1730. Visits may be possible outwith this period by prior arrangement. The castle gardens are open throughout the year. Admission fee applies: tickets are available for the Castle and Grounds or for the Grounds only. Castle admission includes a fascinating twelve minute audio-visual presentation by the present Clan Chief which deals with the history of Dunvegan and the MacLeods. The Castle also contains a craft shop. For further details, telephone the Castle Office on (0470) 521 206.

Eating Out: MACLEOD'S TABLE. Tel. (0470) 521 310. Licensed restaurant. A variety of foods from tea, coffee and snacks to complete meals are served daily during Castle opening hours. Open from March until October. During June, July and August the restaurant opens in the evening as MacLeod's Table Bistro with table licence and waitress service. A variety of specially prepared "dishes of the day" are offered. Local seafood is often available. Last orders 2130. Credit cards accepted.
CARPARK KIOSK. Located in the castle carpark. Sells filled rolls, sweets etc.

Shopping: CASTLE CRAFT SHOP. Tel. (0470) 521 206. Located in the castle carpark. The wide range of quality items on sale includes glassware, pottery, a good selection of Scottish books, postcards, jewellery, paperweights, shortbread, whisky, O.S. maps, stamps and a good selection of specialty jams and preserves. Open daily, March-October.

On The Road To Claigan

After Dunvegan Castle, the road becomes single track and descends to the coast, giving good views across Loch Dunvegan to the Colbost Islands opposite. Lying just off-shore on the Dunvegan side is Gairbh Eilean (the Rough Island). Both brown and grey Atlantic seals are often to be seen here. The road now descends to cross the attractive reed covered Loch Suardal by means of a small causeway. Immediately after the causeway there is a large parking area on the left. This is the starting point of an easy walk to Dun Fiadhairt broch (see Walks for full details). The road now begins to climb and Loch Corlarach is seen to the left. As height is gained, there are good views across Loch Dunvegan to The Duirinish Peninsula. At the first T-junction, turn left and pass the crofts of Claigan which lie at the foot of Beinn Bhreac. A left turn at the second T-junction leads to a large carpark. This carpark is the starting point of a popular walk to the Coral Beaches and is also a convenient place to park if you wish to visit the Claigan souterrain (see Walks Guide for details).

PORTREE TO STRUAN

The B885 links the east and west coasts of Skye and offers the opportunity of an easy drive across the wild moorland of the interior. The single-track road heads west out of Portree and begins a steady climb to the little settlement of Glengrasco where minor roads branch left to Mugeary and right to Coulnacraggan and Benness. The B885 continues around the foot of Ben Grasco and crosses an area of peat moor, still used by local crofters today. After dipping down to cross the River Snizort, the road begins to climb again and passes through patches of forestry before emerging out onto the open moor.

The watershed is crossed as the road continues through the pass between Beinn a Mhadaidh and Braon a Mheallain and the headwaters of the Allt Mor are soon seen to the left. This small river enters a gorge just before the settlement of Totardor is approached. Ahead there are intermittent glimpses of the sea and the cliffs of Minginish near Ardtreck Point. The road now descends, giving good views down the glen.

Open Farm: HILLCROFT OPEN FARM Tel. (047 072) 242. To the left of the road at Totardor. A 15 acre farm with a variety of common farm animals and some rare breeds including sheep, cattle, ponies, goats, pigs, hens, ducks etc. Admission fee applies, reduced rate for Children. Open daily Easter-October, 1000-dusk.

The B885 joins up with the A863 Sligachan - Dunvegan road 1 mile east of Struan.

PORTREE TO DUNVEGAN

The A850 to Dunvegan leaves Portree in a north-westerly direction and after 3 1/2 miles branches left at the BP Filling Station. After this junction, the road continues west across a rather flat, open landscape. The visitor is now at the heart of the ancient lands of Sgoirebreac which were once a possession of the Clan MacNicol. The MacNicols were originally from Assynt in Sutherland. In the 14th century, the daughter of the last of the Assynt chiefs married Torquil MacLeod whereupon the lands of Assynt passed to the MacLeods of Lewis. At this time it appears that the Clan MacNicol moved across to Skye where the MacLeods held extensive territories. In the early 19th century, Norman, the last Chief of the Sgoirebreac Nicolsons, sold his land to Lord MacDonald and emigrated to Tasmania. Lord MacDonald subsequently evicted the remnants of the clan and gave Sgoirebreac over to sheep.

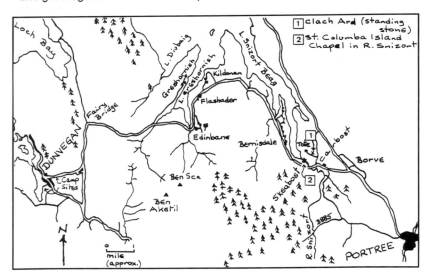

Shortly after the Glengrasco road junction, the A850 passes through the communities of Carbost and Crepkill. The B8036 then branches right, giving access to the Clach Ard symbol stone, a carved slab which dates to the time of the Picts.

The Clach Ard Symbol Stone

To find the Clach Ard symbol stone, turn right onto the B8036 and then take the first left signposted to Tote. After a short distance, the stone can be seen by the right of the road, surrounded by a small wooden fence. The

Clach Ard stone dates to the late 7th/early 8th century A.D. It belongs to the earliest class of Pictish symbol stones, that is boulders or roughly prepared slabs which display groups of incised or pecked symbols. The Clach Ard stone bears the symbols known as the crescent rod and spectacles which are thought to commemorate a marriage alliance between different family groups.

St Columba's Island And The Nicolson Chapel

On a small island in the River Snizort is one of the most important early ecclesiastical sites in the Western Isles. To find the site, return to the A850 and cross the River Snizort. Turn right immediately after the bridge and leave your car in the large parking area behind the old post office building. Walk to the right, in front of the post office building (once an inn on the road from Portree to Uig), go through the gate and cross the river by means of the old bridge. After the bridge, turn left and follow the track which descends to the river bank. Access to the island is by means of a small wooden bridge.

The island takes its name from the Irish missionary St Columba who visited Skye sometime in the late 6th century and is said to have baptised an aged pagan chief near this spot. From 1079 until 1498 St Columba's Island was the location of the ancient burial ground and cathedral church of the Bishops of the Isles. The site is first mentioned in 1079 when Wymond or Hamond was consecrated Bishop of Skye at York. According to various records held in Norway and the Vatican, the island continued to be the seat of the Bishops of the Isles until 1498, apart from a period of 62 years when the bishopric was transferred to the Isle of Man. After 1498, the cathedral church was moved to Iona. Included in the island's colourful history is an event which took place in 1223. Reginald, Bishop of the Isles at that time, was involved in a family quarrel between the Norse King of the Isles and Man and the King's brother, Olav the Black. One day, while staying on the island, the King's son Godric was attacked and captured by his uncle Olav. Despite being subject to the most horrific torture, including having his eyes put out, Godric managed to survive.

The restored mortuary chapel belongs to Clan MacNeacail, the Nicolsons of Sgoirebreac. The stones used in its construction come from the original chapel on the island. Tradition has it that 28 clan chiefs are buried in Nicolson's aisle. Allowing 30 years per generation, this would take the site back at least 840 years. The chapel building was originally cross-shaped, with wings on either side. One of the walls contains an effigy dating to the 15th century which is believed to be that of a MacSween. There is also an effigy of a MacNeacail which was sculpted in the 16th century by the same craftsman who made the famous figure of John MacLeod of Minginish which is in St Clement's Church at Rodel on the island of Harris.

The sculptured stones within the graveyard are believed to date from the 13th century. One flat slab bears an attractive carving of a knight in full armour. Such memorials are often called Crusader's Graves, although it is not known whether those they commemorate actually took part in the Crusades. Also to be found within the burial ground are the graves of the 19th century evangelists Angus Munro, Blind Donald Munro and Murdoch Macdonald. Donald Munro is regarded as being the father of evangelical religion on Skye. Born around 1773 at Achtalean near Portree, Donald lost his site at the age of 14 after contracting smallpox. In later life he was appointed Catechist to the Society in Edinburgh for Propagating Christian Knowledge and he carried out his evangelical work in the parishes of Kilmuir and Bracadale. After falling under the influence of the itinerant preacher John Farquharson who visited Skye in 1805, Donald came to believe that the only way to achieve eternal salvation was to renounce the evils of music. Although he had previously loved music and was one of the finest fiddlers in Trotternish, Donald ordered his flock to gather together all the bagpipes and fiddles in their possession and on a designated day he cast them into a great bonfire at the head of Loch Snizort. Munro died at Bernisdale, Snizort on 1st October 1830.

Although extremely important to Clan MacNicol, St Columba's Island was until recently largely neglected. The chapel walls were broken and the site was overgrown with grass and weeds. Happily, this situation has been remedied, thanks to the Community Council and the Nicolson Trust who now oversee the maintenance of the bridge and the grass cutting.

Skeabost To Edinbane

As you rejoin the A850, immediately on your left can be seen a prominent rocky knoll known as Carolina Hill. This rather un-Skye-like name was given to the area by a Captain MacDonald who emigrated to Carolina in the mid 18th century together with many other members of the clan. After fighting in the American War of Independence, he returned to Skye, bought the little hill and named it after his old home state in the New World. It was in the vicinity of this hill that the Battle of Trotternish or Trouterness took place in 1539. This battle was one of the most important to be fought between the MacLeods and the MacDonalds and it resulted in victory for the MacDonalds. The conflict was a bloody one and it is said that the severed heads of the vanquished were later seen floating down the River Snizort.

Skeabost was the home of the famous Skye poetess, Mary MacPherson (Mairi Mhor nan Oran). Born in March 1821, MacPherson was committed to the crofters' cause and wrote passionately about the Clearances and land reform. She died in Portree in 1898. As the road turns to the north-west, the landscape becomes more hilly and wooded. To the right lies

Skeabost House, originally a Victorian shooting lodge which was converted to a hotel in 1950.

SKEABOST

Clay Pigeon Shooting: SKEABOST HOUSE HOTEL. Tel. (0470) 532 202. By arrangement only.

Eating Out: SKEABOST HOUSE HOTEL. Tel. (0470) 532 202. Non-residents welcome. Buffet lunch served daily from 1200-1330. Afternoon teas. In the evening, a choice of dinner menu is available from 1900-2030. Popular restaurant so booking is advisable. Bar lunches and suppers are also available. Credit cards accepted. Open April-October.

Golf: SKEABOST HOUSE HOTEL. Tel. (0470) 532 202. 9 hole golf course open April-October.

The view to the right now opens up and the long, winding upper reaches of Loch Snizort Beag can be seen. It is into this tidal flat that the River Snizort flows. After crossing the River Tora, the road begins to climb and crosses an open moorland landscape. Minor roads branch right to the scattered communities of Bernisdale, Park and Aird. The A850 now crosses the Treaslane River which drains into Loch Treaslane, seen to the right. Minor roads branch right to Treaslane and Knott and left to Suladale. At this point, the moorland on the left contains a striking rock precipice which resembles the Trotternish Ridge in miniature.

The original road from Snizort to Dunvegan was constructed largely due to the efforts of influential islanders, including Colonel MacDonald of Lynedale and James MacLeod of Raasay, who in 1806 lodged a petition with the Commissioners for Highland Roads and Bridges. There was great need of a road to join Dunvegan with the main thoroughfare at Snizort for this was the route taken by cattle from the Long Island to the market at Portree. Although the Dunvegan-Snizort road was the last to be surveyed on Skye, it was the first to be completed in 1811. Prior to this time, the few tracks that existed on the island were incapable of carrying wheeled vehicles in any quantity and travellers commonly had to walk or go single-file on horseback, accompanied by a guide familiar with local landmarks.

The A850 now becomes single track and crosses a bleak and windswept moorland. A minor road branches right to Kildonan and shortly after this the main road begins to bend southwards to skirt around the head of Loch Greshornish, which can be seen to the right. A minor road branches left to Edinbane, but to visit the craft shops and hotels, take the next small road on the left, signposted "Village Centre". This is a loop road which will bring you back to the A850.

EDINBANE

Eating Out: EDINBANE HOTEL. Tel. (0470) 582 263. Bar meals served 1200-1430 and 1700-2100. A La Carte meals are available in the restaurant from 1700-2100 which specialises in locally caught seafood. Also 8oz, 12oz, 16oz and 24oz prime Aberdeen Angus steaks. Tea, coffee, home-baking and snacks are available in An Coire Dubh (The Black Kettle) Tea Room. Music most evenings in the lounge bar.
LODGE HOTEL & RESTAURANT. Tel. (0470) 582 217. Open daily throughout the year. Steak and seafood restaurant serving dinner from 1900 onwards (last orders 2130). Bar meals are available from 1100-2100. Also morning coffees and afternoon teas. Ceilidh every Saturday and/or Wednesday evening in the Bothan. Regular music nights in the bar.

Indoor Games: THE MARSHALL CENTRE. Tel. (0470) 582 266/326/255. Badminton, snooker, table tennis and pool.

Petrol: EDINBANE STORES. Pump outside shop.

Shopping: EDINBANE POTTERY. Tel. (0470) 582 234. A huge selection of beautiful woodfired stoneware, tableware and other items with unusual glaze finishes, including attractive blues and browns. Many different items at prices to suit all pockets. All made on the premises. The various processes involved in the manufacture can often be seen during your visit. Open 0900-1800, 7 days a week in summer; 0900-1800, Monday-Friday in winter. Access, Visa, Mastercard, American Express and Eurocard accepted. Tax Free Shopping.
EDINBANE STORES. Tel. (0470) 582 261. General groceries and post office.
LOCHVIEW KNITWEAR. Tel. (0470) 582 310. A selection of knitwear including mohairs, Arans and hand knits, most from original designs. Also Harris Tweed from the roll, jewellery and sheepskin items. Access, Visa, Mastercard and American Express accepted. Open daily including Sunday 0900-2100.

Edinbane To Dunvegan

At Edinbane, the main road once again becomes double track. As you descend from the village, there is a parking spot with picnic tables by the right of the road from which there are good views over Loch Greshornish. This stretch of road is particularly beautiful in summer when the grass verges are filled with thousands of wild flowers.

As you cross the Red Burn, look out for the attractive old stone bridge just to the right of the modern one. Just after the burn, a single track road branches right to Greshornish, passing the attractive traditional white-washed croft house of Upperglen. This minor road gives good views down Loch Greshornish and there is room for several cars to pull off about half way down. The latter stretches are wooded and the road ends at the Old House of Greshornish, now a hotel. This was once the home of Kenneth MacLeod, the last of the MacLeods of Gesto, an ancient Skye family who claimed direct descent from King Harold The Black of Iceland. Kenneth spent some time in India and made a great deal of money there as a tea and indigo planter. On his return to Skye he wished to purchase his family's old mansion house at Gesto but was unable to do so and bought Greshornish instead. It was Kenneth who planned the nearby village of Edinbane where he also founded the first hospital on Skye. Greshornish House is said to contain a haunted room frequented by the spectre of an unknown man in a kilt who occasionally startles occupants by whipping off their bedclothes at midnight!

Eating Out: GRESHORNISH HOUSE HOTEL. Tel. (0470) 582 266. Restaurant open to non-residents. Open December-October.

From the Red Burn, the A850 climbs up over a windswept moorland. To the right can be seen the crags of Sron nan Aighean and Beinn na Boineide. The road crosses the watershed and descends towards the Waternish junction and the Fairy Bridge (see Waternish section). There are several parking areas both before and after this junction. The road now bends south and passes to the right of Ben Horneval. This section of road affords good views to MacLeod's Tables on Duirinish. If your destination is Sligachan and you do not wish to visit Dunvegan, much time can be saved by taking the A864 which branches left from the A850. Beyond this junction, the A850 turns westwards and heads towards Dunvegan. As the village is approached, note the fertile croft lands which stand out as islands of emerald green amidst the brown moorland.

DUIRINISH

The peninsula of Duirinish lies at the heart of MacLeod country and contains some of the most dramatic cliff scenery in the Hebrides. Here the tourist can visit several fine museums and craft shops and take in Neist Point lighthouse, the westernmost point on the Isle of Skye. Access to the peninsula is via the single-track B884 which branches west from the A863 just to the south of Dunvegan village.

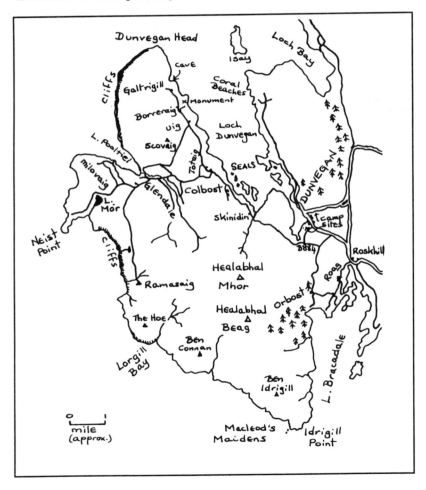

MacLeod's Tables

The first stretch of the B884 crosses a large area of peat banks which are still used by local crofters today. The scenery here is dominated by the huge flat-topped mountains known as MacLeod's Tables. Furthest to the left lies the highest of the two, Healabhal Bheag (1,601 ft) - the Little Table, so named because of the small area of its table-like top, while to the right is Healabhal Mhor, the Big Table (1,538 ft). MacLeod's Tables are comprised of basalt which was laid down as a series of individual lava flows some 60 million years ago. The curious tiered slopes of the mountains are due to variations in the hardness of individual flows. The flat tops of the Tables are formed from a particularly resistant lava flow which has been stripped bare of its covering of soft ash by the forces of erosion.

MacLeod's Tables are said to take their name from an event which occured during the time of the 8th MacLeod Chief, Alasdair Crotach, the Hunchback (1500-1547). While on a visit to Edinburgh, Alasdair was goaded by a group of lowland nobles who insisted that the fine elegance of the capital could not be found in a backwater such as Skye. Alasdair chose to ignore the derogatory remarks until one nobleman asked him whether Skye possessed a roof so lofty, a table so large and candelabra so ornate as those around them then. Alasdair politely replied that Skye could offer far finer facilities and invited the man to the island to see for himself. When the haughty nobleman later arrived at Dunvegan, he was escorted to the top of Healaval Mhor. There, the flat summit was richly laden with food and wine, the stars shone brightly from a cloudless sky and dozens of clansmen stood round bearing flaming torches to illuminate the sumptuous banquet. After they had eaten, Alasdair pointed to the sky and asked was this not a grander roof, or the table before them more commodious, and as to the candelabra, what could be more precious than his faithful vassals? The nobleman was duly shamed and apologised to the MacLeod Chief.

On The Road To Colbost

A small road branches left to Orbost, an interesting detour for the return journey (see below). Shortly afterwards, another road branches right, returning to Dunvegan and then the B884 descends to cross the Osdale River. Just after the river is the turn-off for Uiginish. Here, visitors are often fooled by the extremely lifelike owl which sits atop the sign for the lodge.

Shopping: THE GUN & TACKLE ROOM. Tel. (0470) 521 445. At the Uiginish Lodge Hotel. A variety of equipment for leisure pursuits including hill walking gear, fishing rods and tackle, guns and ammunition, bird books, binoculars, cameras and film, archery equipment, compasses and O.S. maps. Fishing rod hire is also available. Open April to mid October.

Colbost
Folk Museum

4 miles from Dunvegan on the Glendale Road (B884)

(Adjacent to the Three Chimneys Restaurant)

The museum contains implements and furniture of bygone days, has a peat fire burning throughout the day, and is typical of living conditions in the 19th century.

A replica of an illicit whisky still can also be seen to the rear of the Colbost Folk Museum.

TELEPHONE DUNVEGAN 296

• COACHES WELCOME •

OPEN DAILY INCLUDING SUNDAYS 10AM-6.30PM

On a rocky knoll opposite the Uiginish junction lie the remains of Dun Osdale, an Iron Age broch in an extremely ruinous condition. The broch is more noticeable on the return journey. As the road continues, Loch Dunvegan opens up giving views across the Colbost Islands. The scattered white crofts of Skinidin are passed as the road skirts close to Loch Erghallan and heads for Colbost.

In common with many small communities in the islands, Colbost received supplies by sea until earlier this century. Goods would be brought in from Glasgow by steamer which anchored in Loch Dunvegan to unload its supplies. The men of the township would row out to the steamer in small boats and carry back supplies of food, hardware etc. Whisky was transported in large stone jars. The Wee Whisky Shop, next to the Three Chimneys Restaurant, was once the village shop.

COLBOST

Eating Out: THE THREE CHIMNEYS RESTAURANT. Tel. (0470) 511 258. An intimate restaurant, set within a picturesque crofter's cottage. Open Monday-Saturday; closed Sunday lunchtime. Open for Sunday dinner at Easter, Whitsun and during August only. A bistro style lunch is served from 1200-1400 and full dinner menu from 1900. A minimum charge per person applies at lunchtime and dinner bookings are essential. The restaurant specialises in locally caught seafood including wild Skye salmon, oysters, mussels, crabs, scallops, lobsters and langoustines. Highland meat and game and a selection of vegetarian dishes are also offered. Extensive wine list. The restaurant is entirely non-smoking. Credit cards accepted. Open April to October.

Museum: COLBOST FOLK MUSEUM. Tel. (0470) 511 296. An excellent museum which faithfully depicts typical living conditions on the island in the 19th century. The museum was founded in 1969 by local man Peter MacAskill and is set within a reconstructed black house. All restoration work was carried out by local craftsmen. The black house has a thatched roof and real peat fire and contains farming implements and furniture from the period. The displays include a wealth of information on the crofting way of life and how incomers are changing that way of life. The museum also contains a reconstruction of an illicit whisky still & hen roost. Open 1000-1830 daily. Admission fee applies, reduced rates for Senior Citizens.

Shopping: THE WEE WHISKY SHOP. Tel. (0470) 511 258. Adjacent to the Three Chimneys. A must for connoisseurs of whisky. A wide selection of malts and miniatures from all areas of Scotland including rare Taliskers distilled on the island many years ago. Also a small selection of wines and spirits, honey, preserves and gifts and books about whisky. A "Mail-A-Malt" service operates. Credit cards are accepted. Open Monday-Saturday 1000-1800; closed Sunday. Open April to mid October.

The road now climbs, giving good views out across Loch Dunvegan. At low tide, the many islands in the loch are quite colourful with their bands of black algae and orange seaweed. A small road branches right to Borreraig and Galtrigill.

THE BORRERAIG ROAD

This minor road gives good views out across Loch Dunvegan to the little island of Isay. Shortly after the junction the road passes the crofts of Totaig which lie strung out along the foot of Ben Totaig and Beinn Bheag. Soon an area of open moorland is crossed and the scene on the left is dominated by the long line of crags on Ben Ettow. Before long, the township of Uig is reached and here a left turn at the crossroads leads to the Borreraig

Park Exhibition Croft.

Museum: BORRERAIG PARK EXHIBITION CROFT. Tel. (0470) 511 311. A traditional
farm building which contains a fascinating collection of crofting items donated by the people
of north-west Skye. Also an extensive outdoor exhibition of horse-drawn farming machinery
(harvesters etc), all of which have been used locally. The Croft also sells a selection of
knitwear and crafts manufactured on the island. Open throughout the year, Monday-
Saturday from 1000 until dusk; closed Sun. Admission fee applies, reduced rate for Children.

Returning to the crossroads, the Borreraig road continues northwards
and soon the scene on the right is dominated by a large stone cairn which
stands on a hill overlooking the sea. Then, further back to the right, on the
cliffs on the opposite side of the bay, Dun Boreraig comes into view. The
remains of this broch stand on a distinct knoll overlooking the sea. The
houses of Borreraig are soon reached.

Borreraig Piping College And The MacCrimmons

The township of Borreraig lies at the heart of the ancestral land of the
MacCrimmons who were hereditary pipers to the chiefs of Clan MacLeod.
The MacCrimmons were the first composers, players and teachers of the
classical form of bagpipe music known as piobaireachd (pronounced
"pibroch") and it is to this one family that the development of Scottish bagpipe
music is largely due. The MacCrimmons were first patronised by Alasdair
Crotach, or Hunchback, the 8th MacLeod Chief, who in 1540 granted them
rent free land at Borreraig. Here the family set up a piping college where they
instructed pupils only in Ceol Mor, the Great Music of the bagpipe. The
college soon gained a high reputation and attracted students from far and
wide. It is said that training often took ten years and that to gain the coveted
MacCrimmon Diploma pupils were required to memorize and play without
fault 199 compositions in Ceol Mor. Two of the MacCrimmon pipes now lie in
Dunvegan Castle.

The origins of the MacCrimmons are unclear. The name appears
suddenly in Glendale in the 16th century and was apparently unknown before
this time. This suggests that the family came to Skye from some other place
and either changed or were forced to change their name on arrival. If this is
true, every MacCrimmon throughout the world today is descended from this
one family. Scholars believe that the MacCrimmons came either from Harris,
Ireland or Italy. Of these three suggestions, the first is the most likely, as the
MacLeods held lands in Harris and there was at that time a movement of
people between the two islands.

Records in Dunvegan Castle contain references to the family dating
from 1595 to 1801. The first MacCrimmons to be mentioned are Finlay, Iain
Odhar and Padraig Donn. The relationship between these three is not known
but they were all alive in the 16th century. The family at this time lived at
Galtrigill, one mile to the north of Borreraig. The next MacCrimmon to be

mentioned is Donald Mor (c.1570-1640). Donald's compositions include three pieces which were specially commissioned in 1603 to be played at a banquet in Dunvegan Castle marking the end of a long period of hostilities between the MacLeods and the MacDonalds. The pieces, "The MacDonalds' Salute", "The MacLeods' Salute" and "The MacLeods' Controversy", are of the highest technical merit and no great improvement in the art of ceol mor has been achieved since. Donald's other compositions include "The Earl of Ross's March" and "Too Long In This Condition". Donald Mor's brother was murdered in Glenelg around 1610 and to avenge this deed, Donald burned down houses in Kintail, killing several people in the process. Following this event, he spent several years in hiding in Sutherland before returning to Dunvegan to take up the position of hereditary piper to the Chief of MacLeod in 1620.

Donald was succeeded by his son, Patrick Mor (1595-1670), who is generally thought to have been the greatest composer of the MacCrimmon family. Perhaps his most famous pieces are "MacLeod of MacLeod's Lament" (1626) and "Lament For The Children" (1650). Patrick in turn was succeeded by his son, Patrick Og (1645-c.1730), who is considered to have been the best player and teacher of the MacCrimmon line. It was Patrick who moved the piping college from Galtrigill to Borreraig and under his tutelage, the school attained a high reputation.

Patrick Og was succeeded by his son, Malcolm (1690-1760), during whose time as hereditary piper the Act of Proscription was passed. This Act was designed to crush the spirit of the Highlander by making the wearing of tartan and the playing of the bagpipe illegal. Thus, from 1746 onwards, the piping college was a college in name only, although Malcolm continued to teach his sons and a few friends.

Malcolm's sons Iain Dubh and Donald Ruadh each held the title of hereditary piper for a time. Then in 1770, Norman, the 25th MacLeod Chief, aware that the Borreraig lands were now worth a huge sum of money, tried to take back some of the land which had been given rent-free to the MacCrimmons. This so offended the family that Iain Dubh quit Borreraig and moved away from the area. He died on the island in 1822. Donald Ruadh died in London in 1825, thus bringing the famous line of MacCrimmon pipers to an end.

The Memorial Cairn of the MacCrimmons

A memorial cairn to the famous piping family stands on a little knoll overlooking Loch Dunvegan (seen on the approach to Borreraig). The cairn was unvieled by Sir Reginald MacLeod in August 1933 and is visited annually by a large gathering of MacCrimmons. To reach the cairn, take the road on the right, just before the piping museum. The ruins of the original piping college lie to the right of this road, just behind the first white house. The walls are now mainly covered in bracken and not much remains to be seen. The path to the memorial cairn lies a short distance on, to the left of the road. It is signposted and there is room to pull your car off onto the grassy verge opposite (take care not to block the road). Allow 5 minutes each way. The cairn reads: *"Memorial Cairn of the MacCrimmons, hereditary pipers to MacLeods for 10 generations and renowned for composing, playing and teaching Ceol Mor - the classical music of the bagpipe. Near here was the site of the MacCrimmon music school 1500-1800 A.D."*

In the cliffs below the memorial cairn lies a cleft known as the Piper's Cave. Some say that this cave was used by the MacCrimmon pipers when practicing their art. Others say that the cave acquired its name after one of the MacCrimmon pipers disappeared there. Tradition holds that one day a famous member of the family entered the cave with his dog. After a time, the skirl of the pipes became fainter and fainter until eventually the sound disappeared completely. Anxious villagers waited at the mouth of the cave day after day but the piper was never seen again. Some time later the dog reappeared, starving, exhausted, and with the fur flayed from his back. The villagers then knew that the piper had been spirited away by the fairy queen, whose ears he had delighted with his music.

The Silver Chanter
There are many traditions associated with the MacCrimmon pipers, the most famous of which concerns the Silver Chanter. It is said that the MacCrimmons' proficiency with the pipes and their appointment as hereditary pipers to the MacLeods was due to the possession of a magical chanter acquired from a member of the fairy world. One day, Iain Og MacCrimmon, one of the early members of the family, sat playing his pipes on a mound near his home at Borreraig. Iain was sad because his piping was not skillful enough to gain entry to a competition being held by the MacLeod Chief at Dunvegan Castle. As he played, the green mound opened before him and out rose a fairy who asked Iain why he was so sad. On being told the reason, the fairy said, "The sweetness of your music has brought you a faery sweetheart; I give to you this Silver Chanter, which, at the touch of your fingers, will ever bring forth the sweetest music." The fairy gave to Iain a beautiful silver chanter and with it, the art of the pibroch. Iain Og went immediately to Dunvegan and was allowed to play before the Chief. The judges were astonished by Iain's piping and declared him to be the best of the assembled musicians. The MacCrimmons were subsequently awarded the position of hereditary pipers to the MacLeod Chiefs.

The Silver Chanter is also said to have been the cause of the demise of the great MacCrimmon family. When the fairy first gave the chanter to Iain Og, she cautioned that if he or any other member of the family ever treated it with disrespect, the gift of the fairies would disappear forever. Centuries later, the Chief of the MacLeods was returning home by boat from Raasay accompanied by one of Iain's descendants who occupied the traditional piper's seat at the head of the galley. The crossing was rough and the swell on the tide made piping difficult. As MacCrimmon tried to play, his fingers continually slipped from the chanter and eventually he threw down the pipes and gave voice to his annoyance. The Silver Chanter immediately detached itself from the pipes, rose up from the galley and then plunged into the sea where it remains to this day. The charm was broken and in a short time the supremacy of the MacCrimmon pipers declined and their college at Borreraig fell into decay.

BORRERAIG

Museum: THE PIPING MUSEUM. A fascinating museum containing displays on the history of bagpipe making and the history of the MacCrimmons, hereditary pipers to the Chiefs of Clan MacLeod. The museum also contains many tales of the MacCrimmon pipers and the fairy legends associated with the pipes. All the while you can listen to the music of the piobaireachd and there is even a practice chanter to try. A souvenir section sells chanters and cassettes of bagpipe music. Admission fee applies, reduced rate for Children. Open April-October, Tuesday-Sunday 1200-1800; closed Mondays except during July and August.

Shopping: SCOVAL SHEEPSKINS. Located at 18 Borreraig, on the minor road to the piping cairn. Wool and rugs. Unusual coloured wool from Swedish Gotland Sheep (look out for the flock in the vicinity of the memorial cairn or Galtrigill village). Gotland sheep produce excellent wool for hand spinning.

Galtrigill Deserted Village

After Borreraig, the road continues on to the settlement of Galtrigill. It is possible to park at the end of the road here, but do not block the turning circle. Beyond the modern houses lies the old village of Galtrigill. Access to all parts of the village is possible via wooden ladders which climb up and over the electric fences. The remains are well preserved, with many of the house walls standing to their original height. One house near the road still has its chimney stack completely intact. All of the outbuildings and field boundaries are still extant.

Galtrigill was the home of Donald MacLeod, the boatman who aided Prince Charles in his escape from the Redcoats following the Battle of Culloden in 1746. MacLeod piloted the Prince and his companions from Borrodale to Benbecula and guided them during their subsequent travels up and down the Long Island before giving the Young Pretender into the care of Flora MacDonald. He was later captured by the militia and spent many months on board a prison ship. Although he stood to gain the Government reward of £30,000 for information leading to the capture of the Prince,

MacLeod would not speak out against the Young Pretender. Conditions were so terrible on board the prison ship that when Donald was eventually released in 1747, he returned to his home at Galtrigill close to death.

As to Galtrigill village itself, the people began to desert their homes in the 19th century due to the hardships caused by living in such a remote place. At that time, there was no road to the village and no piped water. The village peat bank lay downhill some distance from the houses so that every piece of fuel had to be laboriously carried up to the village on the backs of the crofters. Gradually, over a period of several generations, the people drifted away to other areas. Still lying amidst the ruins is the Manners Stone, a large flat stone upon which the villagers of old carved their initials. Tradition holds that naughty children were made to walk to this stone and to sit upon it three times to "find their manners". To locate the stone, walk behind the ruin with the prominent chimney stack and continue right along the fence until you descend to a style. Cross the fence here. The Manners Stone lies in the middle of the field, just a short distance from the style. From Galtrigill village (if you are keen eyed), the trig point on Biod an Athair can be seen to the east. To reach these impressive cliffs, the highest on Skye, is simply a matter of slogging straight up the hill behind the village.

In the bay below Galtrigill lies a cave known as the Piper's Cave. It is said that here too the MacCrimmons practiced the art of the piobaireachd. To reach the bay, continue straight ahead from the carpark through the village ruins until you reach an attractive wooded gorge. Follow this down towards the sea, looking out for a faint path which descends into the gorge via a small cleft. There are a few rock cut steps, but stout shoes or boots are recommended. This path will take you down to the shore. Once at the bay, the Piper's Cave is located to your right.

THE GLENDALE ROAD

After the Borreraig junction, the B884 continues on to Glendale. About 1/3 mile past the junction, the old Colbost schoolhouse is seen to the right. This is now the home of Skye Silver.

Shopping: SKYE SILVER, Colbost. Tel. (0470) 511 263. Beautiful gold, silver and enamel jewellery in eye-catching Celtic and Pictish designs. All made on the island. Also Celtic ceramic tiles and cheeseboards. For a unique souvenir of Skye, check out the Coral Beach range of jewellery which is cast from coral originating on the Coral Beaches north of Dunvegan (see Walks for details). All items are attractively displayed in a large showroom. The jewellery workshop is also located on the premises but is not open to the public. A mail-order service is available - ask for the free colour brochure. Open 1000-1800 daily. Access, Visa, American Express, Mastercard and Eurocard are accepted.

skye sílver

Established 1974

The Old School, Colbost, Dunvegan, Isle of Skye.
Telephone. Glendale (047 081) 263.

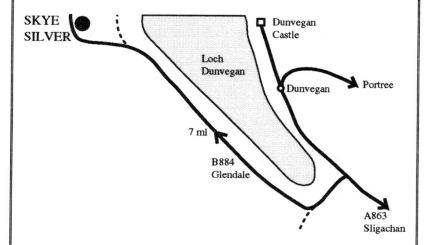

The original silver and gold jewellery from Skye. Visit our shop at Colbost near Dunvegan - full of delightful jewellery and other gifts to bring back memories of your visit to our island.

Friendly mail-order service available - please send S.A.E. for our free, full-colour brochure.

Seven miles from Dunvegan on the B884 to Glendale.

Open 7 days a week, 10.00am to 6.00pm.

The Glendale Land Leaguers

The B884 now begins to climb the steep pass between Ben Totaig and Beinn na Creiche. About half way up the hill, to the right, lies a memorial cairn to the Glendale Land Leaguers. There is room to pull off in front of the monument. The inscription reads: *"To commemorate the achievements of the Glendale Land Leaguers 1882-1886. Locus where 600 crofters challenged the government forces. Imprisoned John MacPherson Glendale Martyr, Rev. D. MacCallum, Donald MacLeod, John Morrison."*

The people of Glendale were instrumental in bringing about the passing of the Crofters Act in 1886 which greatly improved the lot of the crofter by guaranteeing security of tenure, fair rents and fair compensation for outgoing tenants. Like their counterparts at Braes, the Glendale crofters suffered great injustices at the hands of their landlord and in 1882 they decided to stand up for their rights. In their struggles, the crofters were led by John MacPherson of Milovaig who later became known as the Glendale Martyr.

As elsewhere in the Highlands, many of the crofters' grievances arose from the introduction of sheep to the area. As the size of flocks increased, so the people found their status as crofters being steadily reduced until soon they had lost much of the land anciently possessed by them. The townships of Lowerkell (Lorgill), Ramasaig and Hamara were cleared early on to make way for sheep and many of the tenants were forced to emigrate. As the evicitons continued, outgoing families were moved to other townships where existing tenants were required to give up a portion of their holdings to the newcomers. By the latter part of the 19th century, the townships of Glendale were greatly overcrowded and many families were squeezed onto half crofts, forced to turn their hands to other industries in a desparate attempt to make ends meet. Additionally, crofters were faced with high rents and incoming tenants were compelled to pay the arrears of their predecessors. The flames of discontent were fanned even higher when the Glendale crofters were deprived of the ancient right to collect and get salvage for driftwood. They were also forbidden to keep dogs and a half of their alloted quantity of seaweed, essential fertilizer, was taken from them and given to friends of those in high places in the district.

The Glendale crofters met at Glendale Church on 7 February 1882 to decide which course of action they should take to air their grievances. At this time, the Glendale Estate was in the hands of the Trustees of the late Sir John MacPherson MacLeod. The estate factor was unsympathetic to the plight of the crofters and often dealt with them in an arrogant and dictatorial manner and so the Glendale people decided to get up a petition and approach the Trustees direct. It was resolved that each township would make one demand so that no one person would bear the brunt of any subsequent punishment. As a mark of their honour, each crofter entered his name in a book and the petition was then forwarded to the Trustees in Edinburgh.

As a means of forcing the landlord to consider the grievances of the people, the crofters subsequently withheld their rents and re-occupied the land which had been taken from them previously. Their actions were incited by John MacPherson, a leading figure in the land agitations of the 1870's and 80's, and the great bard and clergyman, Reverend Donald MacCallum of Glendale, who was later imprisoned and persecuted for supporting the crofters' cause. MacPherson declared, "It would be as easy to stop the Atlantic Ocean as to stop the present agitation until justice has been done to the people." By the autumn of 1882, there was civil unrest throughout the area and eventually the gunboat H.M.S. Jackal was dispatched to deal with the situation and to force the surrender of the ringleaders.

In March 1883, three crofters, John MacPherson, Donald MacLeod and John Morrison, were sentenced to two months' imprisonment by Lord Shand in the High Court in Edinburgh for organizing the defiance of an interdict forbidding the grazing of cattle on Waterstein farm. Many people considered this to be an unnecessarily harsh punishment for what was generally viewed as a justified stand against oppression and there was subsequently great pressure for government reform. Eventually, Prime Minister Gladstone was forced to bow to public opinion and set up a Commission of Enquiry early in 1883 to look into the Highland land question. The Commission was headed by Lord Napier, a well-known landed gentleman, and comprised Sir Kenneth MacKenzie and Donald Cameron of Lochiel, both landowners, Donald MacKinnon, Professor of Celtic at Edinburgh University, the radical M.P. Charles Fraser-Macintosh and Sheriff Alexander Nicolson of Skye. The Commissioners spent the summer of 1883 travelling around the Hebrides, listening to the grievances of the crofters and recording their evidence.

It was no great surprise that the crofters were wary of the composition of the Commission and land seizures and rent strikes continued throughout the Highlands and Islands. At this time, the Highland Land Law Reform Association (later called the Highland Land League) was formed in London. John MacPherson played a leading role in this active crofters' movement which demanded security of tenure, fair rents and fair compensation for outgoing tenants. The Crofters Act which was eventually passed in 1886 fulfilled these demands and effectively brought the clearances to an end. In 1904, the Congested Areas Board acquired the 18,000 acre Glendale Estate and then gave the people the right to buy their own land. The Glendale crofters subsequently became the first in Skye to own their own title deeds.

The cairn to the Glendale Land Leaguers was funded by money collected after the death of John MacPherson in 1924. After a long delay, it was finally unveiled in 1970 on the spot where the marines attempted to arrest the ringleaders of the Glendale crofters.

GLENDALE

As you continue through the pass between Ben Totaig and Beinn na Creiche, keep an eye out for the wild deer which often wander close to the road here. The scattered settlement of Glendale is entered as you reach the crest of the hill. From this vantage point there is a spectacular view over all the croft lands to Loch Pooltiel ahead. On a clear day, the Outer Hebrides are visible out to sea. The road now descends steeply and minor roads branch right to Glasphein and Feriniquarrie and left to Fasach.

Just after the Fasach turnoff, a small road branches right to Glendale graveyard. You can take your car along to the carpark just outside the graveyard wall. This is the burial ground of Cille Chomgain, the Church of Comgan. Lying against one of the inner walls is a medieval grave slab, now badly worn, which depicts a great two-handed sword. The burial ground also contains a twisted elder tree which is said to grow out of the grave of a Norwegian Prince whose body was washed ashore at the head of Loch Pooltiel. Tradition holds that bad luck will befall anyone who harms this ancient tree.

GLENDALE

Eating Out: AN STRUPAIG CAFE. Tel. (0470) 511 204. Licensed restaurant/cafe. Tea, coffee, snacks, home-baking and full meals are served throughout the day. Locally caught fish and seafood is often available. Children's menu also available (including beefburgers & chips) and a good selection of vegetarian meals. Open Monday-Saturday 0930-2030 (last orders). Evening meals are served from 1830. Open January-December.

Holistic Therapy: THE CRYSTAL CROFT. Tel. (0470) 511 386. Treatments in reflexology, aromatherapy and electro cystal therapy available by appointment only. Also tuition in aromatherapy. Books, tapes, crystals and oils for sale.

Museum: HOLMISDALE HOUSE TOY MUSEUM. Tel. (0470) 511 240. Situated down the Holmisdale Road (first left after the Hamara River). A must for children and adults alike. A fascinating and unique collection of toys, dolls, puppets, games, Meccano, trains, boats, tin-toys and books from the distant and not-so-distant past. The museum's owner has dispensed with the "look but don't touch" thinking of most museums and instead encourages visitors to touch and play with some of the games. A small shop sells a selection of home-made toys, dolls, board games, books and pictures. Open throughout the year, Monday-Saturday 1000-1800; closed Sunday. Admission fee applies, reduced rate for Children.

Shopping: GENERAL STORE. General store, post office and newsagents all in one. Sells books, crafts and O.S. maps.
GLENDALE GALLERY. A selection of original oil paintings of Skye and the Scottish mainland. Open Monday-Saturday.
GLEN STORES. Tel. (0470) 511 204. Spar supermarket. Licensed grocers, greengrocers, bread, milk, frozen foods. Open 0900-2000.
WHOLEFOOD SHOP. Sells a selection of fresh fruit in season e.g. raspberries and melons.

Glendale Mill

Close to the shore of Loch Pooltiel lies the beautifully restored Glendale Mill, an attractive dry-stone building complete with thatched roof and working water wheel. To find the mill, continue past the Glendale shops on the B884 and take the first right. Follow this for a short distance and then take the first left and continue to the parking area at the end. The Glendale Mill dates to the latter part of the 18th century and was last used commercially in 1914. Several grinding stones can be seen outside the building and there is also a peat-kiln nearby. Local crofters would bring their oats to be dried in the kiln and then ground into meal at the mill. As payment, the miller would receive some of the produce. The Glendale Mill was restored to its original state in 1971-72 but burnt to the ground the following year on the same day that several old millstones were being brought across from Skeabost. This was a rather curious occurrence for a legend associated with the Skeabost millstones says that disaster strikes whenever these are moved. The mill was subsequently restored for a second time and is now occasionally open to the public between March and mid October. On purchasing a ticket you can enter to view the interior mechanisms and watch flour being ground. It is possible to climb up onto the grassy clifftops behind the mill for superb views over Loch Pooltiel.

Glendale To Waterstein

Returning to the B884, the main road continues westwards and passes Borrodale Primary School. As the road bends right, a left turn leads to Borrodale and the remote croft of Ramasaig. Ramasaig is the starting point of a walk to the clearance village of Lorgill (see Walks for full details). After the Ramasaig turn-off, the B884 bends to the right, giving views to the white crofts of Upper and Lower Milovaig which dot the hillside ahead.

A small road branches left to Waterstein. This gives good views back across Loch Pooltiel to the stunning cliffs of Biod an Athair and the waterfall on the far side of the loch. The road continues to climb across an area of moorland and at the crest of the hill Loch Mor comes into view to the left. This loch is said to be the haunt of a terrifying *each uisge* or water-horse. There is a large parking area on the left from which you can admire the view. On the steep descent to the crofts of Waterstein, the Outer Hebrides can be seen peeking through the cleft ahead. The scene to the left is dominated by the striking cliffs of Waterstein Head which rise to a height of 296m (971 ft). You can follow the road all the way round to the end where there is a parking area with room for several cars. From this vantage point there are spectacular views of the cliffs to the south - Waterstein Head with An Stac lying just offshore, Ramasaig Cliff and the stunning waterfall which drains Loch Eishort and finally Hoe Point, beyond which lies the clearance village of Lorgill. If the weather is clear, there are also good views west to the islands of the Outer Hrbrides. The Waterstein carpark is the starting point of popular walks to the lighthouse at Neist Point, the most westerly point on Skye, and the old coastguard station (see Walks for full details).

Waterstein To Milovaig

As you retrace your route from Waterstein, take the left turn at the bus stop to reach the crofts of Upper Milovaig. At the crest of the hill, this elevated road gives spectacular views across Loch Pooltiel to the cliffs of Biod an Athair opposite. At 313m (1,028 ft), these are the highest sea cliffs on Skye and some of the most impressive in the Hebrides.

> **Shopping:** RAVEN PRESS, Milovaig. Tel. (0470) 511 367. Situated in croft house by left of road. Wood engravings and miniature books by Kathleen Lindsley. A large selection of finely detailed bird, animal and landscape limited edition prints on hand-made papers. Available both framed and unframed. Printed by the artist directly from the woodblock using an Albion hand press of c.1840. Kathleen's engravings are also available at the Struan Craft Workshop (see Sligachan to Dunvegan).

The road now begins to descend, passing the crofts of Lower Milovaig and giving views to Lewis, Harris and North Uist. Keep right, descending round the hairpin bend to the lochside and Meanish Pier. Loch Pooltiel was once the centre of life in Glendale and received regular visits from both passenger and cargo steamers. Around 1840, the 25th MacLeod Chief tried to start a fishing station here, but like similar attempts elsewhere in the Highlands and Islands, the project soon met with failure. At this point, the road becomes the B884 which ascends steeply above the loch and pulls away from the shore to return to Glendale.

The Scoval Transmitter Road

This scenic moorland road provides an alternative route for the return journey. From Meanish Pier, continue on the B884 until you pass Borrodale Primary School on the left. About 1/3 mile beyond the school a small road branches left. Take this, keeping right at the fork (the left fork leads to Glendale Mill - see above). This road continues around the head of Loch Pooltiel and then turns eastwards towards Feriniquarrie. At Feriniquarrie, take the left fork which climbs up over a high moorland. If you feel that your vehicle is up to the task, you may wish to ascend the very steep road which branches left to the Scoval Transmitter Mast. From this vantage point can be seen Loch Dunvegan and the Dunvegan Peninsula to the east, the edge of the Biod an Athair cliffs to the north, the crofts of Upper and Lower Milovaig to the west and the distinctive shape of Waterstein Head to the south-west. There is also a stunning bird's eye view of Loch Pooltiel. After the transmitter turn-off, the road descends towards Uig, giving beautiful views over the moor and Loch Dunvegan to the white sands of the Coral Beaches opposite. The Exhibition Croft is passed on the left (see above). At the crossroads, a right turn will bring you back to the B884 just north of Colbost.

DAVID & MARION ROBERTS INVITE YOU TO VISIT ORBOST GALLERY

started in 1977 to provide a changing selling exhibition of framed paintings and prints of Skye and the adjacent Highlands. The new gallery and studio is a few hundred yards from the old one at Orbost House on the loop-road through Roag, south of Dunvegan. All works are by professional painters and printmakers who either live on the island or are frequent visitors. On show are landscape paintings in oil by David Roberts, watercolours prints and calligraphy by Marion Roberts, the only complete range of Paul Kershaw's wood-engravings, works by Sir Roderick Macdonald, Angus Stewart's watercolours and other invited artists. A selection of antique prints is usually on view. A comprehensive picture framing and restoration service is available and artists' materials are on sale—

Telephone : Dunvegan (047·022) 207

The Orbost Road

As you head back towards Dunvegan, a pleasant detour is to be had by taking the minor road to Roag which branches right from the B884 about 1 1/2 miles past the Uiginish turnoff. This minor road heads south and shortly after entering a patch of trees at Orbost, a left turn leads to Roag (the Orbost road continues south to Orbost House and the start of a strenuous walk to MacLeod's Table South - see Walks for full details). The Roag road now continues eastwards.

Shopping: ORBOST GALLERY. Tel. (0470) 521 207. Situated by right of road. Exhibition of original paintings, drawings and prints of Skye and the Highlands by professional artists. A picture framing and restoration service is available and there are artists' materials on sale. Visa, Access, Mastercard, Eurocard and American Express accepted. Open daily 1000-1800, April-October.

The road now bends north and passes the strangely shaped peninsula of Ardroag which shelters the stretch of water known as Pool Roag. It is said that King Haakon's Viking fleet anchored here as it sailed home following defeat at the Battle of Largs in 1263. Haakon's men came ashore and laid waste to the surrounding countryside in their search for supplies. At Roag, look out for the attractive thatched croft house with rounded gables. This minor road joins the A863 at Herebost, 2 miles to the south of Dunvegan.

Eating Out: DUNORIN HOUSE HOTEL, Herebost. Tel. (0470) 521 488. Licensed restaurant open to non-residents for a la carte dinner. Specialising in traditional home-made island recipes. Open April to October.

WATERNISH

The long, thin peninsula of Waternish (pronounced "Vatternish") stretches out into the Little Minch giving wonderful views to the long chain of islands which make up the Outer Hebrides. Historically, the area seems to have had more than its fair share of tragic events and this perhaps accounts for the air of sadness which still lingers in some parts today. But there is much to delight the visitor, including several craft shops, a cosy restaurant and the picturesque lochside settlement of Stein.

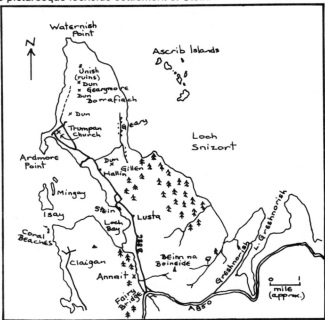

The Fairy Bridge

The B886 single-track road branches north from the main Dunvegan-Portree road at the famous Fairy Bridge. This attractive stone bridge is now no longer used to carry traffic, but it gives a good impression of how the older roads of Skye once looked. There is a parking area with an information board shortly after the junction from which the bridge can be viewed. In the 19th century, the Fairy Bridge was the meeting place of local crofters who came together to discuss the injustices of the Clearances. Here, the assembled crowds would listen to the speeches of the great John MacPherson, the Glendale Martyr, who was a leading figure in the land agitations of the 1870's and 80's. History aside, the bridge is probably better known for its long associations with the Fairy Folk. The most famous tale concerns William, the 4th MacLeod Chief who married a fairy woman. After the birth of their son, the woman was commanded by her kin to return to her own people. The couple took leave of one another on the Fairy Bridge and this event later led to the acquisition of the famous Fairy Flag by Clan MacLeod (see Dunvegan Castle).

The Cats' Cairn

A short distance on from the Fairy Bridge, just before crossing a metal bridge, a small pile of stones can be seen by the right of the road (Grid Ref. 277518). This is known as the Cats' Cairn and is said to derive its name from a strange incident that occurred here around the middle of the 18th century. One day, a twelve year old boy was sent from Dunvegan by his parents to convey a message to his grandmother in Waternish. All went well on the outward journey, but as he returned home, a violent thunderstorm broke out which caused him to take shelter in an old ruined cottage near the roadside. It was quite late by this time and the boy was tired and soon fell fast asleep. Some hours later he was awakened by a strange scrabbling sound and upon opening his eyes he beheld a large black cat sitting quite close to him. The cat was staring up at a hole in the roof through which two other black cats were descending. When all three had reached the floor, they changed into three old women, two of whom the boy recognised as neighbours from Dunvegan. Realising that the women were powerful witches, the terrified lad lay quite still and hoped that he would not be noticed. However, the three soon spotted him and drew close to determine whether the boy had witnessed their transformation. The lad continued to feign sleep until eventually one of the witches said, "If he is truly asleep he knows nothing and if he is awake he will not dare to say anything." She then addressed the boy directly: "For if you do, we will know about it and we will kill you." The three women then resumed their cat form and scrambled back up through the hole in the roof. When all was quiet, the frightened boy ran out of the cottage and hurried back to Dunvegan, resolving to keep the incident to himself. However, it did not take long for his mother to realise that something was amiss, for the boy could not eat or sleep and refused to leave the house. At last he was persuaded to recount the whole story, in the course of which he named two of the witches. His mother, desperate for advice, confided in a neighbour and soon the whole village knew the tale. For a time the boy lived in fear of retribution but nothing happened and soon the family forgot the incident entirely. A year later, the boy was again sent to Waternish with a message for his grandmother. On the return journey he was again caught in a thunderstorm and took cover in the same ruined cottage. The next day his body was found on the spot now marked by the cairn. He had been torn to pieces by long, sharp claws.

Annait

A short distance on from the Cats' Cairn, at the base of the forestry to the left of the road, there is a round depression of very green grass on a little ridge between two tributaries of the Bay River (Grid Ref. 274527). This is the ancient site of Annait, an important early Christian monastic settlement which is over a thousand years old. The name "annait" derives from the Irish *annoid*, signifying a church containing the relic of its founder. The site comprises a narrow triangular enclosure some 200ft long and 165ft across the base which contains the remains of several beehive cells and what may be the foundations of a church. Annait was visited by James Boswell on Friday 17 September 1773 during his tour of the Hebrides with Samuel Johnson at which time the locals believed the site to be the remains of a temple dedicated to the pagan goddess Annaitis. The old custom of burying unbaptised babies at Annait continued up until the end of the 19th century.

Annait To Stein

As the road continues, there is a beautiful view left across Loch Bay to the islands of Isay, Mingay and Clett and Ardmore Point beyond. A small road on the left leads to the little settlement of Bay and then the houses of Camuslusta can be seen clustering around the loch to the left. The B886 continues through Lusta and heads towards the village of Stein. The original road from Sligachan to Stein owed its existence to a recommendation by the great civil engineer Thomas Telford who in 1803 was asked by the Commissioners for Highland Roads and Bridges to plan a road network for the Highlands. The Stein road proved more difficult to construct than had been imagined and the final cost of £40,000 greatly exceeded the original estimates. The 24th MacLeod Chief, John Norman MacLeod, contributed £15,000 towards the work and the road was named MacLeod's Road in his honour. Construction was carried out by the renowned engineer Joseph Mitchell and the road was completed in 1829.

STEIN

After Lusta, the B886 reaches a T-junction. A left turn here will take you down to the shores of Loch Bay and the picturesque settlement of Stein. There is room to park by the jetty. Stein was planned by the British Fisheries Society, a semi-charitable organisation which was founded in 1786 to develop the herring fishing industry. The Society set up several fishing stations on the west coast and islands, providing all the necessary equipment for the work and giving each family a house and small parcel of land. The location of the stations was determined by the London bookseller and philanthropist John Knox, who was commissioned by the Society to seek out the most advantageous sites. Knox travelled up and down the west coast and around the islands observing the movement of the herring shoals and then recommended 29 suitable locations. Land at Ullapool and Tobermory was bought through public subscription and contributions from expatriate Scots. On Skye, Knox originally considered Dunvegan but soon changed his mind when the locals informed him of the favourable conditions at Stein. He later recorded, "The advantages of this coast are many and important. A good country, and very improveable; abundance of limestone; a numerous people already fishermen; waters, harbours, and fish on every side; lying in the track of shipping which pass and repass through the outer channel and having an easy communication, in moderate weather, with the Long Island." The Society followed Knox's recommendations and in 1787 built a quay, stores and houses to establish a fishing industry at Stein. The village was planned by Thomas Telford. However, as elsewhere in the Highlands and Islands, the local crofting population had difficulty in adopting fishing as their main source of livlihood and soon the industry was in trouble. Further problems were caused by poor catches and the largely unpredictable movements of the herring shoals. Additionally, the scarcity of salt and its high cost when available created problems in preserving the catch for shipment. Gradually, the workers and their families began to leave the area and the project was finally abandoned in 1837.

The house at top of the brae leading down into Stein, together with the schoolhouse and some other properties in the area were once owned by the folk singer Donovan. He purchased them back in the 1960's with the intention of setting up a small community dedicated to living off the land. The attractive white-washed buildings on the water front include the Stein Inn, the oldest inn on the island, established in 1648.

STEIN

Diving: HEBRIDEAN DIVING SERVICES. Tel. (0470) 592 219. Located in the old Stein schoolhouse. Various diving services are offered to certified sports divers and sub aqua clubs. Compressed air is available daily between 0800 and 2100 by prior arrangement. For dives in the north-western area of Skye, a 23ft Fastworker boat is available for hire. If you wish to dive elsewhere on the island there are also a number of local fishing and pleasure boats. Hebridean Diving Services also offer self-catering accommodation to diving parties. Telephone for details.

Eating Out: THE LOCHBAY SEAFOOD RESTAURANT. Tel. (0470) 592 235. Licensed restaurant specialising in fish and shellfish dishes, including lobster, king prawns, scallops, oysters, halibut, hake, monkfish and shark when available. Open 1100-1600; evening meals served from 1800-2030. Closed Saturday. Very popular with locals and visitors alike - reservations are highly advisable. Open March to November.

Stein To Hallin

From the Stein T-junction, a minor road continues right, climbing up above the loch to the crofts of Hallin. Just before the village is reached Dun Hallin broch is visible on a knoll on the hillside on the right. The church building and former manse at Hallin, now occupied by Skye Frocks, was designed by Thomas Telford.

HALLIN

Shopping: SKYESKINS, 17 Loch Bay. Tel. (0470) 592 237. Located shortly after the T-junction, by the right of the road. A selection of beautiful hand-combed Highland fleeces. Also slippers, a selection of goatskin rugs and leather wallets, keyrings etc. Credit cards accepted. Open daily 1000-1800, January-December.
DUNHALLIN CRAFTS & KNITWEAR. Tel. (0470) 592 271. Situated in a croft house up farm track to the right of the road, before the Gillen turnoff. Knitwear workshop and showroom. Open daily throughout the year.
SKYE FROCKS, Old Church, Hallin. Tel. (0470) 592 307. Situated in the old village church at the Gillen turnoff. A variety of unusual handmade clothing in natural fibres including printed dresses for adults and children. Also local woollens, woodwork and paintings. Credit cards accepted. From Easter to October open Tuesday-Saturday 1000-1700; from November to Easter open Tuesday-Thursday 1000-1700 (closed all February). Skye Frocks also incorporates the Waternish Craft Workshop which offers short classes in watercolour, oil and silk painting, spinning, decorative wood burning (pyrography) and hand and machine patchwork. Beginners welcome, all materials provided. Prices include lunch and tea/coffee. Tel. (0470) 592 307/253 for details.

The Island Of Isay

After Hallin, the road passes through Halistra and continues north-west along the coast, giving superb views over the islands of Isay, Mingay and Clett to the dramatic cliffs of Dunvegan Head beyond. The now deserted island of Isay has a long and bloody history. In the early 16th century, Roderick MacLeod of Lewis, whose daughter had married twice, decided to eliminate two entire families so that his own grandson could inherit the lands of Raasay and Gairloch. MacLeod invited the members of the two families to a banquet on Isay, telling them that once there, they would hear something to their advantage. This inducement had the desired effect and all turned up eagerly at the appointed time. During the meal, Roderick announced that he would like to hear their views on a matter of great importance. Retiring to an adjacent room, he then bade each of the guests to visit him privately. As each entered the room, they were stabbed to death.

In the early 18th century Rory Neimheach, who was known as "bitter and malicious Rory", massacred a band of the MacLeods of Raasay on the island. Later in the same century, Isay became the property of MacLeod of MacLeod and on 23 September 1773 the Chief offered the island to the renowned traveller Dr Samuel Johnson, on condition that he reside on it for three months each year. Dr Johnson, a great lover of comfort, never took up this generous offer. In the 19th century, Isay contained a thriving fishing station and had its own general store. By 1850 there were 17 families on the island. The entire population was cleared in 1860. The remains of the old blackhouses can still be seen today along the shoreline. In more recent times, the island was purchased by the folk singer Donovan.

Ahead can be seen Ardmore Bay, formed by the encircling arm of Ard Mor. It was here that Bonnie Prince Charlie and Flora MacDonald first tried to land on Skye after their journey across the Little Minch from Benbecula on the morning of 29 June 1746. Their boat was spotted and fired on by the MacLeod militia stationed on the Point after which they headed north and eventually landed near Kilbride Bay on the west coast of Trotternish. The road soon forks and the left branch descends and continues along the coast. Soon, a sharp right bend is reached and a short distance on from this, Trumpan Church is seen to the right. There is a large parking area opposite which has excellent views out to sea.

Trumpan Medieval Churchyard

Trumpan Church is known in the Gaelic as Cille Chonain, the Church of Conan. It takes its name from the 7th century Saint Conan, Bishop of the Southern Isles. The present building dates from the late Medieval period and is thought to have replaced an earlier church which stood on the same site. The walls are held together with a thick cement made from crushed sea shells and lime. When the church was being renovated in 1989 by Skye and Lochalsh District Museums Service, a tomb was discovered within the south wall. This can still be seen today. Such tombs appear only rarely in the Western Highlands and it is thought this feature was introduced sometime after 1500. Within the church can be seen an attractive medieval grave slab which depicts a claymore flanked by beasts and foliage. Also lying in a corner of the church is a small baptismal font which, according to tradition, never runs dry. A communion cup used at the church during the 16th century can be seen in the folk museum at Kilmuir.

Cille Chonain churchyard was originally circular in shape. The present stone wall dates to the late 19th century. Lying in the graveyard immediately behind the church is a second medieval grave slab which depicts a fully vested figure in a gothic alcove below a circle of rosettes. Also within the churchyard, to the right of the church as you enter the gate, is the Clach Deuchainn or Trial Stone. This large upright stone has a small hollow on one face. Tradition holds that villagers accused of a crime were brought blindfolded to this stone by the local priest. If they could successfully put their finger into the hollow on the first attempt they were declared innocent. If not, a verdict of guilty was passed.

The Battle of the Spoiling of the Dyke

One of the most tragic events ever to have occurred on the island of Skye took place at Trumpan Church in 1578. At that time the MacLeods and MacDonalds were engaged in a tit-for-tat clan feud which resulted in many bloody killings and reprisals. The MacDonalds were seeking revenge for the massacre the previous year of 395 of their kinsfolk on Eigg who had been smoked to death by a raiding party of MacLeods as they hid in a cave. One Sunday morning in May 1578, while some of the local MacLeods were at prayer, eight MacDonald galleys sailed round Ardmore Point concealed in fog and beached in the bay just to the west of the church. Climbing quietly up towards Trumpan, the MacDonalds proceeded to bar the door of the church and set fire to the thatched roof. It is said that only one old woman escaped the inferno by climbing out through a window. She managed to struggle towards a group of villagers to raise the alarm before dying on a bog that has ever since been known as "Margaret's Bog". Driven by outrage, a mob of angry MacLeods gathered up their weapons and set off from Dunvegan in pursuit of the MacDonalds. The MacLeods caught up with the murderers just before they could reach the safety of their ships and a bloody battle ensued. It is said that the Fairy Flag was unfurled to ensure victory and every single MacDonald was put to the sword. The MacLeods refused to give a Christian burial to the MacDonalds because of the horror of their crime and instead tore down the dyke beside which their foes had fallen and cast the stones and rubble over their bodies. This event has ever since been known as Blar Mhilleadh-garaidh - the Battle of the Spoiling of the Dyke. This sad event subsequently became the inspiration of a famous MacCrimmon piobaireachd. Today, the gloomy Bay of Ardmore still retains a tangible air of tragedy.

Lady Grange

Lying just in front of the church door can be seen a simple headstone dedicated to Rachel, Lady Grange. This tragic figure was swept up in the political machinations which surrounded the Jacobite cause in the first half of the 18th century. Born Rachel Chiesley, she married James Erskine of Grange, the Lord Justice Clerk, in 1707. It is said that she was an excessively temperamental woman and not the easiest of persons to get along with and by 1730 Lord Grange could stand her no longer. He sent her off to the country, together with their children and a sum of £100. To make matters worse, Rachel, a protestant, was bitterly opposed to her husband's politics. Lord Grange was sympathetic to the Jacobite cause and indeed his brother, the Earl of Mar, had led the 1715 Rising. One night in 1731, during a brief stay at Lord Grange's house in Edinburgh, Rachel hid behind a sofa and eavesdropped on a group of Jacobite conspirators. She then made the mistake of revealing her presence and threatened to turn her husband and his friends over to the authorities. Lord Grange knew his wife to be capable of this and so to protect the lives and reputations of several prominent families, he arranged for Rachel to be kidnapped and removed to a remote part of the country where her silence could be ensured. It is said that during the struggle to abduct her, the poor woman lost two of her teeth. Lord Grange then spread the story that his wife had died from fever and a mock funeral was held for her in Greyfriars Cemetery in Edinburgh.

Meanwhile, MacLeod of Dunvegan and MacDonald of Sleat had agreed to hold her on remote parts of their properties. Rachel was first taken to Skye where MacLeod sent her to lodge in a cottar's hut at Idrigill on Duirinish. She was next held by Lord MacDonald on the tiny island of Heiskir to the north-west of North Uist for a period of two years. Then, in 1734, MacLeod sent her to the remote island of St Kilda and there she remained for a total of seven years, living miserably amongst a Gaelic-speaking people with whom she could not communicate. Although the St Kildans were kind to her, giving her the best peat for her fire and ensuring that she had enough food, Rachel's refined habits kept her aloof from the islanders. It is said that she spent her days asleep and her nights weeping and composing letters for help. These she bound with yarn to pieces of cork and cast into the sea.

As danger was thought to lessen, Lady Grange was brought back to Uist, then to Assynt, then to Skye again, where she was imprisoned in a cottar's house in Waternish. Here, conditions were kinder and the lady of the house taught her to spin wool. Rachel was allowed to send her produce to market in Inverness along with that of her neighbours and in this way she was at last able to smuggle out a plea for help hidden in a hank of her own wool. The letter was written in her own blood as she had no ink. The buyer of the wool forwarded the letter to relatives in Edinburgh who were appalled by the whole story and immediately pressed the Solicitor General for assistance. At last a ship was sent to search the island but MacLeod got wind of its coming and immediately moved Rachel to a remote cave at Idrigill, used by local fishermen for curing and drying their nets. Soon this too was felt to be unsafe and MacDonald shipped her back to Uist accompanied by a boatman with a rope noose attached to a large boulder who had orders to throw her overboard should a ship approach. After a long period on Uist, Lady Grange was again returned to the Waternish peninsula. By this time the long years of imprisonment and the hopelessness of her situation had caused Rachel to lose her mind and in 1745, after 15 years in captivity, she died alone. The conspirators were at last rid of their burden but, fearful that an exhumation could still bear witness against them, they filled a coffin with stones and turf and staged a second mock funeral in the churchyard of Duirinish. Meanwhile, Lady Grange's body was interred without ceremony in an unmarked grave in Trumpan churchyard, the exact whereabouts of which still remains a mystery today. In the 1880's one of the Trumpan Church Elders, believing that Rachel should be commemorated in some way, erected a simple stone over the grave of his father. Several items associated with Lady Grange - the accounts detailing her board while on St Kilda and her funeral expenses in Skye, the iron lamp used in her hut on St Kilda and the quern stone used to grind corn for her food - are today preserved at Dunvegan Castle.

Trumpan To Gillen

The road continues on from Trumpan Church and takes a sharp right turn. At this point, a farm track heads north along the coast giving a long but easy walk to the deserted village of Unish and the lighthouse on Waternish Point (see Walks for details). The road now heads south and soon rejoins the outward route by the little hill known as Hangman's Knoll. To the left lies Ben Geary, the highest point on north Waternish. As you return to the village of Hallin, a pleasant detour is to be had by taking the road which branches left to Gillen and Geary. This minor road travels across to the east coast of Waternish from where there are fine views to the Ascrib Islands in Loch Snizort. A right turn leads to the crofts of Gillen.

Shopping: GILLEN KNITWEAR (CLOSED FOR 1994 SEASON). Tel. (0470) 592 267. On right as you travel down into Gillen. Showroom in yellow roofed shed by side of croft. A selection of knitwear manufactured on the premises. Open Tuesday-Saturday 1000-1800; Sunday 1100-1700. Closed Monday. Open June-September. A mail order service is available - send an S.A.E for details.

TROTTERNISH: THE EAST COAST VIA STAFFIN

The great peninsula of Trotternish is known to locals as The North End. The journey up the the east coast is dominated by the 22 mile long Trotternish Ridge which produces some of the most striking cliff scenery in Britain.

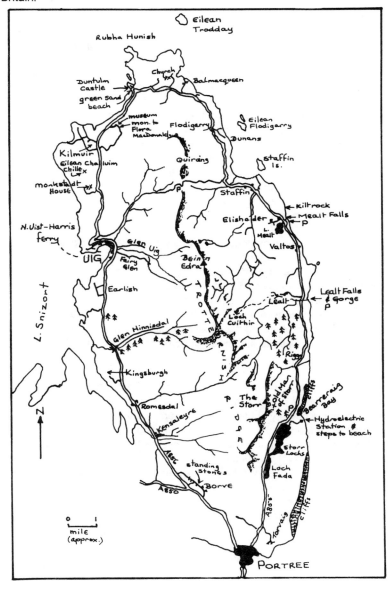

Portree To The Storr Lochs

The A855 heads north from Portree centre and makes its way through the town, giving glimpses of the Isle of Raasay through the narrow harbour entrance. Before long, the sign for the Cuillin Hills Hotel is seen. The hotel was built in the 1870's by Lord MacDonald of Sleat and was originally a shooting lodge. Today, one of the first floor windows still retains an etching of the MacDonald coat-of-arms. Torvaig Caravan and Campsite is passed and beyond this point the road becomes single track.

The A855 now traverses a large area of peat bog which is still cut today to provide fuel for local crofters. In summer, the landscape is dotted with the piles of black turfs, set out to dry in neat stacks. The peats are collected each autumn and provide a valuable source of fuel for the coming year. As the open boggy grassland is crossed, height is gained giving magnificent views ahead to the fantastically shaped pinnacle known as the Old Man of Storr. Much of the eastern coastline of Trotternish is comprised of a series of magnificent crags which stretch in an almost unbroken line from Portree in the south to Staffin in the north. The coastal cliffs at this point are some of the most inaccessible on the island and contain a cave known as Prince Charlie's Cave, which is said to have been used briefly by the Young Pretender as he made his way back to Skye from the adjacent island of Raasay. The cave can be reached only by boat.

The road now dips down close to the shore of Loch Fada which flows into the adjacent Loch Leathan by means of a narrow channel. Collectively, these two lochs are known as the Storr Lochs. From here on, the other-worldly shape of the Old Man looms ever closer. If you wish to take a photograph of the pinnacle, continue along the lochside until you reach a small parking space with a picnic table by the left of the road. An excellent shot is obtained by climbing the small rise just behind the parking area. This small picnic spot, with its attractive river cascade, is a pleasant place to stop for refreshments.

It was from Loch Fada that Bonnie Prince Charlie was able to make his escape to Raasay on the night of 30 June 1746. This journey was made possible by the bravery of two of his followers, the young Laird of Raasay and his brother Dr MacLeod, who were then in hiding at their sister's house near Portree. After agreeing to shelter the Prince on Raasay, the pair debated as to how to convey him across the Sound. They did not own a boat and dared not borrow or steal one for fear that the Redcoat troops would discover their plan. Then, they remembered that a small rowing boat was usually kept on Loch Fada. Under cover of darkness, the pair made their way to the loch and, although Dr MacLeod was recovering from a wound sustained at Culloden, they were able to drag the boat across two miles of rough moorland

and lower it by rope over the steep cliff to the shore below. The Laird and his brother then rowed across to Raasay and returned with a larger boat and a trustworthy crew to transport the Prince to that island.

The Trotternish Ridge

After the Loch Fada picnic area, the road once again becomes double track and continues on past Loch Leathan. In the loch are to be seen the salmon cages of Strathaird Farm, one of the many enterprises owned by Iain Anderson, singer with the rock group Jethro Tull. To the left of the road at this point there is an excellent view of the Old Man and the massive escarpment of the Trotternish Ridge. The ridge is formed from lavas which originated in the great Cuillin volcano some 60 million years ago. These hard volcanic rocks are underlain by soft Jurassic clays which, because of their weakness, are continually giving way. Huge blocks of lava are gradually sliding downhill towards the sea, leaving a high line of cliffs behind and creating the largest landslip in Britain. Subsequent erosion of this jumbled terrain has resulted in a fantastic landscape of pinnacles and ravines which has featured in both films and television commercials. This surreal country was also much loved by Victorian travellers who flocked to the area to capture the scene on canvas or to write about their wanderings amidst the strange rock spires. The poet Robert Buchanan, writing in 1873, described his visit thus: "The whole coast from Aird Point to Portree forms a panorama of cliff-scenery unmatched in Scotland. Layers of limestone dip into the sea, which washes them into horizontal forms, resembling gigantic slabs of white and grey masonry, rising sometimes stair above stair, waterstained, and hung with many-coloured weed; and on these slabs stand the dark cliffs and spiral columns; towering into the air like the fretwork of some Gothic temple, roofless to the sky; clustered sometimes together in black masses of eternal shadow; torn open here and there to show glimpses of shining rowans sown in the heart of the stone, or flashes of torrents rushing in silver veins through the darkness; crowned in some places by a green patch on which goats feed small as mice and twisting frequently into towers of most fantastic device, that lie dark and spectral against the grey background of the air."

Storr Lochs Hydro-Electric Scheme And Bearreraig Bay

As you pass the end of Loch Leathan, a small single track road branches right to Bearreraig Hydro-Electric Dam. A short distance down this road there is a large grassy verge on the left where there is room for several cars to pull off (please do not block the passing places). From here, it is an easy five minute walk to view the fish farm buildings and the impressive dam. The Hydro-Electric Scheme was officially opened in June 1952 and uses water from the nearby Storr Lochs to power a station which is situated on the beach some 500 feet below. Prior to 1949, the only electricity on the island was that generated by a diesel engine owned by the Portree Hotel which provided a very small local supply for the town. There were also a few generators dotted about the island at the larger houses and hotels. The first mains electricity became available in 1949 when a submarine cable was laid across the Kyle to provide a supply for Broadford and the south of Skye. The Storr Lochs scheme was then devised to provide electricity for the rest of the island. To obtain an adequate head of water to power the turbines, a concrete dam 180ft long and 36ft high was built across the north end of Loch Leathan to raise it to the same level as Loch Fada. Sadly this put an end to one of the most beautiful waterfalls on Skye which once flowed out of Loch Leathan and plummeted sheer over the cliffs to the beach below. But the station has been of great benefit to the island and is today linked to the National Grid which provides a back up when water levels are too low to produce an adequate supply.

Bearreraig Bay is one of the few places on this rugged stretch of coastline where shore access is possible. You can reach the attractive pebble beach by walking over the dam to the end of the road and then descending a narrow and incredibly steep flight of 640 steps. This will take approximately 25 minutes from your present parking spot (the stairs alone will take at least 25 minutes on the return journey!). The steps descend alongside the humming hydro-electric pipes and an unusual pulley-operated cliff railway used by employees to reach the station on the beach below. As you make your way down there are good views over the wide sweep of the bay to the striking columnar basalt coastal cliffs of Rubha Sughar. The walk is worth it for this view alone. From the bay itself you can see south to the rocky lump of Holm Island lying just off-shore and east across the Sound to the islands of Rona and Raasay with the hills of Applecross and Torridon beyond. Trickling down over the cliffs behind the power station is a small cascade, all that is left of the once mighty Bearreraig waterfall. Shortly after crossing the river, look out for the remains of the old boulder shelter and iron winding gear once used for pulling fishing boats up out of the water. About halfway along the bay lies a fisherman's bothy and another winding gear. Here, note the sandy channel just offshore which would have been regularly cleared of stones to provide safe access for the boats.

Bearreraig Bay contains sedimentary rocks of Jurassic age which are rich in fossils and has long been a favourite haunt of palaeontologists and collectors. It was here that the finest Scottish specimen of an Ichthyosaurus was discovered in 1966 by the engineer of the Storr Lochs power station. The Ichthyosaurus is a type of fish-lizard, rather like a porpoise, that lived around 70 million years ago. The engineer, Mr Gillies, was out fishing one day when he spotted something unusual outlined in the rock as he reached down for his kife. At first he took it to be the backbone of a sheep, but on closer inspection he saw that it was much too large. Mr Gillies contacted the

Royal Scottish Museum in Edinburgh and a team was sent to cut the fossil from the rock. It turned out to be the backbone of a headless Ichthyosaurus, 10ft long and with 21 vertebrae, the first vertebrate fossil to be found on the island. The most commonly found fossils today are tube-shaped worms known as belemnites and ammonites. The worms occur in the light brown mudstones and are often seen in section as a lighter glassy grey material anywhere up to a 5p piece in diameter. The ammonites are found in the steel grey/blue limestones.

The Storr Lochs To Lealt

Shortly after the turn off to Bearreraig, the main A855 begins to ascend and a carpark is seen to the left of the road. This is the starting point of one of the walkers' routes to The Old Man Of Storr (see Walks for full details). Next, an area of forestry is passed on the left and just beyond this lies the main route to the Old Man. It is possible to pull off by the side of the road here but this area is usually very busy and it is often better to park in the official carpark mentioned above. From this point, the Old Man is normally well camouflaged against the similarly coloured ridge behind. When weather conditions are right however, a rather ghostly scene is created when mist descends from the ridge behind and outlines the surreal shape of the pinnacle. Almost directly behind the Old Man lies The Storr which at 2,358ft is the highest point on the ridge.

The road now passes a large expanse of forestry on the right and draws close to the shore. To the left, the Trotternish Ridge with its crumbling basalt pillars begins to recede inland. Out to sea there are fine views to the islands of Raasay and Rona and the mainland hills of remote Applecross beyond. As you continue northwards, the gap between the two islands opens up and the smaller island of Eilean Tigh can be made out lying just to the north of Raasay. Until the time of the Clearances, Rona was owned by the MacLeods of Raasay. In the 16th century, the island was thickly wooded and was a well known hiding place of those seeking to escape the attentions of the law. It became the home of a band of robbers who used the natural harbour of Acairseid Mhor as a base from which to raid passing ships and pillage the surrounding islands and adjacent mainland villages. For these activities, Acairseid Mhor became known as Port nan Robaireann, the Port of the Robbers. In the 19th century, the island contained thriving crofting communities at Acairseid Mhor (Big Harbour), Acairseid Thioram (Dry Harbour) and Doire na Guaile. The islanders had two schools and worshipped in a huge cavern on the east coast known appropriately as Church Cave which contained an altar and seats of natural rock. By the end of the First World War, the crofters were facing economic ruin and in 1919, seven desperate families shipped their sheep and cattle across to the adjacent island of Raasay and seized fertile land there. Soon, there was only one family left on Rona and eventually it was deserted completely. At the north end of the island can be seen Rona lighthouse, which was established in 1857. This is one of the two major lights guiding shipping in the Minch, the other being at Neist Point on the west coast of Skye.

The A855 continues past the fertile valley area of Rigg which was cleared of its crofters in the 19th century. The road begins to climb steadily and soon the white crofts of Lealt are seen scattered on the hillside ahead. On the coast at this point is a huge rock known as the Eaglais Bhreagach, or False Church, so called because it contains a hole shaped like the door of a church. Tradition holds that here Clan MacQueen raised the devil using an ancient ceremony called Taghairm which involved the roasting of live cats. The road now descends to cross the Lealt River just beyond Lower Tote.

Lealt Gorge And The Diatomite Works

The Lealt River contains one of Skye's most impressive waterfalls which is often missed by the tourist in a hurry. It is well worth while pulling into the large carpark by the right of the road here to view this spectacular natural phenomenon. For a quick look at the falls, go through the gate adjacent to the carpark and walk along the left side of the gorge for a couple of minutes. From here there are fine views back to the river which flows under the bridge and plummets into the ravine in a pretty double waterfall. Note the basalt columns on the bank opposite.

Lealt was once the location of an unusual industry involving the processing of diatomite, an earth-like material consisting of the remains of microscopic aquatic plants known as diatoms. The cell walls of these tiny plants are comprised of almost pure silica which sinks to the bottom of the water when the diatoms die. When dried and processed, this material is highly absorbant - capable of holding three times its weight in water - and can be used for a variety of purposes including pressure filtration (e.g. sugar refining, malt extracts), heat and sound insulation, toothpaste, cosmetics, explosives and high grade polishes. Diatomite occurs at several locations on Skye, but by far the most extensive deposits are those at Loch Cuithir, some three miles inland from the Lealt Gorge. These deposits were first worked at the end of the 19th century, the diatomite being transported by narrow gauge railway from Loch Cuithir to a crushing mill on the shoreline at Inver Tote. Here, the earth was dried and ground before being shipped to the mainland. Further extraction was carried out at the turn of the century and during the First World War the industry provided work for many local people. Between the wars, cheaper German imports rendered the Loch Cuithir deposits uneconomic and production ground to a halt. The enterprise was revived after the Second World War, with the diatomite being taken to Uig by lorry. This too proved uneconomic and the industry gradually wound down in the

1960's. Many people still believe that the Loch Cuithir deposits could be successfully worked on a small scale, despite the fact that a feasibility study carried out in 1969 and a subsequent assessment by the Highlands and Islands Development Board indicate that the industry would have to be highly mechanised to be economic. Today, Britain's requirements for diatomite are mainly filled by imports from Denmark and California. The old crushing mill is still standing on the shoreline at Inver Tote and makes a pleasant excursion for those interested in industrial archaeology (see Walks for full details).

Lealt To Elishader

Shortly after crossing the Lealt River, another minor road branches left to the little community of Lealt (the roadsign has been battered by the wind and currently reads "La"). Lealt is the starting point of a fairly long but easy walk to Loch Cuithir, the source of the diatomite processed at the Inver Tote mill (see Walks for full details).

The A855 now enters Culnacnoc and Lonfearn. To the right lies the Rubha nam Brathairean headland, once the site of an early Christian monastic settlement. The remains of the monks' circular stone cells can still be detected when the light is right. Lonfearn has connections with the story of Bonnie Prince Charlie for it was here that MacDonald of Kingsburgh was forced to lie low after sheltering the Young Pretender in his own house on the west coast and accompanying him on foot to Portree.

Eating Out: GLENVIEW INN, Culnacnoc.   Tel. (0470) 562 248.   By left of road at Culnacnoc. Bar meals served throughout the day. Morning coffees and afternoon teas with buttery shortbread, cream cakes, chocolate eclairs and meringues. Evening meals include whisky flamed steaks, chicken stuffed with crab, scallops, hand made chocolates, a tempting sweet trolley. Traditional roast lunches with all the trimmings are served on Sundays.

At Culnacnoc, a road branches left to Grealin, then the A855 passes through Valtos. Here, on a prominent basalt knoll to the right of the road, can be seen the remains of Dun Dearg Iron Age fort. Lying directly inland at this point is Beinn Edra, the highest hill on the northern section of the Trotternish Ridge. Towards the end of the Second World War, this was the scene of a tragic accident involving a Flying Fortress bomber. The bomber was making its way from Prestwick to Iceland in the spring of 1945 when it hit the summit in mid-day mist. The impact hurled two of the engines over the hill-top and caused the plane to burst into flames, killing all on board.

Beyond Valtos, the road begins to descend towards Loch Mealt, one of the last breeding places of the wild otter. Ahead, the cliffs of the Quiraing come into view. At the northern end of the loch, the ruinous remains of Dun Grianan can be seen on a small knoll jutting into the water. A road on the right leads to the Kilt Rock viewpoint.

The Kilt Rock

The Kilt Rock viewpoint contains ample parking space and several information boards describing the flora and fauna of the area and the local geological formations. Sturdy platforms give good views of the spectacular coastline and there are also pay binoculars for a closer look at the cliffs and mainland hills. As the name suggests, the Kilt Rock is a complex geological formation which resembles a kilt. This unusual structure formed when magma rose up towards the earth's crust and became trapped beneath layers of softer sedimentary rocks. So caught, the magma spread out to form a series of horizontal sills. As the molten rock slowly cooled to become the rock known as dolerite, it took on the shape of distinctive hexagonal columns, similar to those seen at the Giant's Causeway in Ireland and at Fingal's Cave on the Isle of Staffa. Erosion at the cliff face reveals a vertical section through the whole structure which, when the light is right, resembles a kilt - the vertical columns being the pleats and the horizontal patterns being the setts of a tartan. Also visible from the Kilt Rock viewpoint are the impressive Mealt Falls which flow out from the nearby loch and plummet over the cliffs to the sea 300ft below.

Museum: ELISHADER MUSEUM. After Loch Mealt, a small road branches left to Elishader. At the junction, in a beautifully restored stone schoolhouse, is a newly opened museum. Collections include local fossils, Bronze Age arrowheads and potsherds, pottery and other artefacts from the Iron Age, a range of 19th century furniture and farming implements & a large array of glass and earthenware bottles. All collected by a local farmer.

STAFFIN

The A855 now enters the crofting community of Staffin. From here, minor roads lead to the scattered settlements of Clachan, Marishader and Garrafad. The lands here were held for several centuries by the MacQueens, a clan that once had traditional links with the MacDonalds. The names MacQueen, MacSween and MacSwan are still fairly common on Skye today.

Staffin Bay can be reached by taking the small road which branches right to Staffin Slipway just after the Stenscholl River. This road gives good views to Eilean

Flodigarry and Staffin Island. The working crofts of Glashvin, Digg and Dunans can be seen strung out along the hillside at the north end of the bay with the cliffs of the Quiraing rising steeply behind. The small road continues around the bay to the slipway at Ob nan Ron. On the way, it passes the little headland of An Corran which contains an important multi-period archaeological site. Here, compacted in the cliff face, lie the remains of a massive mound of discarded shells and other food debris. Such "midden" sites are usually associated with the first hunter-gatherers who began to colonize Scotland as conditions gradually improved in the millennia following the last Ice Age. The An Corran cliff was recently in danger of collapsing and local archaeologists took the opportunity to excavate the site during operations to render the cliff-face safe. In addition to deposits of consolidated shells, the finds included animal bones, various small flint and stone tools, and bird and fish bones worked into points designed to extract winkles from their shells. The artefacts are typical of the Mesolithic, Neolithic and early Bronze Age periods, suggesting that the site was in use from around 5,000 B.C. to 2,000 B.C., which makes it the earliest industrial complex so far discovered on Skye.

Staffin Bay is a pleasant place to stop for a picnic. There is also a picnic table located behind Talla Stafainn, the Staffin Community Hall, which has a glorious view stretching all the way from the Quiraing in the north to the Storr in the south.

STAFFIN

Eating Out: THE OYSTERCATCHER. Tel. (0470) 562 384. Restaurant and tea room. Light snacks, full meals and home baking. Childrens' portions available. Traditional Scottish cooking - vegetarian options available. B.Y.O. wine. Open Monday-Saturday 1000-1930 (until 2030 during July and August); closed Sunday. Last orders 2000.

Shopping: CILMARTIN CRAFT CENTRE.   Tel. (0470) 562 384.   Located at the Oystercatcher. A selection of Scottish and local crafts and gifts. Opening hours as above. VG STORES. Access, Mastercard, Eurocard accepted. Open Monday-Saturday 0900-1300 and 1400-1730 (open until 2000 on Fridays); closed Sunday.

Petrol: BP FILLING STATION. Situated just to the north of Staffin at Stenscholl, by left of A855. Also general store.

Toilets: In the Community Hall. Also, just north of Staffin, by left of A855, shortly after the Quiraing turnoff. A drinking water tap is located on the outside wall of this toilet block.

Staffin To Flodigarry

After Staffin, the A855 travels through Stenscholl and Brogaig where a minor road branches left to the Quiraing. The main road continues northwards and soon becomes single track, passing the working crofts of Glashvin and Digg. Immediately behind these settlements rises the striking bluff which contains the fantastically-shaped towers and pinnacles of the rock formation known as the Quiraing. At the centre of this formation, completely hidden from view, lies an elevated grassy plateau known as "The Table" which is surrounded by an amphitheatre of black shattered rocks. The Table was used by local people in the 15th and 16th centuries to hide their cattle from raiders. This surreal landscape has featured in several science fiction films, including the recent production "Highlander". A small road branches right to Dunans and then there is a good picnic spot and parking area by the left of the road, overlooking a lochan, with the impressive ridge rising behind. A short distance on from this point a footpath ascends to the Quiraing. This route is more strenuous but considerably quieter than the usual tourist approach from the Staffin-Uig road (see Walks for full details). The A855 now continues on to Flodigarry, a small crofting settlement with ancient Clan Donald connections.

Flodigarry And Flora MacDonald

A small road branches right from the A855 to the Flodigarry House Hotel, in whose grounds lie the remains of Dun Flodigarry Iron Age broch and Flora MacDonald's cottage. The broch is located about 100m to the north of the hotel, at the base of a crag. To find Flora's cottage, walk to the left around the seaward side of the hotel (there are magnificent panoramic views over Eilean Flodigarry and Staffin Island from the terrace), and continue on to the staff area. The attractive white cottage is seen just to the right. For her part in aiding Prince Charles's escape from Benbecula to Skye in June 1746, Flora was taken on board the notorious prison ship "Furnace" and then held captive in London for a time. When she was eventually released, Flora returned to Skye and married Allan MacDonald of Kingsburgh. She and her husband moved into the Flodigarry cottage in the spring of 1751 and spent 8 years farming the rich land here. Flora had five of her seven children at Flodigarry. The couple later moved to Kingsburgh House on the west coast of Trotternish which Allan inherited in 1760. The Flodigarry cottage was recently converted to holiday flats by the owners of the adjacent hotel.

The present Flodigarry Hotel was built as a private residence in 1895 by one of Flora's descendants, Major R.L. MacDonald. The house was converted to a hotel in 1928. This interesting building still retains many of its original features and is worth a visit. The Moorish decor was inspired by the Major's stay in the Middle east and the great billiard room is now the hotel bar. It is said that the hotel grounds are frequented by the Little People and a legend associated with the area holds that Eilean Flodigarry once had its corn reaped in two nights by seven score and ten fairies. Surprisingly, the owner of the island was not grateful for their help and wished to be rid of them, so when the fairies asked for more work, he set them the impossible task of emptying the sea with a sieve.

Eating Out: FLODIGARRY HOUSE HOTEL. Tel. (0470) 552 203. Bar and conservatory meals are served daily from 1100-2300. A selection of local Scottish dishes are available, including Staffin Bay prawns. The Water-Horse Restaurant offers a Table d'Hote menu specialising in seafood, game and local produce. The restaurant is open daily from 1900-2200 and at Sunday lunchtimes from 1230-1430. Booking is advisable. Morning coffees and afternoon teas are available in the Conservatory or Lounge. Children welcome.

Flodigarry To Duntulm

1 1/2 miles on from the Flodigarry turnoff, a derelict World War II building is seen by the right of the road. For a panoramic view of the surrounding countryside, park in front of this building and walk up the dirt track just to the left. This leads to another deserted building on the hill top from which there are spectacular views to the mainland hills of Wester Ross, Assynt and North Sutherland. On a clear day the hills of Harris and Lewis, the Shiant Isles and Eilean Trodday can all be seen out to sea, while behind lies the Trotternish Ridge. This short walk to the hilltop takes only 5 minutes each way. On the shore to the left of the viewpoint is a small sea stack known as Stacan Gobhlach - the Forked Stack. There are some wonderful cliffs to explore on this section of coastline and once at the viewpoint you can walk all the way back to Flodigarry if you wish.

The road now curves westwards over the top of Trotternish and passes through an area of neat croft lands. There are parking spots on both sides which give great views back to the Ridge. Minor roads lead to Balmacqueen, Connista and Port Gobhlaig. The A855 crosses a grassy moor before entering the settlement of Kilmaluag which takes its name from the Celtic missionary Saint Mo Luag of Lismore who established a church here in the 6th century. Kilmaluag is the starting point of an attractive moorland walk to the cliffs above Rubha Hunish, the most northerly point on Skye (see Walks for full details).

Shopping: TROTTERNISH ART GALLERY, Kilmaluag. Tel. (0470) 552 302. Signposted. Situated in croft house by right of road in Kilmaluag. Beautifully detailed local scenes in pencil and pen/ink by Bill and Susie Lawrence, many inspired by the dramatic scenery of the Trotternish peninsula. Also a selection of greetings cards. Commissions accepted. Open daily all year.

After Kilmaluag, a road branches right to North Duntulm and then the distinctive white walls of the Duntulm Hotel are seen to the right. Ahead, the ruins of Duntulm Castle come into view. To the right can be seen Tulm Island, nestling in Tulm Bay.

Duntulm And The Other Lord MacDonald

In the early years of this century, the MacDonald clan found itself in the embarrassing situation of having two Clan Chiefs. This unusual state of affairs came about because of the stigma that was then attached to illegitimacy. In December 1799, Godfrey MacDonald, the brother of the 18th Chief, eloped with a girl whose acquaintance he had made while out riding near Hampton Court. This girl was the child of the Duke of Gloucester and the illegitimate daughter of Sir Edward Walpole and a milliner's apprentice. Godfrey MacDonald succeeded his brother as 19th Chief, but on his death, the title passed to his second son, for in the eyes of English law, his first born was illegitimate. Godfrey's eldest son instead inherited the family's estates at Thorpe in the East Riding of Yorkshire.

In 1886, Alexander Wentworth MacDonald Bosville of Thorpe and Gunthwaite, a decendant of the 19th chief, married a woman called Alice Middleton. When Alice discovered her husband's family history, she determined that he was the rightful heir to both the chiefship and the peerage. Largely due to her perseverance and determination, the stigma of illegitimacy was removed and Alexander was able to prove his grandfather's legitimacy. In 1910, he was legally declared the 21st Chief of Sleat and Alice became Lady MacDonald of the Isles.

The new Lord and Lady decided to take up residence on their ancestral lands in Skye, but as Armadale was then occupied by Lady Edith MacDonald, the couple instead looked to Duntulm, the ancient seat of the clan. They at first tried to purchase Duntulm Castle, but their request was turned down by the Secretary of State, Lord Pentland, who believed that the castle should remain in the hands of the nation. Lord and Lady MacDonald then decided to lease a nearby house, now the Duntulm Hotel, together with 4,000 acres of land and here Alice contented herself with adding a large kitchen and new servants' quarters.

This situation proved rather awkward for clan members who were unsure as to which Chief loyalty was due. The problem was unexpectedly solved by the outbreak of the First World War which caused Lady Alice and Sir Alexander to return to their Yorkshire estates. The Chiefship has to this day been left in the hands of the Armadale MacDonalds.

Eating Out: DUNTULM CASTLE HOTEL.   Tel. (0470) 552 213.   Snack lunches served from 1200-1400. Also teas and dinners.

TROTTERNISH: THE WEST COAST VIA UIG

The western side of the great Trotternish peninsula exhibits a landscape quite different to that seen on the east. Here the countryside alternates between gentle moorland and rich crofting land dotted with small townships. Much of the journey up the east coast gives spectacular views across the Little Minch to the Outer Hebrides.

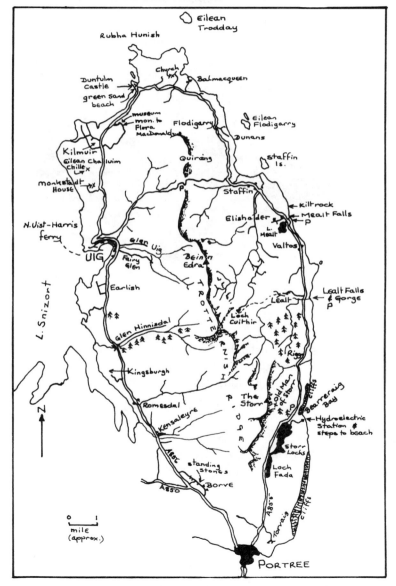

Portree To Kingsburgh

The A850 (signposted to Dunvegan) leaves Portree in a north-westerly direction and crosses a flat and mainly treeless landscape. This is known as A' Mhointeach Mhor, the Great Moss. Before the arrival of coal and electricity to the island, this area used to supply all the peats required by the village of Portree. After a couple of miles a small road branches left to Drumuie. At this point, the beginnings of the Trotternish Ridge can be seen to the right, although it is not recognisable as such from this angle. Here we are looking at the gently sloping western aspect which attains a maximum height of 2,358ft at The Storr before dropping away to form an impressive east-facing escarpment.

Shortly after the turn-off to Drumuie, another small road branches right to Borve. This road leads to the Dun Studio and one of the most accessible prehistoric sites on the island.

Shopping: THE DUN STUDIO, 30 Borve. Tel. (0470) 532 402. Follow the Borve road and then take the first right. The studio is situated at the end of this small road. A striking selection of limited edition prints taken from paintings by John Bathgate, including tiny prints of various Scottish views which make ideal souvenirs. Many of the paintings are inspired by the landscapes of Skye and North-West Scotland. Commissions accepted. Open daily throughout the year from 1000-1900. The studio takes its name from Dun Borve, a very ruinous broch which is perched on the hillside behind the house.

After you have visited the studio, rejoin the Borve road and continue on round until you come to a group of standing stones on the grass verge by the left of the road. Three stones - two tall, one squat - are immediately obvious. Four smaller stone segments are hidden by the long grass. Such standing stones first begin to appear in Scotland around 2,000 B.C. and are associated with the arrival of new groups of people from the European continent who brought with them knowledge of copper and bronze working. Several functions have been suggested for these monuments: route or boundary markers; memorial stones; calendrical or astronomical indicators. There is certainly plenty of evidence to support the last theory, for many such stones are clearly related to the movements of the sun, moon and stars and in particular mark the passing of mid-summer and mid-winter. Such concerns are indicative of an agricultural community to whom the turning of the seasons would have been of great importance. When you have finished looking at the stones, continue on the Borve road and take the first left. This will bring you back on to the main road, now classified as the A856, just beyond the Dunvegan junction.

Petrol: THE FERRYWAY. Located at the junction of the A850 and the A856. Open Monday-Sunday, until 2100. Ice-cream, sweets, videos for rent. Credit cards not accepted.

At the BP station, the A850 branches left to Dunvegan, while the main road north now becomes the A856. After the junction, the A856 begins to descend and Loch Snizort Beag comes into view to the left. The single-track B8036 branches left, providing another opportunity to turn back to Dunvegan. A small road branches right to Annishader and then the main road crosses the River Haultin at Rhenetra.   Shortly afterwards, another minor road branches right to Keistle.   The A856 now continues through Kensaleyre and passes close to the shore of Loch Eyre, a small branch of the much larger Snizort Beag.   Just as the road begins to pull away from the water, two standing stones can be seen on a little knoll to the left, overlooking the loch. Legend has it that there were originally three stones here which were used by a race of giants called the Fiennes to support great cauldrons of venison stew.

Shopping: CARN LIATH STUDIO.   Tel. (0470) 532 405.   Located by right of A856 at Kensaleyre.   Original landscape photographs of the Isle of Skye and surrounding areas, both framed and unframed.   Also landscape and mountain photography courses on a daily or weekly basis (brochure available - phone for full details).   The studio has a small tearoom overlooking Loch Snizort which serves tea, coffee, home baking and light lunches.   Open Easter to October, Monday-Saturday 1000-1700.

A minor road branches left to Romesdal and then the A856 begins to ascend once again over rolling moorland.   On clear days Harris and the southern part of Lewis can be seen out to sea beyond the mouth of Loch Snizort Beag.

Kingsburgh House

Another single track road branches left to Kingsburgh, a township that has long associations with the MacDonalds. "Kingsburgh" is an anglicisation of the Norse *cisborg* which means "tax-town". As the name suggests, this settlement was originally built at the entrance to Loch Snizort for the purpose of extracting tolls from passing ships.

The old house of Kingsburgh, now gone, saw many famous visitors over the years. It was here that Bonnie Prince Charlie sheltered for a night when he first arrived on Skye on 29 June 1746 with a price of £30,000 on his head.   He was brought to the house disguised as Betty Burke, an Irish serving woman, by the brave Flora MacDonald who had previously sought help at Monkstadt further to the north. After the Prince left for Portree the following morning, Mrs MacDonald folded away the sheets he had slept in to be used as shrouds, one for herself and the other for Flora.

Flora herself was later to become the mistress of Kingsburgh House, for in 1750 she married Allan MacDonald, the heir to the property.   After farming at Flodigarry for eight years, the couple moved here when Allan inherited the house and lands in 1760. While at Kingsburgh, Flora and Allan entertained the renowned traveller Dr Samuel Johnson and his companion James Boswell during their visit to the island in 1773. The pair arrived on Sunday 12 September en route from Portree to Dunvegan and were given a welcoming dram by the fire in the parlour. Boswell though highly of Allan and later recorded in his *Journal*, "Kingsburgh was completely the figure of a gallant Highlander...He had his Tartan plaid thrown about him, a large blue bonnet with a knot of black ribband like a cockade, a brown short coat of a kind of duffil, a Tartan waistcoat with gold buttons and gold button-holes, a bluish philibeg, and Tartan hose. He had jet black hair tied behind, and was a large stately man, with a steady sensible countenance." At supper, the travellers at last met with the famous lady of the house. Boswell wrote, "She is a little woman, of a genteel appearance, and uncommonly mild and well-bred. To see Dr Samuel Johnson, the great champion of the English Tories, salute Miss Flora MacDonald in the isle of Skye, was a striking sight; for though somewhat congenial in their motions, it was very improbable they should meet here." The pair were later conducted to a chamber on the upper floor where each had a neat bed with tartan curtains. It was here that Prince Charles had spent the night while at Kingsburgh 27 years previously and indeed Johnson's bed was the very bed in which the Young Pretender had slept. The travellers left Kingsburgh the next day, accompanied by Allan who ferried them across the loch to Greshornish where they met up with their horses.

The Prince At Hinnisdal

Returning to the A856, the road soon reaches the River Hinnisdal. It was here that a potentially disasterous but nevertheless amusing incident took place concerning Prince Charles Edward Stuart. While crossing the river dressed as Flora's serving woman Betty Burke, the Prince lifted his skirts so high that he revealed more than he should have done to a passing youth. The astounded boy ran home to tell the tale of a brazen "wild Irish girl". Fortunately it seems that no-one paid much heed to the story and the Prince was able to continue on his way.

Just beyond the River Hinnisdal, another small road branches right to Balmeanach, Peinlich, Peinaha and Glenuachdarach. This single track road passes an area of forestry and follows the River Hinnisdal into an attractive glen. At the head of the glen the hills rise to form the precipice of the Trotternish Ridge. Glenuachdarach was the home of Donald MacDonald, the first person to record the classical bagpipe music of the Highlands in writing. MacDonald was born here around the year 1750 and bacame a pupil of the MacArthurs, the hereditary pipers to Clan Donald. In 1822 he published the first ever book of piobaireachds and this achievement is commemorated by a small cairn by the right of the road.

Caisteal Uisdean

From the Glen Hinnisdal junction the A856 continues north and, as Lynedale Point is passed, a clear view is obtained left across Loch Snizort to the Waternish Peninsula beyond.   The main road now traverses an undulating landscape of tussocky grass.   Lying on the coast at this point is Caisteal Uisdean or Hugh's Castle, the grim stronghold of Uisdean MacGillespuich Chleirich.   Hugh was the son of Archibald, a half-brother of Donald Gorm, the 5th Chief of the MacDonalds of Sleat.   Throughout his life, he was known as a violent and treacherous man and spent much of his time engaged in acts of piracy up and down the west coast.

Hugh began building the castle shortly after the long-standing fued between the MacDonalds of Sleat and the MacLeods of Dunvegan came to an end in 1601.   Tradition holds that at this time Hugh anchored his great birlinn An Ealadh (The Swan) at Cuidreach, a couple of miles to the north, in the bay still known as Poll na h-Ealaidh, the Pool of the Swan.   While the castle was being built, Hugh spent his days contemplating ways of gaining yet more power for himself and before long he fell to plotting the overthrow of his Chief.   When the construction work was nearing completion, he decided to invite Donald Gorm Mor to a house-warming banquet at the castle and to have him murdered at the end of the festivities.   To assist with this evil plan, Hugh enlisted the help of one William Martin of Trotternish and at this point fate took a hand in the proceedings.   The cordial house-warming invitation to Donald Gorm and a letter detailing Hugh's murderous plans were placed in the wrong envelopes and so the Chief received the instructions intended for the accomplice.   Donald Gorm acted promptly and engaged Donald of Eriskay, a renowned swordsman, to capture Hugh and bring him back to Duntulm dead or alive.   Hugh meantime had managed to board his birlinn and set sail for North Uist where he took refuge at Dun na Sticir, a fort situated on a small island in a freshwater loch.   Despite enduring a long siege and disguising himself as an old woman to escape the attentions of Donald's men, Hugh was eventually captured and taken to Duntulm.   There, Donald Gorm had him thrown into the dungeon, telling Hugh that it was now his turn to be the guest of the Chief.   As Hugh sat in the darkness, tired and hungry from his exertions, a small slot in the wall opened up, through which something was pushed towards him.   Drawing close, Hugh discovered a platter containing a large lump of salt beef and this he ate gratefully.   Next through the slot came a pewter jug and, to his horror, Hugh found this to be empty. And so Uisdean MacGillespuich Chleirich died an agonizing death, driven mad by a thirst he could not quench.   It is said that when the dungeon was finally opened up many years later, inside lay the skeleton of a man clutching a jug with a chewed and broken rim.   Hugh's skull and thigh bones were for centuries displayed in a window at Kilmuir Church and were objects of local curiosity because of their huge size. The bones were eventually given burial in 1827.

In form, Hugh's Castle is a traditional rectangular medieval keep, rather like Castle Moil at Kyleakin, but without any kind of adornment. The sturdy walls are comprised of huge blocks of basalt bound together with heavy lime mortar. Tradition holds that the material was quarried from the nearby Ascrib Islands. Originally, the castle contained a basement and two upper levels and the only entrance was via a door set high in the west wall. This was probably accessed by a wooden ladder which could have been drawn up inside the castle in times of trouble. The castle can be entered today via one of the basement windows in the north wall. Even in its present ruinous condition, the fortification is still a formidable structure. To reach Caisteal Uisdean, take the farm track to South Cuidrach which branches left from the A856 3/4 mile north of the River Hinnisdal. Park well before the farm buildings and continue on foot through the gates. Follow the track past the steadings which emerges on the coast near the castle.

Glen Hinnisdal To Uig

Returning to the A856, the main road continues north and another minor road branches left to Cuidreach. After this, and just before Earlish Post Office, there is a parking spot on the left which gives a panoramic view across Loch Snizort to the hills of North Uist, Harris, the islands in the Sound of Harris and the southern part of Lewis. Suddenly, Uig Bay and the impressive cliffs of Ru Idrigill come into view ahead.

On the final descent to the village of Uig, a single track road branches right to Sheader. This road leads to the Fairy Glen, a small valley filled with strangely shaped mounds and pinnacles which are the result of an ancient period of landslip activity. This miniature landscape is always of great fascination to children and makes an ideal place for a picnic. The first stretch of road gives fine views back across Uig Bay. There is room for several cars to park on a large grassy verge by the left of the road, just before the main area of mounds (Grid Ref. 412633). From here, its fun to explore the area on foot. One of the most striking parts of the landscape is Castle Ewen, a flat topped hill which rises up behind an attractive lochan. The farm buildings at the end of this road are the starting point of a long and strenuous walk to Beinn Edra, the highest point on the northern part of the Trotternish Ridge (see Walks for full details).

Shortly after rejoining the A856, a small tower is seen in a field to the left of the road. This folly was built in the mid 19th century by Captain Fraser, a gentleman who owned part of Snizort and the whole of Kilmuir. Captain Fraser also built a fine villa for humself overlooking Uig Bay. Access to the folly is through a gate opposite the Uig Hotel.

UIG

The A856 now descends into Uig and crosses the rivers Conon and Rha before terminating at the village pier. The village takes its name from the Norse *vik* which means simply "Bay". Uig was visited on 1 September 1902 by King Edward VII and Queen Alexandra who came to preside over the official opening of the new pier. A monument adjacent to the pier carpark commemorates their landing. Today the sheltered bay is the departure point for the Caledonian MacBrayne ferry to the Outer Hebrides.

On 14 October 1877, the Uig area experienced a violent storm which had rather macabre consequences. Incessant torrential rain swelled the waters of the Rivers Rha and Conon causing them to overflow. The two rivers became one seething mass of water which poured down the hillside and carried away part of the village burial ground. For many weeks afterwards, the beaches on either side of bay were littered with coffins and the bones of the dead.

UIG

Bike Hire: NORTH SKYE CYCLE HIRE. Angus Mackenzie, 5 Glenconon. On the Glen Conon road, first right after crossing the River Conon from the south. Follow the signs. Daily hire or longer.

Community Hall: UIG COMMUNITY HALL. Snack bar, badminton and other indoor games. Open afternoons and evenings, weekdays only.

Cruises: CALEDONIAN MACBRAYNE offer a variety of full-day and half-day cruises from Uig Pier to Tarbert (Harris) and Lochmaddy (North Uist) on board MV Hebridean Isles. Some trips include optional coach tours which take in some of the famous landmarks of the Outer Hebrides (St Clement's Church at Rodel, Callanish Stones, Dun Carloway Broch, Arnol Black House, Harris Tweed weaving demonstrations and beautiful sandy beaches). MV Hebridean Isles has a licensed bar and a self-service restaurant which serves tea, coffee, snacks and main meals. Packed lunches are available on the ferry. For tickets and further details, contact the Uig Ferry Terminal Office on (0470) 542 219. For details of coach tours available, contact Harris Coaches on (0859) 2441.

Eating Out: THE FERRY INN. Tel. (0470) 542 242. Restaurant open to non-residents. Dinner served from 1800-2030. Tea and coffee served throughout the day. Bar meals also available daily from 1100-1430 and 1700-2300.
UIG BAY BISTRO. Tel. (0470) 542 234. Located at the pier. Licensed restaurant and cafe. Snacks, tea and coffee available all day. Also breakfasts, lunches and evening meals. Children welcome. Open Monday-Saturday 0800-2100.
SGITHEANACH RESTAURANT. Tel. (0470) 542 212. Located at the pier. Morning coffee, afternoon tea, lunches and dinners. Children half price. Bar snacks are also available in the Bakur Bar: open Monday-Saturday 1100-2300; Sunday 1200-1430 and 1830-2300. Tel. (0470) 542 324.
UIG HOTEL. Tel. (0470) 542 205. Morning coffee, bar lunches, afternoon tea. The hotel is open from Easter until mid-October.

Shopping: JOHN RANKIN. Tel. (0470) 542 213. Grocer, baker, newsagents, post office.
Filled rolls, bread, fruit, cakes and scones. *(Continued)*

UIG POTTERY. Tel. (0470) 542 424. Located near the pier, next to the BP Filling Station. A selection of ceramics, knitwear, books and cards.

WHYTE WOODS CRAFTS. Tel. (0470) 542 417. Location: Follow the A855 out of Uig and take the left branch to Idrigill. The craft shop is situated on the right, a short distance down this road. Signposted. A selection of gifts and toys hand-made in Uig.

Petrol: BP FILLING STATION. Open Monday-Saturday 0900-1800. Credit cards are not accepted.

Pony Trekking: UIG HOTEL. Tel. (0470) 542 205. The hotel organises morning, afternoon and full-day treks on docile Highland ponies which are descended from the native Garron, the traditional working pony of the Highlands. Hats provided, fully supervised.

Toilets: Located adjacent to the pier carpark. Separate facilities for the disabled.

Water and Outdoor Sports: WHITEWAVE. Tel. (0470) 542 414. Canoeing, windsurfing, archery and guided walks. Introductory and action courses for all ages and abilities.

Uig To Linicro

The single-track A855 branches right from the A856 in Uig village centre and climbs high above the bay. The road rounds an incredibly tight hairpin bend and at the top of the hill, a minor road branches right to the Quiraing. A few yards down this road it is possible to pull off onto the grassy verge by a wooden picnic table. From this point there is an unhindered view out over Uig Bay - a great vantage point from which to watch the CalMac ferries come and go.

The A855 continues north across an area of moorland and enters Kilmuir Parish. This stretch of road gives superb views out across the Little Minch to the Outer Hebrides. About 1/2 mile on from the Quiraing junction, a convenient parking spot by the left of the road allows you to take in the view at your leisure and there are several picnic tables on a little knoll opposite. From this viewpoint can be see from left to right Eaval and North and South Lee on Harris, the Sound of Harris, the hills of South Harris, Clisham on North Harris and Beinn Mhor on Lewis. The small island of Fladda-chuain can also be made out just off the north-west tip of Trotternish. Lying in Loch Snizort between Trotternish and the Waternish Peninsula are the Ascrib Islands, famous for their sea-birds and rich fishing grounds. Closer to home, the remains of Dun Skudiburgh can be seen on a prominent coastal knoll just to the left. This Iron Age dun exhibits an interesting building technique known as timber lacing which first began to appear in Scotland around the 7th century B.C. Timber lacing involved the building of substantial dry-stone walls in and around a framework of pegged timbers. This had the effect of binding the walls together, creating a durable and substantial structure. Dun Skudiburgh and many other such early fortifications exhibit signs of vitrification, that is the stones and rocks have become fused together as a result of intense heat. This occurred when the timbers within the walls were set alight. Whether this was done deliberately to improve the strength of the walls, or whether it was the act of an aggressor is not known.

As the A855 continues, the scattered houses of Totscore can be seen to the left. The view right is dominated by the little rounded hill of Reieval and the crags of Creag Collascard. The large sweep of bay seen immediately to the left is Port Kilbride, bounded on the south by Kilbride Point which juts into Loch Snizort. At the northern end of the bay there is another finger of land which is called Prince Charles's Point. It was here on 29 June 1746 that Bonnie Prince Charlie lay in hiding in the small boat which had carried him from Benbecula while Flora MacDonald sought help at nearby Monkstadt House.

Monkstadt House

As the settlement of Linicro is entered, the ruins of Monkstadt House can be seen on the hillside to the left. The house is reached by taking a small sealed road which branches left from the A855. There is room to pull off onto the verge just after the ruins. Monkstadt was built by Sir Alexander MacDonald, the 14th Chief, to replace the old fortress of Duntulm as the family seat. Construction of the grand two-storey house was begun in 1732 using stones from the old castle and the work was finally completed in 1741. Sir Alexander settled here on his return from St Andrews and devoted himself to farming the surrounding fertile countryside. The great house of Monkstadt was to become in effect an independent township for the MacDonald Chief employed not only household staff and gardeners but also a grieve, tailor, cooper, blacksmith, grooms, salmon fishers, herdsmen and other skilled men. It was here on Boxing Day 1741 that Sir Alexander's son James was born. James, the 8th Baronet of the MacDonalds, was an enlightened man who did much to influence the early development of the town of Portree.

Monkstadt figures prominently in the story of Bonnie Prince Charlie and Flora MacDonald. On the night of 29 June 1746 Flora came to the house to seek help from the Chief's wife, Lady Margaret, in finding shelter for Prince Charles who was waiting in a boat at nearby Kilbride Bay. Flora was dismayed to find that a number of Royalist troops were being entertained at the house but she bravely managed to convey her message to Lady Margaret, a fervent Jacobite, and word was soon sent to the Prince. Charles was subsequently taken south to Kingsburgh House where he spent the night.

Monkstadt was abandoned by the MacDonalds around 1790 when the First Lord MacDonald decided to re-establish the family seat at Armadale and began work on a grand mansion there. The house was subsequently lived in by various tacksmen and then gradually fell into ruin.

Loch Chaluim Chille

Just after Monkstadt, to the left of the road, lies an extensive marshy depression known as Loch Chaluim Chille (St Columba's Loch). This was once a large body of water, some 2 miles in length, at the centre of which stood the small island of Eilean Chaluim Chille. Tradition holds that when St Columba visited Skye in 585 A.D. he founded a small chapel and tower here. Whatever the truth of this story, Eilean Chaluim Chille was the site of an early Christian community of some size. A monastery was also built there at a later date, giving rise to the name "Monkstadt". Today, the island can still be distinguished as a small raised area at the centre of the marsh which contains the tumbled remains of the monks' beehive cells.

It had long been thought by local crofters that much fertile agricultural land could be gained by removing the water from Loch Chaluim Chille. Attempts were made to drain the loch in 1715 and 1760 but success was only temporary and the water soon came seeping back. The venture was finally accomplished in 1824 by the renowned Alexander MacLeod, An Doctair Ban, who succeeded in digging a wide outlet to the sea after six year's hard work. The reclaimed land was then divided up amongst the local crofters who devoted much time and effort to removing the stones and tilling the soil. The final result was a huge tract of excellent arable land that was envied throughout the island. But as in so many other instances, the crofters' hard work went unrewarded, for the landowner promptly took the land away from them and added it to the large sheep farm at Monkstadt.

Balgown To Kilmuir

As the road continues north through the crofts of Balgown, the Shiant Isles come into view intermittently on the horizon. The broad expanse of flat coastal land here is often referred to as the Granary of Skye because of the high fertility of the soil. The Kilmuir Estate, like that of Glendale, was purchased by the Congested Districts Board in 1904 and was subsequently divided up amongst the local crofters. Small roads branch from the A855 to Bornesketaig and Heribusta. An interesting detour is to be had by taking the left branch to Borneskataig. Note the beautiful thatched house and barn on your left. The road curves to the right and then continues on to a crossroads. Turn left here. In a white building by the right of the road is Macurdie's Exhibition.

> **Exhibition:** MACURDIE'S EXHIBITION. A rather oddball and humerous collection of fishing memorabilia and pickled sea creatures. Mr Macurdie describes himself as the last in a long line of master craftsmen, creelmakers, fishermen and lunatics who roamed the Kilmuir district. Open daily until 2100. Admission free - donations accepted.

The Bornesketaig road terminates at the Sgeir Lang Slipway where there is a large turning circle and room to park. From this quiet spot there are fine views to Lewis, Harris and North Uist. Lying closer to shore are the rocks of Sgeir nan Ruideag, An t-Iasgair, and An Dubh Sgeir, while across Camas Mor, the Big Bay, can be seen the remains of Bornesketaig broch, perched on a little knoll. Also on the Ru Bornesketaig headland opposite lies Uamh Oir, the Cave of Gold. Tradition holds that this cave once contained a fabulous hoard of treasure which was guarded by a terrible monster. This horrifying creature wandered further and further afield in its search for food until at last the whole neighbourhood lived in fear of its raids. Eventually one of the MacArthur pipers decided to put an end to the beast and, with pipes skirling, he set off into the dark recesses of the cave. Anxious neighbours, gathered around the entrance, heard the pipes grow fainter and then suddenly stop. Next came the sound of a great conflict and the piper was heard to shout in Gaelic, "Pity me, without arms three, two for the pipes and a sword hand free." MacArthur was never seen again, but it seems that he succeeded in his efforts, for the monster never troubled the district again.

Bornesketaig was the setting of an incident which is said to have given the MacDonalds their clan motto "Per Mare Per Terras". Donald, son of Reginald MacSomerled, was engaged in a feud with the rival MacLeods over a piece of contested land in Trotternish. To settle the dispute, it was eventually agreed that the two clans would stage a boat race and that whoever touched land first would have rightful title to the territory. As the two galleys raced off, it seemed for a time that the MacDonalds would win the day, but as they drew near the coastline, the MacLeod boat nosed ahead. In desperation Donald drew his dagger and as the galleys rounded Ru Bornesketaig, he cut off his hand and threw it onto the shore. Donald's victory cry, "On Sea, On Land" became the MacDonald's motto thereafter.

To return to the main road from Bornesketaig, retrace your route past Macurdie's Exhibition and continue straight on at the crossroads. The road forks right and passes the ruins of an old church before rejoining the A855 just south of Hungladder. Until the close of the 18th century, the lands of Hungladder were occupied rent-free by the MacArthurs, hereditary pipers to the MacDonalds in Trotternish. The last of the MacArthurs, Angus, died in 1800.

KILMUIR

Eating Out: THE CROFT TEAROOM. Situated to left of A855, behind the Crafts Shop.

Museum: THE SKYE MUSEUM OF ISLAND LIFE. Right turn shortly after The Crafts Shop. Signposted. The museum comprises a range of traditional thatched buildings which recreate a crofting settlement or clachan of a century ago. The Croft House contains traditional furniture and a real peat fire, and a display of historical items including the chalice from Trumpan Church and Flora MacDonald's egg cup. There are various items for sale including a good selection of Scottish books, Clan bookmarks and postcards, preserves, sweets, knitwear and a guide to the museum. Other buildings include The Weaver's Shed - loom and associated implements; The Ceilidh House - an excellent display of photographs and postcards depicting crofting life; The Barn - a good selection of original farming implements; The Smiddy - forge, bellows and anvil. If you visit on a Tuesday or Thursday, there are spinning and carding demonstrations at 1400.   Open Monday-Saturday 0900-1730. Admission fee applies, reduced rates for Senior Citizens and Children.   *(Continued)*

Shopping: THE CRAFTS SHOP. Tel. (0470) 552 279. To left of the A855. Established in 1950, this was the first craft shop to be opened on the island. Excellent selection of tweed caps and hats, knitwear, tartans, blankets, knee rugs, sheepskin items, preserves and honeys (Arran Provisions and Struan range), shortbread, postcards, ties, jewellery and a wide selection of Scottish books. Open Monday-Saturday 0900-1800.

Toilets: There is a small toilet block by the right of the minor road which leads to the Skye Museum of Island Life. Facilities for the disabled.

Kilmuir Churchyard and Flora MacDonald's Monument

The small road which leads to the Skye Museum of Island Life also gives access to Kilmuir Churchyard. The old burial ground is dominated by the imposing Celtic Cross which marks the final resting place of Flora MacDonald. Here, beneath a large slab of granite, Flora lies wrapped in one of the sheets used by Prince Charles while at Kingsburgh house. Her gravestone is inscribed with Dr Johnson's words of tribute: "A name that will be mentioned in history, and if courage and fidelity be virtues, mentioned with honour." The present monument was erected in 1955 by Major Reginald Henry MacDonald O.B.E., a great, great grandson of Allan and Flora. The marble slab that originally covered Flora's grave was completely removed by souvenir-seeking tourists.

The famous encounter with Prince Charles Edward Stuart was not the only period of adventure in Flora's life. When she and her husband Allan saw that their Kingsburgh farmlands would not pay their way, they decided to emigrate to America. In 1774, shortly after Johnson and Boswell's visit, the couple set sail for North Carolina. There, Allan and two of his sons held commissions in the Royal Highland Emigrant Regiment and fought in the War of Independence. Allan, one of the boys and Flora herself were subsequently taken prisoner and the family lost most of their possessions. It is said that Flora was in danger of her life. In 1779, she returned to Skye with her daughter Fanny and the pair were later joined by Allan. Flora died at Peinduin, on the shore of Loch Snizort, in 1790.

Kilmuir burial ground is also the last resting place of many generations of Martins, MacDonalds, MacArthurs and Nicolsons and it is worth taking time to walk around the many interesting graves. Lying flat on the ground, to the south of Flora's monument, is a memorial slab which contains the following curious inscription: "Here ly the remains of Charles MacKarter whose fame as an honest man and remarkable piper will survive this generation for his manners were easy & regular as his music and the melody of his fingers will..." Two stories are told as to why this inscription was left unfinished. One says that the mason refused to complete the work because he felt that he had not been paid enough. The second story holds that Charles's son, who had commissioned the stone, drowned at sea while shipping cattle across to Duntulm from the Uists; on hearing this, the stone mason abandoned his task for he knew that he would not be paid for the work.

Towards the east end of the cemetery is a long thin slab which bears the effigy of a mailed warrior. This ancient stone marks the burial place of the Martin family, the greatest of whom was Martin Martin, author of *Description of the Western Islands of Scotland*, published in 1703. It is said that the stone once covered the grave of a Scottish King on Iona and was brought to Skye by Aonghas na Gaoithe, Angus of the Wind, the first of the Martin family. Angus is reputed to have been so strong that he was able to carry the stone up from the shore on his own back.

Beyond Kilmuir Churchyard lie the crofts of Peingown. It was here that the MacArthurs, hereditary pipers to Clan Donald in Trotternish, established their piping school.

Kilmuir To Duntulm
The main road continues north from Kilmuir and skirts around Lub Score. Here, on the narrow strip of land between the sea and the road, lie the scattered remains of dry-stone cottages. These were once the homes of crofting families who were evicted from the fertile lands of Kilmuir at the time of the Clearances. If you wish to stop to admire the view to the islands, there is a small picnic area with a barbecue by the right of the road overlooking the bay. The A855 now passes an area of striking weathered basalt cliffs. On this section there are benches by the left of the road and a parking spot on the right which gives excellent views to the islands and the smaller skerries close in.

Duntulm Castle soon comes into view ahead. As the road begins to ascend from Lub Score and takes a sharp right, there is room to park on the large grassy verge on the left, next to the sheep fanks. To reach the castle, follow the line of the fence downhill and go through the gate. An easy 5 minute walk along short springy turf will take you to Duntulm.

Duntulm Castle
The ancient castle of Duntulm occupies a position of strength atop a small promontory of basalt jutting out into the Minch. Although the fortification changed hands many times throughout the centuries, it was as the seat of the MacDonald Chiefs that Duntulm gained prominence.

Given the strategic advantages of the site, it is likely that the headland was occupied by an earlier fortification, perhaps an Iron Age dun. Tradition holds that this was the location of Dun Dhaibhidh or David's Fort, the residence of a powerful Viking lord during the days when Skye was a possession of the Norwegian Crown. Following the Treaty of Perth in 1266, the island was ceded to Scotland and thereafter the fortification, now known as Duntulm, passed to and from the MacLeods and the MacDonalds on numerous occasions. MacDonald possession of the castle came to an end for a time when the Lordship of the Isles was surrendered to the Scottish Crown in 1493. The MacDonald territories passed to the Crown and King James IV eventually granted Duntulm to Torquil MacLeod of Lewis in 1498.

The 16th century saw many skirmishes between the rival MacLeod and MacDonald clans and during this time tha lands of Trotternish changed hands several times. Duntulm was once again occupied by the MacDonalds following their victory at the Battle of Trouterness in 1539. The following year, King James V undertook a great procession through the troubled Highlands and Islands in an attempt to pacify the warring clans and was much impressed by the strength and charm of the castle. The fortification subsequently underwent further refurbishment to create a residence befitting a Clan Chief, but despite this, the castle was abandoned for a time in the late 16th century when it appears that Donald Gormson decided to return to the MacDonald's territories in Sleat.

On 11 January 1613, the MacDonald lands of Trotternish, Sleat and North Uist were granted to Sir Rory MacLeod on condition that he reside at Duntulm. This led to another period of claims and counter-claims concerning the castle until, in 1618, the two clans decided to turn their charter lands over to the King. The lands of Trotternish were subsequently granted to Sir Donald Gorm Og, the 9th Chief of Sleat, on condition that he pay adequate compensation to the MacLeods. The charter also stipulated that Sir Donald must reside at Duntulm and carry out any necessary repairs. All this Sir Donald agreed to and Duntulm Castle thereafter became the principal residence of the MacDonald chiefs.

In 1695, the chiefship passed to Sir Donald MacDonald, the 4th Baronet. Sir Donald was imprisoned for a time on suspicion of being a Jacobite sympathiser and on his release he went to live at Duntulm where he died on 1 March 1718. The estate was confiscated by the Crown as punishment for the Clan's part in the 1715 Rising, but when it was put up for sale in 1723, it was bought by the creditors and the castle was eventually returned to the MacDonalds in 1726. By this time it seems that the building had fallen into a state of disrepair and was no longer considered suitable to be the seat of a clan chief. The 14th Chief, Sir Alexander, who was used to fine lowland residences in Edinburgh and St Andrews, began to look for a suitable site for a new house and in 1732 work was begun at Monkstadt. The old castle of Duntulm was broken up to provide stone and timber for the new residence, the building materials being shipped south by boat. A substantial part of the structure was still standing when William Daniell made a sketch of

Duntulm in 1819, but since then the castle has undergone a steady process of decay and is now in a very sorry state indeed. Care should be taken when wandering about the ruins.

Duntulm Castle is a classic medieval fortification, comprising a stout curtain wall which originally enclosed the summit of the headland, giving protection to the buildings within. The earliest surviving structure is a sturdy square tower of four storeys which dates to the 14th or 15th century. The vaulted basement of this structure, once used as the castle kitchen, can still be identified today. In the early 16th century, more space was created by building a smaller three storey tower against the north wall of the original structure. Incised in the mortar adjacent to one of the windows of this later tower was the representation of a ship, believed to be the great birlinn of the MacDonald chief. Sadly, this line drawing was lost when the window arch collapsed in 1985. Sometime in the latter part of the 16th century, the castle was refurbished and a new curtain wall with artillery platforms was added. The last building to be erected on the site was a large rectangular hall lying in the north-western corner of the enclosure. This dates to the 17th century and may have functioned as a banqueting hall. Lying just outside the castle is a modern memorial cairn dedicated to the MacArthurs, hereditary pipers to the MacDonalds of the Isles.

As with Skye's other castles, the ancient stronghold of Duntulm is the subject of many tales and legends. There are two traditions concerning the reasons behind the final abandonment of the fortification. One states that the infant heir of Donald Gorm Og was being cradled by a window overlooking the Minch one day when he suddenly wriggled free from the nurse's arms and fell onto the rocks below. The Chief was greatly affected by this tragic event and was no longer able to live at Duntulm. The second reason given for the abandonment of the castle is that it is haunted by the ghost of Donald Gorm Mor, the blacksheep of the MacDonald family. Although Donald died in Edinburgh, it is said that his ghost, together with two companions, returned frequently to the castle to raid the cellars. Such was the noise and fear created by these apparitions that the residents of the castle were forced to move elsewhere. Duntulm is also supposedly haunted by the ghost of Uisdean MacGillespuich Chleirich who died a barbarous death in the early 17th century, sealed up in one of the castle's vaults.

Lying to the south-east of Duntulm is a prominent rounded hill known as Cnoc Roll, the Knoll of the Rolling. In the days of the MacDonald chiefs, local people found guilty of a crime would be placed inside nail-studded barrels and then rolled down this hill. Any criminals who managed to survive this horrifying punishment were subsequently released.

TROTTERNISH: STAFFIN TO UIG
VIA THE QUIRAING

The single track road to the Quiraing branches left from the A855 at Brogaig just north of Staffin. This route involves a steep climb up and over the Trotternish Ridge and is therefore unsuitable for caravans.

After the turn-off, the narrow road climbs up over the moor and passes the old and new village burial grounds on the left. Sections of this high peat moor are still cut for fuel today and here and there you may see the little stacks of turfs piled up to dry. The road continues to climb and becomes quite twisty as the Trotternish Ridge is approached. There are spectacular views right to the rock formations of the Quiraing which, in misty weather, take on a rather ghostly appearance. As the road levels out above the ridge, there is a parking spot on the left. This is the starting point of the "tourist" route to the Quiraing (see Walks for full details). If you are reasonably fit, it is well worth making the effort to see this fascinating array of pinnacles and rock formations. At the heart of the towers and pillars, completely hidden from view, lies an elevated grassy plateau known as "The Table" which was used in the 15th and 16th centuries to hide cattle from raiders.

As the road continues across the high moor, the headwaters of the River Rha can be seen just to the right. The river is crossed via a little bridge as you continue towards Uig. This high moorland area is subject to heavy rainfall and experiences frequent flash floods - note the deep drainage ditches on either side of the road. The land on the left begins to fall away and the River Rha disappears from sight. Soon the first crofts of Uig come into view ahead followed by the deep sheltered anchorage of Uig Bay. The road rejoins the A855 above Uig village.

WALKS DESCRIBED

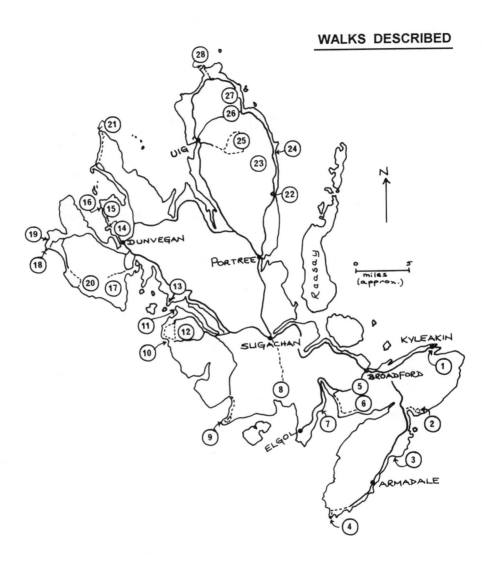

WALKS GUIDE

The Isle of Skye is justifiably famous for the impressive peaks of the Red and Black Cuillin which draw thousands of walkers and climbers to the island each year.   These well-known mountains contain a variety of crags, ridges, peaks and crevasses to tax even the most experienced hill-walker and there are a number of specialist books on the subject readily available from retail outlets on the island.   However, the Cuillin represent only a tiny part of the island and it would be a pity to come away from Skye without having sampled some of the other possibilities on offer.   The following is a selection of the finest walks on the island which take in areas of scenic, historical and archaeological importance.   All are within the capabilities of reasonably fit people and many are suitable for families.   Each individual entry gives details of the distance and time required for each route, together with an indication of the state of the paths and a recommendation on footwear.   Although a general location map is included here, it is strongly advised that the appropriate 1:50,000 Landranger map should be carried on the moorland and hill walks.   O.S. Sheets 23 and 32 cover most of the walks detailed here.

Weather Forecast: For an up-to-date guide to mountain conditions in the West Highlands, telephone (0898) 654 665.

Country Code: When out walking, please observe the Country Code: Guard against risk of fire; Keep dogs under control; Leave gates as you find them; Keep to paths across farmland; Do not damage hedges, fences or walls; Leave no litter; Do not contaminate water supplies; Do not harm animals, plants or trees; Be careful on country roads; Respect the life of the countryside.

Cairns: Please resist the temptation to build cairns.   Existing cairns have been erected for good reason - to mark a division of the path or to guide walkers over indistinct ground in mist.   Adding to them can be confusing and is certainly unsightly.

1. CASTLE MOIL

The seaward approach to Kyleakin is dominated by the striking profile of Castle Moil, the ancient stronghold of the MacKinnons of Strath.   This popular walk takes you around the bay to view the castle, from which there are superb views up and down the narrows which separate Skye from the mainland.   The route follows a gravel footpath along the shoreline and is suitable for any type of footwear.   **Distance:** 1/2 mile (3/4 km) return.   **Time:** 30 minutes for the round trip.

Step By Step: Heading west from Kyleakin Pier on the A850, take the first road on the left marked to South Obbe.   Continue over the bridge and turn left. A short distance on, there is a small parking area by the left of the road, just before a sharp right bend. It is also possible to park at the end of the road, taking care not to block the turning circle (Map Ref. NG 755 264). Walk along to the pier at the end of the road from which there are good views across the old village harbour. A well made gravel path leaves from the right of the turning circle and skirts around the little bay and past a boathouse to the castle. It is well worth while climbing up to the ruin for the superb views up and down the Kyle. The castle is a simple rectangular tower with crenellated battlements and originally had three stories. As you ascend, you are actually climbing over accumulated rubble which conceals a basement level with kitchen and storage area. The present ground floor level is therefore actually the first floor. This originally would have contained the castle entrance and main hall. On the inside walls can be seen joist holes which would have supported an upper floor of private rooms. For historical details, see Kyleakin to Broadford. Retrace the route to your car.

2. LEITIR FURA DESERTED VILLAGE

A relatively easy walk through attractive oakwoods and conifers to the deserted village of Leitir Fura. The route gives periodic views across the Sound of Sleat to Sandaig opposite. The outward section is mainly by a rough footpath which can be very muddy in places and the return journey is by a good Forestry Commission road. Walking boots highly recommended. **Distance:** 4 3/4 miles (7 1/2 kms) return. **Time:** Allow 2 hours for the round trip.

Step By Step: Take the A851 which branches south at Broadford. After 5 miles, take the first road on the left after the Drumfearn junction. Follow this through the trees until you come to a fork. Take the left branch (sharp right descends to the Kinloch Hotel) and continue for a short distance. There is room for a couple of cars to park by the right of the road, just before the forestry gate (Map Ref. NG 703 162). Go through the gate and continue along the well made forestry road which passes through an attractive area of natural woodland, in summer dotted with wild foxgloves. Here you may also spot the beautiful iridescent common blue butterfly. This early section of the walk gives views south down Loch na Dal to the tidal island of Ornsay. There are also periodic views across the Sound of Sleat to the mainland hills opposite. After about ten minutes walk, just before you reach a second gate, a small wooden post by the left of the forestry road marks the start of a footpath. Take this path and ascend through the attractive broad-leaved woodland. This eventually gives was to conifer plantations and the path soon levels out and continues along a cutting in the trees. There are many open stretches on this upper part which allow superb views across the Sound to the mainland hills. One stream along the way is crossed by means of a handy bridge constructed by the 108 Royal Monmouthshire Royal Engineers in June 1991.

After about an hour, the footpath becomes faint and a large clearing is seen down the hill to the right. Descend the slope to this area. Here, amidst the long grass and bracken lie the ruins of Leitir Fura village. Up until the end of the 18th century, this was the home of a large family of MacInneses. The remote settlement was finally deserted in 1782. From the village there are superb views across the Sound to the little white house at Sandaig and the lighthouse on Eilean Mor. Skirt to the right of the ruins where you can join a faint footpath which makes its way downhill through a clearing between a line of conifers and a line of broad-leaved trees. After about 5 minutes another clearing is reached and here the footpath joins a grassy vehicle track. Turn right and follow the track up the gentle slope. This track soon becomes the well made forestry road taken at the start of the outward journey and gives good walking all the way back to your car.

3. CAISTEAL CHAMUIS

A pleasant riverside walk to the ruins of Caisteal Chamuis or Knock Castle which look out over Knock Bay. The route follows a farm track and rough footpath, suitable for any type of footwear. The path can be muddy after rain. **Distance:** 1/2 mile (3/4 km) return. **Time:** 20 minutes for the round trip.

Step By Step: Take the A851 south to Sleat. A short distance beyond the Toravaig House Hotel, a farm track branches left. Park on the grass verge by this track (Map Ref. NG 671 092), taking care not to block farm access. Walk down the track past the white cottage and veer left to cross a small bridge. Immediately after crossing the river, turn right and go through a wooden gate which gives access to a pleasant woodland walk. In summer this shady glade is filled with ferns, purple orchids, foxgloves and yellow flag irises. Keep left after the boathouse and pass through a second wooden gate to reach the pretty ivy-covered ruins of the castle (see Sleat section for historical details). The grassy knolls adjacent to the castle are ideal for a picnic and at low tide there are plenty of nooks and crannies to explore on the rocky coastline.

Caisteal Chamuis is today in a sadly ruinous state. The ivy-covered walls which remain standing at the eastern end of the site were once part of a great rectangular three storey tower or keep, the oldest part of the castle. The surviving seaward wall still retains one of its windows. Lying opposite the tower, across a large courtyard, there was once a second rectangular building of two rooms. This building was linked to the tower by means of a curtain wall which ran along the cliff edge. Virtually no trace now remains of this building or the wall. Sometime in the late 16th or early 17th century, a small rectangular house was built in the courtyard, abutting onto the tower. The seaward wall and gable end of this structure which survive today belong to the basement level of the house. This apparently non-defensive structure also originally contained upper rooms lit by large windows and perhaps an attic level.

4. POINT OF SLEAT

A popular walk to the lighthouse at the southernmost tip of Skye which gives excellent views to the nearby islands of Rum and Eigg. Most of the walk is along a well-made track with narrow footpaths and rough moorland in the later stages. Boots are essential. Dogs must be kept on a lead. Unfortunately, part of the route is currently the subject of an access dispute. If you have any problems, contact the Clan Donald Country Ranger on (04714) 305. **Distance:** 5 miles (8 kms) return. **Time:** Allow 2 1/2 hours return.

Step By Step: Park in the small carpark at the end of the road just beyond Aird of Sleat (Map Ref. NG 588 007). Go through the gate and follow the rough vehicle track across the moor which soon gives fine views west to the island of Rum. The track descends and eventually comes to an end at a wooden bridge. Here, a pleasant detour is to be had by following the right bank of the small river down to the shore where there is an attractive pebble beach. From here, there are excellent views to Rum and this tranquil bay makes a fine place to stop for refreshments. To continue on to the Point, retrace the route to the track, cross the wooden bridge and go through the farm gate. Follow the distinct footpath which soon veers left and reaches a second gate. Go through this, passing close to a house on the right, and cross the small burn at the head of the creek. At this point, the path becomes indistinct. Ascend the rocky slope to the left to reach a fence and follow this south. Shortly after the fence turns left, the path peters out completely and the easiest way ahead from this point is to follow the low ridge which runs south-east to the saddle overlooking the little bay of Camas Daraich. This route avoids the low-lying area of moorland which can be boggy in wet weather. From the saddle, a distinct but narrow path heads back across the moor to the west coast where a flight of concrete steps descend to a small rocky bay. The path continues left around the beach and then a narrow isthmus gives access to the Point. Ascend a further flight of steps to reach the lighthouse which sits atop a rocky headland. The Point of Sleat lighthouse was established in 1933 and is now unmanned. From here, the southernmost point on Skye, there are fine uninterrupted views across the Cuillin Sound to the islands of Rum and Eigg. The scene is particularly beautiful at sunset.

5. CILL CHRIOSD & BEN SUARDAL MARBLE QUARRIES

A short walk to the remains of Cill Chriosd village and the old marble quarries at the foot of Ben Suardal. The route follows a farm track and open grassland, suitable for any type of footwear. **Distance:** 1 1/2 miles (2 1/2 kms) return. **Time:** 40 minutes for the round trip.

Step By Step: Take the A881 which branches south at Broadford and follow it for 2 1/2 miles to the old Cill Chriosd churchyard. A short distance beyond the church, just before the start of the loch, there is room for a couple of cars to park by the left of the road (Map Ref. NG 615 205). A short distance on, an old cart track cuts diagonally up the hillside by the left of the road, following the line of the fence. Follow this uphill as it veers to the left, keeping left at the fork and then cross the moorland. Make directly for the ruins of the large house which can now be seen ahead. This beautifully constructed building is still in a very good state of preservation, with four fireplaces and five windows still largely intact. Above the fireplace to the right as you walk in the door, note the maker's mark "CGJ '73". About eight feet from the ground on the interior wall you can still see the line of joist holes which would have supported an upper floor, a building style which was attemped only by the well-to-do. Surrounding this grand house lie the remains of the single storey dry-stone crofters' cottages. The site for the village was carefully chosen, for this area is underlain by a limestone band which renders the soil fertile. This can be seen in the land immediately surrounding the croft houses which is very green and lush compared to the brown moorland.

On the ridge to the south-east of the village can be seen the spoil tips of the old Ben Suardal marble quarries. To reach the quarries, follow the rough path to the east of the village and then head across the moorland and up the flanks of the Ben. The Ben Suardal quarries were worked in the 19th century and extraction continued until 1912. From here, the famous Strath marble was transported by narrow guage railway to the pier at Broadford and then shipped to the mainland. The company which ran the venture brought in workmen from as far afield as France, Belgium and the Scottish mainland. From the quarries, retrace the route to your car.

6. SUISNISH AND BORERAIG CLEARANCE VILLAGES

A long walk to the ruins of the remote villages of Suisnish and Boreraig. The route gives fine views across Loch Slapin to the Cuillin and in the later stages across Loch Eishort to the Sleat peninsula. The first part of the route as far as Suisnish follows a well-made track which gives good walking. The final 2 miles to Boreraig is by a rough footpath. Walking boots essential. **Distance:** 9 miles (14 1/2 kms) return. **Time:** Allow 4 hours for the return journey.

Step By Step: Take the A881 which branches south at Broadford and follow it for 3 1/4 miles to Loch Cill Chriosd. About 3/4 mile after the loch, take the left fork to Kilbride and then left again after "Ashbank". Follow this track all the way to the bay at Camas Malag and park on the grassy foreshore (Map Ref. NG 583 192). From here the track continues south for 2 3/4 miles to Suisnish. This well-made route was constructed shortly after the First World War when the Board of Agriculture briefly tried to re-settle crofters at Suisnish. As the track begins to climb, the distinctive weathered grooves of the steel blue/grey limestone which underlies this whole area are soon apparent. The limestone is particularly noticeable at a small concrete bridge by a waterfall. The track continues south, giving spectacular changing views of the Cuillin mountains across Loch Slapin and later the islands of Eigg, Muck and Rum. After about 1/2 hour, shortly after crossing a bridge, the road turns right and crests a hill and the first crofts of Suisnish can be seen to the right. The track continues down into the village and veers left by the substantial remains of a later croft house. This section of the village displays the tradition pattern of crofting land use, with each croft being delineated by turf and stone dykes running all the way down to the sea. Continue to the end of the track and go left through the gate by the modern hut. Ascend the hill, crossing a small stream, and pass through the gate in the fence at the top. Bear right and join the good footpath which soon gives easy walking over short springy grass. As the path turns eastwards, it passes below the crags of Carn Dearg and then descends steeply to the shoreline. This final approach to the village of Boreraig can be very muddy in places. The walk from Suisnish to Boreraig will take about 50 minutes and gives good views out across the many islands in Loch Eishort to the Sleat peninsula.

The villages of Suisnish and Boreraig were once thriving crofting communities, peopled mostly by families of MacInneses and MacRaes. Here the people grew potatoes and barley, fished in the tranquil inshore waters and grazed their stock on the surrounding hillsides. This peaceful way of life came to an end for ever in September 1853 when the 32 families here were evicted by Lord MacDonald's factor and a body of police. Lord MacDonald was in debt to the tune of £200,000 and had been forced to place his affairs in the hands of Trustees. The notorious Messrs. Brown and Ballingall cared nothing for MacDonald's tenants and wished only to extract the maximum possible revenue from the estate and to this end they determined to evict the people and convert the land into a large sheep farm. The evictions were carried out when most of the men of the villages were engaged on seasonal work on the mainland and no quarter was given to the elderly or the infirm. The Boreraig and Suisnish clearances were witnessed by several prominent people, among them the lawyer Donald Ross who described the dreadful events in a letter to the Northern Ensign: "The scene was truly heart-rending. The women and the children went about tearing their hair, and rending the heavens with their cries. Mothers with tender infants at the breast looked helplessly on, while their effects and their aged and infirm relatives were cast out, and the doors of their homes locked in their faces. No mercy was shown to age or sex - all were indiscriminately thrust out and left to perish." The ground officers used the villagers' precious milk to douse the peat fires and then wrecked or nailed up the cottages so that the people could not return. Three local men who tried to stop the proceedings were taken in irons to Portree. Eye-witnesses also recounted tales of terrible individual cruelty and hardship. When Neill Kelly's wife asked the evicting officers where her small sons were to sleep that night, she was told, "Throw them into the loch!" At the house of John and Duncan MacRae, the factor shouted at their 81 year old mother to take up her bed and walk. When she made no reply, she was dragged outside on her blanket. The widow Flora Robertson, aged 96, was thrown out of her house and had to be helped to an adjacent barn by her three grandchildren and there she lived for several months. She was later joined by her son on his return from seasonal work on the mainland. Such were the cold and damp conditions in the barn that the son soon fell ill and died, and there he lay, head to the door, his black hair waving in the wind, until arrangements could be made for his burial.

When the ground officers finally left, many villagers had no choice but to seek shelter in outbuildings and sheep fanks and there they lived amidst terrible hardship into the winter months. Lord MacDonald's factor and his men came again five days after Christmas and carried out a second eviction. The elderly and infirm were dragged out onto the snow on blankets and left to perish. When Donald Ross visited the area in February 1854, bringing food and clothing, there were still people clinging to life amidst the ruins of the crofts. He came across seven children, all under the age of eleven, huddled together in a shed on "a collection of rubbish, fern, meadow-hay, straw, pieces of old blanket and rags of clothing." The rain and snow fell in on them and they were so emaciated that Ross believed he could have carried them all in his arms for a quarter of a mile without feeling their weight. The tragic scenes he encountered that day later led Ross to write, "Surely in a country boasting of its humanity, liberty, and Christianity, such conduct should not be any longer tolerated in dealing with the infirm and helpless poor."

By the summer of 1854, the villages of Suisnish and Boreraig were at last deserted and the Trustees set about finding a new tenant for the land. Some of those evicted later emigrated to Australia, others moved to Isleornsay, Drumfearn, Tarskavaig, Breakish and to poor land at Strollamus. In defence of the evictions, the Trustees argued that Lord MacDonald had been over-indulgent to the villagers and one Patrick Cooper went so far as to issue a circular stating that the MacDonald Chief's actions had been "prompted by motives of benevolence, piety and humanity, because they were too far from the church."

7. DUN RINGILL

An easy walk to the well-preserved stronghold of Dun Ringill which look out across Loch Slapin. The route lies along a distinct grassy footpath which is boggy in places. Suitable for wellingtons or shoes with care. **Distance:** 1 1/4 miles (2 kms) return. **Time:** 40 minutes for the round trip.

Step By Step: Take the A881 which branches south at Broadford and follow it for 11 miles to the village of Kirkibost. Just after Kirkibost, take the small road to Old Kilmarie Graveyard which branches left immediately after the bridge. Follow this down until you reach the old house of Kilmarie, a large white mansion by the right of the road. There is space for a couple of cars to park just outside this house, but take care not to block the entrance (Map Ref. NG 553 173). Walk back along the road for a short distance and you will see a gate in the fence above the river. Go through and follow the path across the wrought iron footbridge. Turn right and continue along the riverbank through the attractive woodland filled with rhododendrons and foxgloves. After passing through a second gate, the grassy path follows the coastline at the mouth of the river. Cross the over the fence on your left via the stile and continue on the path which winds its way around the coast. In summer this boggy shoreline is filled with cotton grass, bracken, bog asphodel and foxgloves. The prominent mound of Dun Ringill is soon seen on the coast to your right. From the fortification there are fine views to the Cuillin, the Sleat peninsula, the islands of Eigg and Muck and the hills of the mainland.

Dun Ringill started life as an Iron Age fortification some 2,000 years ago. Although not truly circular in shape, the structure exhibits many of the features seen on brochs elsewhere on Skye, i.e. intra-mural chambers, mural passages and a long entrance passage with bar-holes. It may be that the original builders considered the steep seaward cliffs to be a sufficient deterrent to aggressors, for the sturdy enclosing walls terminate at this side. Centuries after the original abandonment of the fortification, the structure was refurbished to improve the defences. These medieval alterations included reducing the height of the passage walls to create a deep and narrow entrance, adding an internal steep flight of stairs and constructing two small rectangular internal buildings. To the west of the fortification lie several houses and enclosures, some of which may be contemporary with the medieval re-occupation. Tradition relates that the later refurbishments were carried out by the MacKinnons to create a residence for their Chief. This ancient clan seat was known to the MacKinnons as Castle Findanus and remained in occupation until the late 16th century when the Chief moved to the more spacious Castle Moil at Kyleakin.

8. LOCH CORUISK VIEWPOINT

The sparkling waters of remote Loch Coruisk have provided inspiration for many artists over the years. If you love breathtaking wilderness scenery, this walk is not to be missed. The route follows a distinct path all the way which can be very wet in places. Walking boots are essential. Do not underestimate the effort required here - this is a long and tiring route which should only be attempted by properly equipped and experienced walkers. **Distance:** 14 1/2 miles (23 kms) return. **Time:** Allow 8-9 hours for the round trip.

Step By Step: Park in the carpark on the A863 adjacent to the Sligachan Hotel (Map Ref. NG 485 298). The route into Glen Sligachan is signposted just opposite the hotel. Cross the footbridge over the River Sligachan and you will soon see the distinct path which follows close to the eastern bank of the river. The path is good but can be very wet in places and there are numerous small streams to cross. As you continue southwards the mountains begin to close around you, first the lesser slopes of Druim na Ruaige on the left and then the crags of Nead na h-Iolaire on the right. Ahead lie the brooding masses of Marsco and Sgurr nan Gillean. After about an hour, at the Allt na Measarroch which flows down the bealach between Ciche na Beinne Deirge and Marsco, the path bends left and then backtracks right for a short distance along the bank of the stream. A cairn marks the point where the stream can be forded, although there are so many stones in the burn that, except in times of spate, there should be no problem in crossing. Once on the far side, an obvious muddy path lead on to the stony path once more.

After rounding the flank of Marsco, the spectacular Black Cuillin Ridge begins to open up. As the path passes the Lochan Dubha, there is a good view right into the huge Harta Corrie which is bounded on the north by Sgurr nan Gillean and Sgurr na Bhairnich and on the south by the long ridge of Druim nan Ramh. Lying at the near end of the corrie, just to the left of the river, is a huge rock known as the Bloody Stone. This marks the site of an ancient clan battle between the MacLeods and the MacDonalds which lasted for a whole day and only came to an end when the last MacLeod had been put to the sword. The bodies of the slain were piled around the base of the Bloody Stone and it is said that the fairy folk fashioned bows and arrows from the ribs of the dead. Shortly after the lochs, the track forks at a large cairn. Take the right fork (the left continues through Srath na Creitheach and emerges on the coast at Camasunary). This next section of the walk is the most difficult. Distance is deceptive and the path crosses numerous streams and marshy areas which make for slow going. The wet areas provide an ideal environment for moisture loving plants such as bog asphodel, bog cotton and the green star-shaped florets of bogbean. The end of Loch an Athain can be seen to the left as the footpath, now a broad track of yellowish scree, winds its way up the Druim Hain Ridge. This is the part of the track that is visible from Sligachan. The ascent takes about 3/4 hour and is not arduous. At the top of the ridge there are views east to Loch na Creitheach.

As you reach the highest point on the bealach between Druim Hain and Sgurr Hain, you will see a large cairn on a rock slab to your right. Shortly after this, a very large cairn, also on the right, marks a fork in the path. Take the left fork which continues on to the viewpoint (the right fork descends to Loch Coruisk). The path to the viewpoint is well marked by cairns which is particularly useful on the return journey if the weather is misty as the path is vague in places and can be easy to miss. To the right can be seen Loch a' Choire Riabhaich which nestles in a little hollow before the final descent to Coruisk. The tip of Loch Coruisk also comes into sight shortly. A short distance along this path, a large pyramidal cairn comes into view on the right. This was erected in memory of a Captain Maryon who went missing in the Cuillin after setting out on a walk from Sligachan. Some eighteen months later his skeleton was found on this spot. About 45 minutes on from here, the viewpoint is reached. This takes the form of a basalt platform which has seemingly been designed by nature for viewing Loch Coruisk. Here you can gaze out over the blue-green waters of the loch and take in the panorama of the mountains behind. Loch Coruisk, the "Water Kettle", was scooped out of the solid rock by the pressure of ice during the last Ice Age. The loch attains a maximum depth of 125ft, 100ft deeper than the adjacent sea loch. This famous stretch of water has been visited by many eminent landscape painters over the years, including J.M.W. Turner, Horatio MacCulloch and George Fennel Robson. Sir Walter Scott's outing to the loch in 1814 resulted in the following lines in "Lord of the Isles":

> *Rarely human eye has known*
> *A scene so stern as that dread lake,*
> *With its dark ledge of barren stone,*
> *Seems that primeval earthquake's sway*
> *Hath rent a strange and shattered way*
> *Through the rude bosom of the hill;*
> *And that each naked precipice,*
> *Sable ravine and dark abyss,*
> *Tells of the outrage still.*

The Coruisk viewpoint is perched on the flank of Sgurr na Stri, The Peak of Strife, which is said to have derived its name from a long-standing dispute between the MacLeods and MacKinnons over possession of the lands in this area. In 1730, the two chiefs eventually agreed on a boundary line running north from the bay of Port Sgailen where the Coruisk stream enters Loch Scavaig. So that this boundary should be remembered in the years to come, the chiefs brought an unfortunate lad across from the island of Soay, showed him the spot and then gave him a severe thrashing so that he should never forget Port Sgailen. As you return to Druim Hain, take care not to lose height - the cairns are useful markers for the path. Turn right at the large cairn and shortly afterwards the cairn resting on a slab to your left is a good marker that you are on the right track in mist. Thereafter the footpath is easily followed all the way back to Sligachan.

9. RUBH' AN DUNAIN

The remote Rubh' an Dunain headland to the south of Glen Brittle gives glorious uninterrupted views south to the island of Rum. This route follows the coastline for the most part and takes in several sites of archaeological interest. The early stages are by vehicle track, followed by a distinct footpath and then some sections of open hill. Walking boots essential. No dogs allowed. **Distance:** 7 1/2 miles (12 kms) return. **Time:** Allow 5 hours for the round trip.

Step By Step: Take the B8009 which branches west from the A863 at Drynoch. After 1 3/4 miles, take the left branch to Glen Brittle and follow this to the end. Park in the carpark just before the camp site (Map Ref. NG 412 205). Walk through the site and head behind the toilet block where a stile gives access over the fence. Ascend the slope to join the well-made upper track which heads south along the coast. Soon, a sizeable stream is reached. When in spate, this can be crossed via a wooden footbridge which lies just to the right of the track. Several more streams are crossed and the track gradually diminishes to a distinct footpath. As the crags of Creag Mhor are passed, the path swings left away from the sea and a dry-stone wall comes into view ahead. Here, the path forks. Take the left fork and continue left along the wall until you reach a small gap. Cross the wall here and then fork left again (the right path simply heads straight up a little knoll). A short distance on, the path forks yet again. Take the left branch which now heads up and over a boggy area filled with bog asphodel, spotted purple orchids and heather. After about 15 minutes, the path swings right and climbs a small rise to give stunning views to the islands of Soay, Rum and Canna. A small loch is seen to the left while directly below, in a beautiful setting, lie the remains of a large house. Make directly for this. This fine residence was once the home of the MacAskills who farmed the surrounding area as tacksmen of the MacLeods. The house has two storeys, a building style attempted only by the gentry and quite different from the single storey black-houses occupied by the general populace.

From the house, follow the indistinct track to the right of the burn which veers right (south-west) through the bracken and heads towards a distinct line of crags. Here a more distinct path is joined which soon drops down onto a flat grassy area, in summer filled with flag irises. From this small platform a faint path now descends left (eastwards) and follows a trickle of water across a large boggy depression filled with bracken. On reaching the other side of this depression, turn right to join the distinct sheep track which heads south along the base of the crags. Keep watching the crags on your left as you continue. After a couple of minutes, on reaching a small clearing in the bracken, a gully in the first line of crags reveals a second crag beyond, in which a cave can clearly be seen. A track heads left through the bracken and ascends the gully to reach the cave. This cave has yielded fragments of beaker ware, a type of pottery which is largely dateable to between 2,500 B.C. and 1,500 B.C. Traces of later ironworking have also been discovered here.

From the cave you can see a knob of headland directly below the island of Canna. Retrace your steps to the base of the crags and make directly for this, taking advantage of the good sheep tracks which give easy walking across the rough grassland. Once at the hillock there is an excellent view down to the sturdy defensive wall which runs across the neck of the small promontory. To reach this impressive Iron Age fortification, follow the sheep track which winds to the left of the base of the hillock. This gives access to the promontory. The Rubh' an Dunain dun is of a type known as a galleried promontory dun or semi-broch, a building style which is thought to have led to the development of the broch. The curved length of wall which cuts off the promontory is constructed of massive squared stone blocks and is in a remarkable state of preservation. The entrance lies to the right and still retains its door checks while a ledge scarcement and the door to a mural gallery can be seen on the inner face. Tradition holds that this impressive stronghold was once occupied by the Clan MacAskill. It is said that the MacAskills were forced to leave their ancestral home in Ireland and subsequently sought protection from the MacLeods of Harris who granted them lands on Skye. They subsequently rose to the position of hereditary Lieutenants of the Coast to MacLeod of MacLeod. From the great stronghold of Rubh' an Dunain the MacAskills protected the MacLeod territories in the south of Skye against the raids of the Norsemen and the birlinns of Clan Ranald. The dun makes a fine place to stop for refreshments, with excellent views to the islands of Soay, Canna, Rum and Eigg.

When you have finished looking around the dun, head north towards Loch na h-Airde, following the well constructed boat channel which joins the loch to the sea. This can be crossed via some rocks near the loch side. From this point on, keep left and follow the coastline, taking advantage of the various sheep tracks which appear and disappear. Continue round until you reach the point of Rubh' an Dunain, from which you can look north-west across the mouth of Loch Brittle to the remote headland opposite. There is no distinct path on the next section of the walk. Keeping left, head north-east and follow the coastline over the grassy cliffs and lines of crags until you begin to descend to the bay of Camas a' Mhurain where a distinct path is joined once again. Shortly after passing through the gap in the dry-stone wall, the remains of a fairly well preserved Neolithic chambered cairn can be seen just to the right of the path. This tomb is of a type known as a passage grave, that is a simple round cairn containing a burial chamber which is entered by a short passage. In this particular case, the lintelled passage leads to a small ante-chamber and an inner polygonal burial chamber. The burial chamber is now open to the sky but would originally have had a corbelled roof. The entrance lies on the east, set in a crescent-shaped forecourt which is faced with upright stones and sections of dry walling. It is thought that such forecourt areas would have functioned as venues for the ceremonies associated with the burial of the dead. The Rubh' an Dunain cairn was excavated in 1931-32 by W. Lindsay Scott. Finds from the lowest level included Neolithic pottery, fragments of several human skeletons and animal bones, the latter possibly deposited to consecrate the burial chamber. A well-preserved comb-decorated beaker of Early Bronze Age type indicates later use of the site.

From the chambered cairn, return to the main path by the gap in the wall, continue north and bear left, following the left hand path which curves around the shore and ascends to an area of old ridge and furrow cultivation strips. This marshy area is a pretty picture in summer with bog asphodel, cotton grass and spotted purple orchids. Ahead can be seen a striking basalt dyke which ascends the slope in a series of steps. Follow this uphill and at the top join the distinct eroded and boggy path which heads north across the moor. This section gives stunning views to the Cuillin hills whose massive flanks reach down like a great five fingered hand. Continue over the moor and descend to cross the stone wall seen on the outward route. Rejoin the original path and head north back to the campsite.

10. TALISKER BAY

The wide sweep of Talisker Bay contains an unusual black sand beach, derived from the basalt rocks which predominate in the area. The bay is an ideal spot for a picnic. The route follows a farm track and distinct footpath and is suitable for any type of footwear. Cyclists are also welcome. **Distance:** 2 miles (3 1/4 kms) return. **Time:** 45 minutes for the round trip.

Step By Step: Take the B8009 which branches west from the A863 at Drynoch. Follow this to Carbost and then take the minor road to Gleann Oraid. Continue along to the end and park by the side of the turning circle, just before the private road to Talisker House (Map Ref. NG 326 306). Take care not to block the turning circle or farm gates. On foot, continue down the road signposted to Talisker House and go through the gate. Just after you pass Mary Ann's Cottage, note the old cheese press by the right of the track. The route passes alongside Talisker House, an elegant mansion that was traditionally possessed by the son of the MacLeod Chief. This sturdy square building dates from the latter half of the 18th century and is roofed with thick Ballachulish slates. The present garden was laid out in the 1920's. Over the years, this house has received many famous visitors, among them the Welsh traveller Thomas Pennant in 1772 and the intrepid duo Johnson and Boswell in 1773. Dr Johnson and James Boswell arrived at Talisker on Thursday 23 September and stayed for two nights as guests of Colonel MacLeod, an officer in the Dutch service who was then on leave from his regiment. While there, Boswell climbed the rocky knoll of Preshal More which overlooks the bay and greatly admired the view from the top. The fine hospitality to be found at Talisker was also praised by the eminent Swiss geologist L.A. Necker de Saussure who stayed at the house on 26 September 1820 while on a scientific excursion: "During dinner, the piper played, in the hall, on the bag-pipes, the Pibrochs, or marches of the tribe of MacLeods; and these romantic airs, for a long time resounded in the vaults of the castle of Talisker."

Shortly after passing Talisker House, a small footpath branches right from the farm track, marked "Scenic Route To Beach". This path passes through an arch of graceful wind swept trees and follows a small drainage channel through a beautiful wild flower meadow. In summer this low-lying area is packed full of roses, lady's mantle, flag irises, nipplewort, ragwort, self-heal, thistles, valerian, marsh woundwort, meadowsweet, red campion and hogweed. The footpath continues out onto a huge mass of storm pebbles and from here you can descend to the shore. The beach at Talisker Bay is comprised mainly of sand derived from the surrounding basalt rocks which gives it an almost black appearance. At the southern end of the bay is a large sea stack which can be reached at low tide. On a hot summer day, this attractive bay makes a fine place for a family picnic. To return to your car, walk along to the southern end of the bay and pick up the farm track which heads east along the foot of the cliffs. A short easy walk will take you back past Talisker House to your starting point.

11. DUN ARDTRECK AND ARDTRECK POINT

An attractive coastal walk to the Iron Age fortification of Dun Ardtreck and the lighthouse beyond. The route mainly crosses open grassland with short sections of gravel and grassy paths, suitable for any type of footwear. **Distance:** 2 1/2 miles (4 kms) return. **Time:** Allow 50 minutes for the round trip.

Step By Step: Take the B8009 which branches west from the A863 at Drynoch. After 5 3/4 miles, turn left at Portnalong, following the signs for Fiskavaig. About a mile after this junction, turn right onto the minor road signposted "Coilleghuail" and follow this to the end. There is room to pull off by the side of the road just before the last house (Map Ref. NG 336 348). From here, take the gravel footpath which heads north through a small gate. This follows the coast and gives fine views back to the scattered houses of Fiskavaig. Across Loch Bracadale the scene is dominated by the flat tops of MacLeod's Tables and the rock pinnacles of MacLeod's Maidens at Idrigill Point while out to sea can be seen the hills of South Uist, Barra and Mingulay. Just as the footpath turns to the right and begins to go uphill, fork left onto the small track which passes through a gap in the dry stone wall and then head across the field and over a farm gate. The path now continues north along the coast, crossing areas of old peat cuttings and ridge-and-furrow cultivation strips. Beyond a wire fence the path becomes vague in places but you can simply head straight for the dun, the walls of which are now obvious.

Dun Ardtreck occupies a position of strength atop a coastal knoll whose western side falls away sheer to the shore below. The fortification is of a type known as a "semibroch", a building tradition which is believed to have led to the development of the broch. Semibrochs are of dry-stone construction and have high galleried walls, but unlike the circular brochs they are "D"-shaped in plan, being comprised of a length of curving wall whose defence is completed by a natural precipice. Excavations carried out by Dr Euan W. MacKie in 1965 revealed that the galleried wall of Dun Ardtreck was built on an artificial rubble platform. There was evidence that the fort had been deliberately destroyed by fire and was subsequently demolished and then re-used as a dwelling for several centuries. Finds dating to the time of the fire included broken pottery and the iron door handle to the fort which was left lying in the entrance passage after the wooden door had succumbed to the flames and been pushed in by hostile visitors.

When you have finished looking around the semibroch, join the distinct grassy path which continues north along the coast to the lighthouse at Ardtreck Point. In summer the boggy grasslands here are filled with moisture loving plants such as the bog asphodel, cotton grass, common spotted orchid and the lesser white butterfly orchid. This area is also a haven for wildlife and you may spot meadow brown butterflies, common blue butterflies, oystercatchers, herring gulls, wheatears, skylarks and blackbirds. The lighthouse at Ardtreck Point was established in 1904. From here there are fine views across the loch to the tidal island of Oronsay which lies just off the tip of Ullinish Point. Retrace the route to your car.

12. FISKAVAIG TO TALISKER BAY

The rugged coastline west of Fiskavaig affords good views across Loch Bracadale to the remote isolated rock pinnacles known as MacLeod's Maidens. This route follows the old Huisgill track south of Fiskavaig for a fantastic bird's eye view of Talisker Bay and then heads north across the open hill for an exhilirating cliff top walk. Walking boots essential. No dogs allowed. **Distance:** 6 miles (9 1/2 kms) return. **Time:** Allow at least 3 hours 15 minutes for the round trip.

Step By Step: Take the B8009 which branches west from the A863 at Drynoch. After 5 3/4 miles, turn left at Portnalong, following the signs for Fiskavaig. Continue for about 2 3/4 miles and park at the hairpin bend towards the end of the road, taking care not to block access to the farm gate (Map Ref. NG 323 331). Go through the gate and follow the well-made farm track which heads south to Talisker Bay. The view ahead is dominated by the rounded lump of Preshal Mor while on either side of the track rise striking rocky bluffs of basalt which mark the edges of ancient lava flows, now weathered into columns. On this first section of the walk there is much evidence of past agricultural activities: peat cuttings (some still in use), turf and stone dykes and the tumbled remains of shielings. The track becomes less defined after 3/4 mile but the way ahead is obvious. About 25 minutes walk from the start, just as the path begins its descent to Gleann Oraid, a hairpin bend is reached. This is a fine vantage point from which to look down on the wide glen with its striking bluffs.

At the hairpin bend, strike right and follow the faint path up the slope. Topping a rise, drop down and then climb over the area of ridge and furrow cultivation, surrounded by a dyke. Keep to the right of the distinct rounded knoll ahead. At the top of the plateau, there are excellent views over Talisker Bay with its striking black sand beach. There is also a sweeping view eastwards to Talisker House and up Gleann Oraid to the hills of Glamaig and Marsco at the head of the glen. From this point, continue to follow the delightful grassy cliff around the sweep of the bay, taking advantage of the many sheep tracks. Suddenly, the dramatic basalt cliffs of Rubha Cruinn come into view ahead. Cascading down these cliffs is a beautiful white mare's tail waterfall and as you continue round you will in all liklihood receive a refreshing shower from the spray which is blown back up over the cliff by the slightest breeze. On hot summer days, Rubha Cruinn is a delightful place to stop for refreshments. Here, serenaded by the song of the skylark, you can take in the fine views across the Sea of the Hebrides to the Outer Isles. There is also an excellent view back to the rugged coastline south of Talisker Bay and the islands of Canna and Rum beyond.

From this point on, the going is rougher and the use of an appropriate map is to be recommended. From Rubha Cruinn, descend north-east across a boggy area and follow the sheep track to the right of the wall to ascend the little hill of Sgurr Mor. Northwards lies Loch Bracadale with its many islands and beyond, the dotted white crofts of Ullinish. To the north-west there is a fine view of MacLeod's Maidens which lie just off the tip of Idrigill Point. Legend has it that these isolated basalt pinnacles derive their name from an incident that took place during the time of the 14th Chief of MacLeod. Following the death of the chief in a clan battle on the island of Harris, the galley carrying his wife and daughters back to Dunvegan was shipwrecked there and all three were drowned. The tallest pillar, around 200ft high, is known as The Mother while the shorter two are The Maidens. From Sgurr Mor, continue north and head across the tussocky grass to the cliff edge once again. The shoreline here consists of flat slabs of rock. In one place a lava flow has been undermined by the sea and has collapsed to form an unusual rock bowl. Although it is possible to descend to the shore here at a couple of places via steep gullies, there is no northern exit route and you must ascend the way you came. North of this point it becomes less easy to follow the coast due to the numerous gullies and bluffs and it is easier to keep inland rather than descending. Continue north until you see a line of cliffs striking inland. Here, keep to the right, following the faint sheep tracks and head to the base of a prominent rocky knoll. From the knoll there is a good view over the low-lying point of Rubha nan Clach to Loch Bracadale and MacLeod's Maidens and Tables beyond. This knoll makes another fine place to stop for refreshments.

To continue, skirt north-east around the rocky knoll, following the faint sheep tracks and then head inland, climbing several rocky platforms. There is no path here, but continually make for the high ground until you see the Trig point on Beinn nan Dubh-lochan to the south-east and head straight for this. From here there is a stunning panoramic view which takes in the coastline beyond Talisker Bay, the Small Isles of Rum, Sanday and Canna, the Outer Hebrides, MacLeod's Maidens and Tables, Loch Bracadale, the Red Hills and the great amphitheatre of the Black Cuillin. From the Trig point, locate the right shore of Loch Dubh to the north-east and descend to it. Continue around the right shore of the loch and descend again through two rocky knolls. Through these knolls can be seen a large rocky prominence with a distinctive pointed cairn which marks the site of an Iron Age broch. Head across the moor and make straight for this. The broch is in fairly ruinous state but the outer entrance passage can still be discerned and there is a mural cell and section of inner wall face intact. From the broch, walk eastwards to the adjacent knoll and look down to locate the road and adjacent stock fence. Descend the grassy slope and head straight for the right corner of the fence. Follow the fence down and go back through the gate to your car.

13. THE TIDAL ISLAND OF ORONSAY

An easy walk to the small island of Oronsay which is accessible by causeway only at low tide. "Oronsay" is Norse for "ebb-tide island". The route is by grassy paths, suitable for any type of footwear. From Oronsay there are good views to the other islands in Loch Bracadale and to the impressive cliffs at Fiskavaig. No dogs allowed. **Distance:** 2 3/4 miles (4 1/2 kms) return. **Time:** 1 hour 20 minutes for the round trip.

Step By Step: Take the A863 at Sligachan and about 1/2 mile beyond Struan turn left onto the single-track Ullinish road. Then, take the first left and follow this minor road to the end. There is room for several cars to park in a large quarry cutting by the left of the road, just before the last house (Map Ref. NG 323 374). Go through the gate opposite the carpark and follow the distinct track. Beyond a second gate, the track skirts round a small bay and terminates at an area of old peat beds. From here, a narrow footpath continues to the left of this marshy area, which in summer is filled with bog cotton, bog asphodel and purple spotted orchids. Bog cotton was once gathered by the islanders and spun like flax or used to fill pillows. The indistinct path now continues to another fence and from here a good view is obtained of the island. Descend to the shore via the rocky defile and then cross the causeway to the sandy beach opposite. From here, continue up onto the island, following the distinct sheep tracks which give delightful walking over the short springy grass. The top of the island is soon reached and from here there are panoramic views to the lighthouse on Ardtreck Point, the Red and Cuillin Hills, the crofts of Portnalong and Fiskavaig, MacLeod's Maidens and the islands in Loch Bracadale. There is also a spectacular view of the striking cliffs and caves at Fiskavaig. The cliffs at the south-western tip of Oronsay are excellent for bird-watching. Here may be seen fulmars, black-backed gulls, herring gulls, shags and gannets. While exploring Oronsay, remember to keep an eye on the causeway. When the tide turns, this little line of pebbles vanishes with astonishing speed and care should be taken lest you become stranded on the island.

14. DUN FIADHAIRT

An easy walk to the well preserved remains of Dun Fiadhairt, an Iron Age broch. The route follows a farm track and crosses open grassland, suitable for any type of footwear. The last section can be marshy after rain. No dogs allowed. **Distance:** 1 mile (1 1/2 kms) return. **Time:** Allow 40 minutes for the round trip.

Step By Step: Take the A850 north from Dunvegan and continue for about 2 1/2 miles until you reach Loch Suardal which is crossed by means of a causeway. Immediately after the causeway there is a large space by the left of the road with room for several cars to park (Map Ref. NG 238 508). Before you set out, take some time to scan the reed-filled shallows of Loch Suardal - this is a favourite summer feeding place of the elegant heron and the wintering ground of various swans and ducks. Go through the farm gate at the back of the parking space and follow the rough track which soon veers right to pass some ruined sheep fanks. The track now becomes a footpath which gives easy walking over short springy grass. Contour left around the base of a knoll and then bear right to descend to the narrow neck of land which joins the tiny Fiadhairt peninsula to the mainland. As you descend there are good views left to Dunvegan Castle. Once at the isthmus, you can look north across Camalaig Bay and Loch Dunvegan to the Outer Hebrides. Continue on the distinct track across the neck of land and as you top a small rise the broch comes into view ahead. Follow the track to the right and then head straight for the broch. This last section can be boggy.

Dun Fiadhairt occupies a classic defensive position atop a small knoll which gives good views in all directions. The broch is of the ground-galleried type, that is it has cells and a gallery within its wall at ground level. The structure is fairly well preserved, with the intra-mural gallery and stairs still partially intact. The main entrance passage contains two opposing guard cells and door-checks to take a stout wooden door. Lying opposite this entrance is a second lintelled doorway which leads through the wall. This appears to be an original feature and is a highly unusual occurrence, most brochs being equipped with only one entrance. Dun Fiadhairt was excavated in 1914 by the Countess Vincent Baillet de Latour. The finds included fragments of pottery, stone whorls for spinning, a section of a steatite armlet, a necklace of amber beads and several individual glass beads, some of which appear to have been made from Roman bottle glass. The excavation also uncovered a rather unusual item. Lying in the lowest levels of the broch was a terracotta model of a bale of hides or fleeces. This small model, 2 inches long by 1 1/2 inches wide, was originally painted bright green on a white slip and is Roman in origin. It was probably intended as a votive offering by a Roman merchant and may have found its way this far north through trade. When you have finished looking around the broch, retrace the route to your car.

15. CLAIGAN SOUTERRAIN

An easy walk along a farm track to an Iron Age souterrain or earth-house. Suitable for any type of footwear. No dogs allowed. **Distance:** 2/3 mile (1 1/4 km) return. **Time:** 30 minutes for the round trip.

Step By Step: Take the A850 north from Dunvegan and continue for about 4 1/2 miles until you reach the T-junction at Claigan. Turn left and then left again at the next T-junction shortly afterwards. Park in the large carpark (Map Ref. NG 232 538). From the carpark, walk back to the junction and continue straight on, passing another minor road on your left. A short distance beyond this, veer right and go through the farm gate which leads to a well-made track. Continue on this track until you pass through a second gate. Shortly after this gate the track bends sharply to the right. The souterrain lies about 50m on from the bend, on the hillside to your left, just behind a large area of excavated ditch. The site is marked by a small raised plinth (this can be picked out from the track by the keen eyed). The souterrain itself can be seen as a small depression in the ground containing a lintelled entrance tunnel. Bring a torch if you wish to examine the interior.

Souterrains are a phenomenon of the Iron Age and belong largely to the 1st-3rd centuries A.D. Around 200 examples have so far been discovered in Scotland and apart from several sites in the east, they are entirely subterranean structures. Souterrains are essentially stone-lined passages, reached by a sloping tunnel whose entrance could be easily camouflaged. The inner chamber provided storage facilities for food and other items. When you have finished examining the site, retrace the route to your car.

16. THE CORAL BEACHES

North of Dunvegan lie two beautiful white beaches of almost tropical appearance. The white "coral" sand is actually the remains of a red algae, Lithothamnion Calcareum, which has been bleached by the sun. This popular walk follows a farm track for most of the way and is suitable for any type of footwear. A good destination for family picnics. **Distance:** 1 1/2 miles return. **Time:** Allow 1 hour for the round trip.

Step By Step: Park in the Claigan carpark as for the Claigan Souterrain walk above (Map Ref. NG 232 538). Walk to the far end of the carpark and go through the gate to join the well-made farm track which gives easy walking to the first small coral beach. From here, cross the burn and head up the slope to the drystone wall. Now follow this wall to its seaward end where it is easily rounded and from this point you can take in the magnificent view to main coral beach ahead. When the sun shines, the deep blue-green of the bay contrasts beautifully with the white of the sand and the bright green of the surrounding grassland - a scene guaranteed to get the cameras clicking! From here it is a simple matter to head down the grassy slope to the delightful bay and explore the sands. Occasionally, sizeable branches of coral are found intact and such treasures are turned into beautiful jewellery by a local manufacturer. The red algae which forms the sand, Lithothamnion Calcareum, lives in sheltered in-shore waters and extracts carbonate of lime to form a hard exterior skeleton. Eventually, these hard secretions develop into a semi-circular cushion some 4in across from which sections are continually broken by the action of the sea and cast ashore. The beaches here also contain tiny cowrie shells which are said to bring luck and happiness. To claim your share of the good fortune, you must collect a handful of shells and return to the same spot exactly a year later and cast them back into the sea, one by one. Beyond the second coral beach, you can continue north around a knoll to reach the headland of Groban na Sgeire which has a fine view to the islands of Isay, Mingay and Clett. Here you may spot mink climbing amongst the rocks or see gannets diving out to sea. Retrace the route to your car.

17. MACLEOD'S TABLE SOUTH

The north-west of Skye is dominated by the great flat-topped masses of Healabhal Mhor (MacLeod's Table North) and Healabhal Bheag (MacLeod's Table South). This walk ascends the highest of the two mountains, Healabhal Bheag, which gives spectacular views of the islands to the south and west. The route follows a farm track and distinct footpath in the early stages and then crosses the open hill, terminating in a steep scramble. Hill-walking boots essential. **Distance:** 5 miles (8 kms) return. **Time:** Allow 4 hours for the round trip.

Step By Step: Take the B884 which branches south-west from the A863 just south of Dunvegan. After 1/2 mile, continue south on the minor road to Orbost and follow this to just beyond Orbost Farm where it is possible to park by the side of the road (Map Ref. NG 257 430). Continue on foot down the farm track which gives fine views out across Loch Bharcasaig. After about 1/2 mile (where powerlines cross the road), the start of a forestry plantation is reached. At this point, turn right and strike uphill, following the edge of the trees until you reach the top of the plantation. Once at the top, turn left and continue to follow the forest boundary in a north-westerly direction for about 1/2 mile until the fence curves distinctly to the south-west. At this point, pull away from the trees and strike uphill to reach a rocky knoll with distinct basalt columns (it is quite a relief to pull away from the mud, flies and bracken at the edge of the plantation!). Continue to ascend diagonally until you reach an obvious break in slope about 2/3rds of the way up the hill. Here there are various sheep-tracks and a turf dyke which give easy walking west towards Healabhal Bheag. When you reach the foot of the final steep slope, strike up towards the grassy gap beyond the bluffs and to the left of the first scree slope and zig-zag up the hill to the plateau. The highest point is marked by a trig point and gives fine views south-east to the Cuillin Hills, south to Eigg, Rum, Canna, Tiree and Coll, west to the Outer Hebrides and east to Dun Caan on Raasay and the Torridon hills beyond. Return to your car by the same route.

18. NEIST POINT LIGHTHOUSE

A deservedly popular walk to the lighthouse at the most westerly point of Skye which has fine uninterrupted views to the Outer Hebrides. The route follows a concrete path, suitable for any type of footwear. The return journey involves the ascent of a steep flight of stairs. **Distance:** 1 1/4 miles (2 kms) return. **Time:** 45 minutes for the round trip.

Step By Step: Take the A863 south from Dunvegan and after 1 1/4 miles turn right onto the B884 Glendale road. After 1/2 mile turn right again and follow the road to Glendale. About 1/2 mile on from Glendale Primary School, turn left to Waterstein (signposted) and follow this road all the way to the end where there is room for several cars to park (Map Ref. NG 133 478). Go through the gate at the far end of the carpark and begin your descent by the concrete steps and path. Near the top note the ingenious pulley system which is used to carry down supplies and luggage to Neist Point Lighthouse and to bring rubbish back up for collection. The steps descend to a plateau and here a large area of ridge-and-furrow cultivation strips can be seen to your left. This method of cultivation improved drainage and increased soil fertility, thus enabling marginal boggy areas to be brought into use. The strips are known as "feannagan" and this form of agriculture continued in use until the mid 19th century. As the path rounds a bend, the attractive yellow and white lighthouse comes into view ahead and another flight of steps descends to sea-level. Neist Point is the main light on Skye guiding ships into the narrow channel of the Little Minch. The lighthouse was built in 1909 and was originally manned by three keepers. The last men to be stationed there left in 1989 and, in common with most others, the light is now fully automated. The keepers' cottages were sold off and are now being operated as self-catering holiday homes. The lighthouse tower is 62 feet high, and the light itself has an intensity of 480,000 candles - so powerful that it can be seen 24 miles away. There is also a foghorn which emits two 3 second blasts every 1 1/2 minutes.

When you have finished looking at the lighthouse, it is worth walking on out past the tower and onto the rocks. Here, sections of the coastline are comprised of rectangularly-jointed columns of weathered basalt, reminiscent of the Giant's Causeway in Ireland. Also to be seen on the shore is the small pier and crane which is used for unloading supplies. Take time to admire the breathtaking views which are particularly stunning at sunset. Out to the west across the Little Minch the skyline is dominated by the Uists and Benbecula while to the south lies Canna. Closer to home across Moonen Bay lie the cliffs of Waterstein Head and the pillar of An Stac, Ramasaig Cliff with its impressive waterfall and The Hoe.

19. WATERSTEIN COASTGUARD STATION

A short walk to the old coastguard station on the cliffs at Waterstein which can easily be combined with a visit to Neist Point lighthouse (see above). The walk crosses open hill dotted with peat banks. The route back across the moor can be marshy after rain and waterproof footwear is recommended. **Distance:** 3/4 mile (1 km) return. **Time:** 30 minutes for the round trip.

Step By Step: Park as for the Neist Point Lighthouse walk above (Map Ref. NG 133 478). Head out from the back of the carpark, just to the right of the small sheds. Here you will see a faint footpath heading across the moor. This will be used on the return journey, but for the outward route veer to the left behind the sheds and continue round until you reach the coastal cliffs (take great care at the cliffs). This section of the walk gives breathtaking views across the Little Minch to the Outer Hebrides. Continue north along the cliffs and after about 15 minutes the abandoned coastguard station is reached. From here there is a panoramic view west over the Minch and north-east to the spectacular Biod an Athair, the highest cliffs on Skye. The coastguard station makes an excellent vantage point from which to scan the Minch for the schools of dolphins and whales which frequent the waters here. Return by the same route or make a circuit by following the footpath which cuts across the moor just behind the coastguard station. This route crosses several peat beds, some of which are still in use today. The path is indistinct in places and can be boggy, but the way back to the carpark is obvious.

20. LORGILL CLEARANCE VILLAGE

A moderately long but easy walk to the deserted village of Lorgill which was cleared of its inhabitants in 1830. The route mostly follows a well-made track with open grassland in the later stages. Boots essential. No dogs allowed. **Distance:** 5 miles return. **Time:** Allow 2 1/2 hours for the return trip.

Step By Step: Take the A863 south from Dunvegan and after 1 1/4 miles turn right onto the B884 Glendale road. After 1/2 mile turn right again and follow the road to Glendale. About 1/2 mile on from Glendale Primary School turn left on to the Ramasaig road (signposted) and continue to the road end. There is room to pull off on the verge just beyond the last house (Grid Ref. NG 165 443). Go through the gate and head south on the well-made track which soon crosses a burn and then skirts to the right of some farm buildings. A second gate is reached and from this point on the track gives an easy walk across the moor, level for the most part, all the way to the outskirts of Lorgill village. The first ruined cottages lie down a grassy slope to the left, just after the third farm gate. From here, you can descend amongst the ruins to the shepherd's hut in the bottom of the glen. The attractive pebble beach at Lorgill Bay can be reached by crossing the Lorgill River and continuing south down the far side of the glen for 1/2 mile.

The tranquil glen of Lorgill, the "Glen of the Deer's Cry", once contained a thriving crofting community of ten families. In the summer of 1830 the entire population was informed that in a month's time they would be cleared from their land and shipped to Nova Scotia in Canada. All those over seventy years of age were to be sent to the County Poorhouse. The eviction order was delivered by the sheriff officer who had travelled to the township in the company of the factor, the local minister and four policemen. The villagers dared not disobey for they were informed that those who did not comply with the notice would be immediately imprisoned. And so on the 3 August, the night before the immigrant ship was due to sail, the Lorgill crofters gathered together to sing the 100th Psalm and the village children picked wildflowers to place on the graves of their forefathers. The following day, at 12 o'clock, the people of Lorgill set out across the moors to join the "Midlothian" under Captain Morrison which was waiting for them in Loch Snizort. As soon as all were on board, the ship started out on the 2 month voyage to Canada. It is said that one of those evicted was a MacCrimmon piper who spent his time on passage composing the pibroch known as "The Lorgill Crofters' Farewell To Skye".

21. WATERNISH POINT

This pleasant walk to the lighthouse at Waternish Point passes several sites of archaeological and historical interest and gives fine views across the Little Minch to the Outer Hebrides. Most of the route lies along a farm track which gives good walking. Boots recommended. **Distance:** 7 1/2 miles (12 kms) return. **Time:** 3 hours 10 minutes for the round trip.

Step By Step: Take the B886 which branches north at the Fairy Bridge and continue for 3 3/4 miles to the Stein T-junction. Turn right and continue for another 2 3/4 miles through Hallin and Halistra. Beyond Halistra take the left fork to the old Trumpan churchyard and park in the large carpark opposite (Map Ref. NG 224 613). Continue on foot north-east along the road until you reach a sharp right bend. Here, go through the farm gate on your left and follow the well-made farm track which heads north across the moor. After about 25 minutes, a small cairn is seen to the left of the track. This is known as Crois Bhain (The White Cross) and it commemorates Roderick MacLeod of Unish, the grandson of Alasdair Ruadh of Trumpan, who died in the Second Battle of Waternish. This battle was fought on the surrounding bleak moorland around the year 1530 and was one of many bloody conflicts between the MacDonalds of Trotternish and the rival MacLeods. In addition to the Crois Bhain, two other cairns commemorate those who fell in the battle. These are set far back on the ridge to the right of the track and are not easily identifiable by the naked eye. The southernmost one is known as Beinn a' Ghobhainn, the northernmost one Crois mhic Alasdair. One of these commemorates John MacLeod of Waternish, the father of the above mentioned Roderick. The memorial cairns were restored in 1985 by the Clan MacLeod Society of the U.S.A. in conjunction with the Clan MacLeod Heritage Trust.

Continue north on the track and after about 10 minutes Dun Borrafiach is seen just to the right. This impressive Iron Age broch sits on a small ridge and it is worth taking the time to examine the beautifully constructed bowed walls at close quarters. A further 15 minutes on, the more ruinous fortification of Dun Gearymore is seen to the right and shortly after this there is a brief glimpse of the lighthouse at Waternish Point. The track now descends and around a bend the ruin of a large house offers a sombre and surprising view. The track peters out as the first deserted cottages of Unish are reached. The main part of the village lies just behind the modern farm wall. For a closer look at the large house, go through the gate on the left and continue on the rough track. After a short distance, cross the wooden gate on the right and make directly for the ruin. This impressive house was built by a merchant adventurer from Fife. It is of multi-storey construction, a style attempted only by the well-to-do and quite different from the single-storey black-houses of the village. To reach the lighthouse from this point, strike to the right of the ruins and follow the fence, crossing it at the foot of the village. Now descend the grassy slope and take advantage of the sheep track which leads through the bracken to a breach in the drystone wall. Cross here and head straight across the moorland to the lighthouse. This section of the walk gives good views east to the Trotternish peninsula and north to the Outer Hebrides. Waternish lighthouse was established in 1924 and is now fully automated. The Point has the distinction of being the place where Prince Charles Edward Stuart first set foot on Skye following his daring escape from Benbecula on the 29 June 1746. The Prince and Flora MacDonald had previously tried to land at Ardmore Bay to the south but here they were fired upon by the MacLeod militia stationed on the Point and had no choice but to pull away and head north. On reaching Waternish Point, the Prince and his companions shelterd briefly in a cave before crossing Loch Snizort to seek help from Lady Margaret MacDonald at Monkstadt. From the lighthouse, retrace the route to your car. The return journey gives breathtaking views west to Dunvegan Head.

22. THE OLD MAN OF STORR

A short but strenuous walk to view the isolated rock pinnacle known as the Old Man of Storr. The route follows a distinct footpath over the open hill. Some sections can be muddy and hill-walking boots are essential. The walk can be extended to take in a viewpoint on a small hill to the north. **Distance:** 2 1/2 miles (4 kms) return; 3 miles (4 3/4 kms) including the extension to the Viewpoint. **Time:** Allow 2 hours for the round trip; 2 hours 40 minutes including the extension to the Viewpoint.

Step By Step: Take the A855 north from Portree and follow it for 6 3/4 miles to the end of Loch Leathan. Park in the carpark to the left of the road, just at the start of the Forestry Commission plantation (Map Ref. NG 508 529). One track to the Storr starts from the back of the carpark but this is not recommended as a route of ascent, being completely enclosed by conifers and stifling hot in summer with thousands of annoying insects. At the time of writing, this track was closed due to severe erosion problems. A more pleasant route is to be found by continuing north along the road for a short distance until you reach the end of the trees. The Old Man is now in view to your left. Go through the gate on your left and follow the well defined track by the edge of the plantation all the way up to the Old Man. This is an enjoyable walk up, with the Old Man straight ahead, looking tantalisingly close. Distance is deceptive however, as part of the route lies in a hollow which is hidden from view from the road.

The Old Man is 160ft high and measures 40ft in diameter. The first ascent of this isolated pinnacle was made in 1955 by Don Whillans, T. Barber and G.T. Sutton who left a coin at the top before abseiling down. This was quite an achievement in climbing circles, for the body of the pinnacle overhangs the base and the rock is a crumbling basalt, notoriously difficult to ascend. After you have walked around the base of the Old Man, there are a variety of other interesting nooks and crannies to explore. One possibility is to continue along the distinct path which heads right (northwards) behind the Old Man, passing a small lochan to the right. This ascends to an obvious saddle from which you can climb up onto a small table-topped peak on your right. This small peak gives glorious views north over the Trotternish peninsula and eastwards to the islands of South Rona and Raasay with the hills of Torridon and Applecross behind. To the south there is a good view back to the Old Man of Storr, a completely different aspect from that already seen. To descend, retrace your outward route or, if open, take the forestry track which begins at the northern corner of the plantation. This latter route will bring you back directly to your car.

23. LOCH CUITHIR DIATOMITE WORKS

A moderately easy walk along an old road to remote Loch Cuithir, the source of the diatomite that was once worked at the Lealt Gorge crushing mill (see below). The road gives good walking all the way but can be very wet after rain. Stout shoes or wellingtons are recommended. This route gives excellent views into the Trotternish Ridge. **Distance:** 4 1/2 miles (7 1/4 kms) return. **Time:** Allow 2 1/2 hours for the round trip.

Step By Step: Take the single-track road to Lealt which branches west from the A855 just to the north of the Lealt River. Continue past the houses for a short distance and park on the grassy verge (Map Ref. NG 505 608). For the first 1 1/2 miles the road follows the course of the Lealt River upstream across a flat boggy moorland giving excellent views ahead to the impressive Trotternish Ridge. Beinn Edra, the highest point on this northern stretch of the ridge, can be seen just to your right. The narrow-guage railway which was used to transport diatomite from Loch Cuithir to the Inver Tote crushing mill lay just to the right of this first section of road. Dismantled some time ago, the line of the track is difficult to pick out, but now and again the grassy embankment which carried the rails can be discerned by the keen eyed. This embankment has in places been later used as a foundation for stock fences. The best view of the rail embankment is to be had some 1 1/2 miles from the starting point where the Lealt River swings left away from the road. At this point, the railway line crossed the road and if you look to your left you can clearly make out the raised embankment as it follows the river for a short distance before heading westwards towards the ridge again.

After a further 3/4 mile Loch Cuithir is reached. Here, if you are quiet, you may spy a heron fishing in the shallows. The loch is now much smaller than it once was, for at the turn of the century the diatomite deposits here covered an area of 22 acres and were 45ft thick. A few traces of the diatomite works can still be seen today: a brick hut by the shores of the loch, an artificial water channel, a brick pillar by the roadside. The rusty remains of the narrow-guage rails can be seen on the little grassy mound behind the brick pillar. From this vantage point you can also see an attractive stone embankment which was built to carry the rails over the stream. Looking towards the coast, Staffin Island can be seen to the north if the day is clear. At Loch Cuithir, the road branches. The right branch continues to the far end of the loch while the left branch crosses a small bridge and leads to an attractive reed-fringed lochan at the foot of the great Cuithir corrie. Here there are spectacular views up into the ridge and on a hot summer's day it is an ideal place to stop for a picnic before you retrace the route to your car.

24. LEALT GORGE DIATOMITE MILL

The Lealt area was once the centre of an unusual industry which involved the processing of diatomite, an algal growth which had many industrial uses (see Trotternish: East Coast for full details). This short walk takes you down to view the diatomite crushing mill at the foot of the Lealt Gorge. The route involves a steep descent and ascent by way of a rough footpath and boots are recommended. **Distance:** 3/4 mile (1 1/4 km) return. **Time:** Allow 1/2 hour for the round trip.

Step By Step: Park in the carpark at the Lealt Falls on the A855 (Map Ref. NG 516 604). Walk back (southwards) across the Lealt River and climb over the farm gate on your left. Follow this track onto the old road and turn left. Continue left for a short distance and cross the fence on the far side of the road, joining the path at the corner marked by a large boulder. Keeping the fence on your left, walk through the low semi-circular earth bank until you see a distinct path to your right. Join this path, climb over a gate, and continue down the gorge until you reach the attractive pebble beach. From this tranquil spot there are good views to the hills of the mainland opposite and you may also spot the bobbing heads of inquisitive seals which frequent the bay here. On the shore lies an old salmon fishermen's bothy and store house. Just behind the bothy is the flat square of the drying green. Here, the fishermen would hang their nets out to dry, draped over long wooden poles. Some of these poles can still be seen today, together with the remains of the old iron winding gears which were used to winch the salmon cobles ashore. From this point you can walk back up the river for a couple of minutes to view the lower Lealt waterfall. Here the river has cut its way down through the rock to form a deep ravine which gradually widens towards the sea. The impressive waterfall is caused by a hard sill of dolerite overlying softer sedimentary rocks.

Except in times of spate, the Lealt River can be crossed by means of stepping stones near the salmon bothy. On the opposite bank lies the grim ruin of the diatomite crushing mill. To the right of the mill building can be seen the yellow brick furnace, with its doors and iron cladding still pretty much intact. In the early 1900's, the mill was visited by Dr J.A. MacCulloch, the Rector of St Columba's Church in Portree, and from him comes this interesting description of the proceedings: "A drying and grinding factory has been erected at the water's edge; great sheds stand on the upper slopes at a precarious angle; while a miniature railway, the continuation of one which runs inland to the diatomite beds, connects the edge of the cliff with the landing-stage and factory far below. When we arrived the work-people were all at the loch and there was scarce a sign of life round this lonely bay. But presently a long train of men and women began to zigzag down the path on the face of the slope and transformed this solicitude into humming activity.

They must get the cargo embarked while the tide served. Each one carried a bag of diatomite from the grinding-house to the boat slip, till the coble was piled up with sacks. Then it made a slow journey to the steamer, where the sacks were transferred to the hold. Meanwhile a second coble was a-filling, and so all day long, for there were hundreds and hundreds of sacks to be removed, the work went steadily on." When you have finished looking around the mill, ascend the path which zig-zags up the hill behind it. This is vague in places, but keep left until you reach the top of the slope and you can't go wrong. The path emerges at an old quarry and from here, keep left to pick up the distinct path which makes its way back up the river to the carpark. There are good views of the upper falls in the latter stages of this ascent.

25. BEINN EDRA

A circular walk with spectacular views which takes in Beinn Edra, the highest point on the northern part of the Trotternish Ridge. The route is mainly across open hill with short sections of rough footpaths and farm tracks. Moderately difficult and strenuous in places. Walking boots essential. **Distance:** 7 1/2 miles (12 kms). **Time:** 4 hours 15 minutes for the round trip.

Step By Step: Take the single-track road to Sheader which branches east from the A856 just south of Uig. Follow this to the end and park in the small cutting by the right of the road just before the last house (Map Ref. NG 418 628). On foot, continue on the road past the house and then take the farm track which branches right through a gate. Keep straight on, ignoring the peat cutters' tracks which branch left now and again. This farm track gives easy walking in the early stages and good time can be made on this section. The track follows the course of the Lon an t-Sratha, a meandering river which shows evidence of ancient silt deposition. Here and there may be seen the outlines of old river bends which gradually became filled with silt and were eventually cut off from the river when the water pushed through a new straight channel. Such features are known as "ox-bow lakes". As you continue on, Beinn Fhuar and Beinn an Laoigh loom up on the right and the great horseshoe of Corrie Amadel closes in around you.

The farm track becomes a footpath which soon peters out. Continue on until you pass a small crag to your far left. At this point you must strike north-east across a marshy area of peat hags until you reach an attractive waterfall on the Abhainn Dhubh on the far side of the glen. The waterfall can only be seen when you are almost at the river. At this point, cross the water and head straight up the slope until you locate a grassy stone and turf dyke which runs all the way up to the cliff edge. This dyke gives easy walking up to the Bealach a' Mhoramhain, crossing several tributaries of the Abhainn Dhubh along the way. At the cliff edge there are spectacular views of the

Trotternish coastline and the great ridge north and south. From here ascend north along the cliff across the delightful short springy turf until you reach the trig point which marks Beinn Edra. As you ascend look out for the delicate leaves of alpine ladies mantle which grows freely on these slopes. The Beinn is a good place to stop for lunch, enjoying beautiful views in all directions.

To descend, continue northwards along the cliff edge over an area of bare soil and rocks. The landscape gradually becomes lusher and about 1/2 mile from the top a rocky crevass gives a breathtaking view down through the cliffs to Loch Dubhar-sgoth and Loch Corcasgill. From this point, continue along the cliff edge for another mile and descend to the Bealach Uige, all the while looking west to locate the cart track which will be used later (this stands out as a green line amidst the brown moorland grasses). This stretch gives good views north along the ridge to the Quiraing and north-east to Staffin across a loch-strewn moorland. At the Bealach head south-west away from the ridge to find the northernmost tributary of the Lon Airigh-uige (difficult to locate). Follow the stream down the hill for about a mile and then strike north-west away from the river until you eventually pass an old shieling and cross some peat beds. The descent gives excellent views down Glen Uig to Uig Bay and the Ascrib Islands beyond.

Beyond the peat beds lies the grassy track mentioned above. This track soon becomes an unsurfaced road and after a short distance a small stream is seen just to the left. When this begins to veer away from the road cross to the left bank and follow the stream down through an attractive gorge. Towards the bottom, the gorge deepens and here you must climb the grassy hill to the left and then begin to descend, contouring left down towards the floor of the glen. There are good views across Glen Uig at this point. Keep left and continue to contour around the grassy hills, passing some old sheep fanks and ruined crofts. A small stream is crossed and then the Lon Airigh-uige with its attractive waterfall is reached. Descend to the river by some wooden fence posts. There are several places to cross but after heavy rain you may have to walk upstream towards the waterfall to cross. Once across, join the prominent sheep track which ascends the steep slope opposite to gain a small rocky hill. From this hill there is an excellent view of a second waterfall. From here, make for the distinct turf dyke and follow this as it makes its way to the right, back towards the original farm track. The dyke disappears at a small stream. Head left here to cross the stream at the head of a small cascade. Beyond this, the original farm track is rejoined and you are only a short distance from your starting point.

26. THE QUIRAING

The strange pinnacles and platforms which make up the rock formation known as the Quiraing have long fascinated visitors to Skye. This route takes the easiest way to the Quiraing, following a distinct level path most of the way but involving a steep scramble in the latter stages. Walking boots are essential. **Distance:** 2 1/2 miles (4 kms) return. **Time:** Allow 3 hours for the round trip.

Step By Step: Take the minor road signposted to the Quiraing which branches west from the A855 at Staffin. Continue along this for 2 1/2 miles and immediately after ascending the rocky bluff, park in the carpark by the left of the road (Map Ref. NG 440 679). The distinct footpath to the Quiraing begins opposite the carpark and skirts below the crags of Maoladh Mor, giving a level easy walk with fine views to the islands of Rona and Raasay and the mainland hills beyond. Ahead can be seen the rock formations of the Quiraing, the detached blocky mass of The Prison being particularly noticeable. The path continues all the way to the scree gulley at the foot of The Prison. The next section of the walk is the most difficult and involves a steep scramble. Keep to the right of the scree as the rocks are larger here and give a better foothold. A rock shelter is passed on the right at the foot of this slope. Climb up until you reach the marker cairn on the saddle and then ascend the steep slope directly on your left. A series of small footholds makes for an easier ascent, but watch out for loose stones. At the top, follow the path which winds to the left around the rock pinnacle known as The Needle and then take the right fork (slightly easier than the left fork). This leads to a narrow passage which rises between two huge walls of rock - take care with the ascent here and use the available hand holds. At the top of the passage, the rocky track continues to ascend and then winds its way amongst a strange collection of rocky and grassy landforms. A further scramble leads up to the large flat grassy top known appropriately as The Table. From this point you can climb up to another small table which looks down upon the whole formation and gives fine views of the mainland hills.

"Quiraing" means "the round fold or pen", a name which derives from the fact that during the 15th and 16th centuries locals hid their cattle here from raiders. It is said that in times of trouble, the rocky recesses could hide up to 4,000 beasts. The lush green platform of The Table never fails to stir the imagination and has been variously likened to a putting green, a billiard table and a football pitch. The sporting connection is not so far fetched, for it was once the venue of an annual midsummer shinty match. This surreal landscape has also featured in both films and television commercials, including a well-known car advertisement where the vehicle in question had to be flown in by helicopter and deposited on The Table. Needless to say, the great pillars and pinnacles of the Quiraing were much loved by the

Victorians and at the height of the season up to 60 visitors a day would set out from Portree to explore the strange formations. As far as climbing is concerned, some of the peaks and pillars of the Quiraing remained unconquered until relatively recent times. The first recorded ascent of the 120ft spire known as The Needle was made in August 1977 by one Kevin R. Bridges who was only 16 1/2 at the time. When you have finished exploring the Quiraing, descend by retracing your outward route, this time remembering to keep to the left of the scree gulley on the way down. Please note that it is not possible to climb to the summit of Meall na Suiramach from the Quiraing.

27. ALTERNATIVE ROUTE TO THE QUIRAING

If you are seeking a quieter route to the Quiraing, this walk provides a pleasant alternative to the masses of people on the "tourist" route above. The rugged path is distinct for most of the way and involves a fair bit of climbing. Walking boots essential. **Distance:** 4 miles (6 1/2 kms) return. **Time:** Allow 3 hours 40 minutes for the round trip.

Step By Step: Take the A855 which branches north at Portree and follow it until you reach the minor road which branches left to the Quiraing. From this point, continue north on the A855 for just over two miles, passing firstly the junction to Dunans, then a small lochan to the left and finally a small stone house with a corrugated iron roof on the right. A short distance on from the house there is a large quarry cutting by the left of the road where there is room for several cars to park (Map Ref NG 711 463). Walk back to the old house and join the peat track opposite which heads inland and skirts around the shore of Loch Langaig (this loch makes a good picnic stop and can be reached after 5 minutes). Just beyond this loch, the track becomes a distinct footpath which begins a steady ascent to Loch Hasco. From here, a path continues up and across the heather clad hill to the west of the loch and ascends to cross a fence. It then contours round and climbs up below the crags on the right. The path gradually swings left and becomes a good sheep track which gives easy walking all the way to the scree gully at the foot of the Prison. Continue until you reach the marker cairn on the saddle and then begin the ascent of the steep slope on your right. At the top, take the path which veers left around the rock pinnacle known as the Needle and from this point on follow the instructions given above for Walk 26.

28. RUBHA HUNISH

A popular walk to the old coastguard station which looks out over Rubha Hunish, the most northerly point on Skye. From the station there are stunning views across the Little Minch to the Shiant Isles and Lewis and

Harris beyond. The route crosses open moorland and hill-walking boots are recommended. **Distance:** 3 miles (4 3/4 kms) return. **Time:** Allow 1 hour 20 minutes for the round trip.

Step By Step: Take the A855 north from Portree for 25 miles to the township of Kilmaluag. Shortly after the township, take the small road which branches right to North Duntulm. There is room for a couple of cars to park immediately on the left by the phonebox at the junction (Map Ref. NG 422 743). Go through the farm gate, keeping to the right of the sheep pens and follow the sheep tracks up onto the small ridge on your right. Continue along the ridge until you reach some old croft ruins on your right. At this point there are views east to the mainland hills and west across Tulm Bay to Tulm Island and Duntulm Castle. At the croft ruins, bear left until you reach the edge of the ridge. The path is indistinct here but there are several sheep tracks which give easier walking across the rough moorland. On the low-lying land between the ridge and the shore can be seen the remains of several houses and associated dykes. Descend north to the stock fence and cross by the style. From here, a faint path heads up the next hill. Don't be tempted to drop down and join the more distinct path which continues through the depression to the left - this comes to an abrupt end a short distance ahead at the cliffs. As there is no distinct path from this point on, simply continue uphill and make for the highest point. The abandoned coastguard station soon comes into view.

Once at the station you can look down upon the low lying point of Rubha Hunish and take in the panoramic views of the mainland hills, the Outer Hebrides and the numerous little skerries and islands in the Minch. Most of the small islands around the coast of Scotland have associated with them various tales and legends and those lying off the tip of Trotternish are no exception. Sitting just to the north-east is Eilean Trodday with its little white lighthouse, established in 1908. This island once supported a herd of dairy cattle which, it is said, was attended by a supernatural being known as a *gruagach*. The Trodday gruagach took the form of a tall girl with flowing yellow hair who spent much of her time ensuring that the cows did not injure themselves on the rocky shore. Up until the end of the 18th century, it was the custom of the local milkmaids to leave out milk each day for the gruagach in the hollow of a stone. It is said that failure to perform this act of respect was rewarded by a painful blow from the reed switch which the gruagach always carried with her. Lying just to the north-west is the long island of Fladda-chuain, the wintering ground of barnacle geese and summer home of thousands of arctic terns. This island contains the remains of a chapel dedicated to St Columba which has an unusual blue altar stone. When local fisherman found their boats becalmed, it was once customary to pour water onto this altar to ensure favourable winds. In 1962 the island was the scene of an incident rather reminiscent of Compton MacKenzie's *Whisky Galore*. In the midst of a southerly gale, a Swedish coaster ran aground on the rocky shore at night.   The ship was so badly damaged that she could not be refloated and rumour soon spread that she was carrying a cargo of whisky and cigarettes. As far as is known, nothing was ever found! Lying just to the south of Fladda-chuain are several smaller islands which are home to thousands of seabirds including storm petrels, fulmars, kittiwakes, guillemots, puffins and black-backed gulls.   One of these islands is known as Bord Cruinn (the Round Table) or Lord MacDonald's Table from an incident that occurred at the time of the first Jacobite Rising in 1715. Here, Sir Donald MacDonald of Sleat hid the title deeds of his possessions before setting out to meet up with the Earl of Mar at Braemar. Also to be seen far to the north of Rubha Hunish, lying closer to the shores of Lewis, are the Shiant Isles. "Shiant" is an anglicisation of the Gaelic "Na h-Eileanan Sianta" which means the Enchanted Isles. Here, amidst the strong and turbulent currents which flow in and around these remote land masses, supernatural beings known as the Blue Men swim with the seals.

LANDSCAPE, GEOLOGY
AND THE SKYE VOLCANO

The underlying rocks exert a control on the landscape of all countries, but nowhere is this more obvious than on Skye where changing rock types produce different landscapes and dramatic scenery. The mountains on Skye display a spectacular range of distinctive shapes which betray their constituent rocks. In Sleat some of the oldest rocks in the world have been eroded into gentle, rolling hills which contrast with the steep jagged ridge of the black gabbro Cuillin Hills. The granite of the Red Hills weathers to classic conical shapes, while the lava flows in the north form the flat-topped, stepped hills of MacLeod's Tables.

In Trotternish Skye boasts the largest landslide in Britain, and this gives rise to inland escarpments and spectacular pinnacle scenery which form The Old Man of Storr and The Quiraing. At the coast, slices of columnar basalt-like rocks lying on flat sediments form The Kilt Rock. To the west of the island, the extensive lava flows, which cover much of the north and north-west of Skye, fall to the sea as high cliffs, often stepped by several flows such as at Dunvegan Head. These flows also give the island in Loch Bracadale their stepped outlines, so distinctive against the setting sun. This contrasting scenery has been moulded by recent geological events, but the development of the Skye landscape started billions of years ago.

ANCIENT LANDS

The oldest rocks in Skye are found in Sleat (they also occur in northern Raasay and on Soay) where they preserve a fossil landscape. Here, rocks of Lewisian, Moine and Torridonian sequences form rolling hills with a characteristic rounded appearance. These rocks are all over 500 million years old, with the striped and banded Lewisian rocks the oldest by far: these were formed deep in the Earth's crust around 2800 million years ago by melting and squeezing even older rocks at high temperatures and pressures. About 1700 million years ago the Lewisian rocks were thrust to the surface of the Earth to form mountains. This must have been a stark and barren landscape of bare rock for no land plants existed at this time, and would not evolve for another billion years. For over 500 million years the Lewisian mountains were exposed and gradually eroded away to form rolling, hummocky scenery in a hot, arid climate. Over this landscape ran large, fast flowing rivers which deposited extensive areas of sands and gravels, particularly near the ancient shoreline, and these gradually covered areas of the Lewisian hills, burying the ancient landscape. It was about 1100 million years ago when these sandy sediments were laid down, later solidifing to form the Sleat Torridonian sequence of rocks which was originally over 3 miles thick. Just where the Moine sequence fits into the picture of this ancient landscape is uncertain. The Moine rocks are of about the same age as some of the Torridonian rocks and were originally located further to the south-east but were thrust into their present position by earth movements along a plane known as the Moine Thrust.

GEOLOGICAL MAP

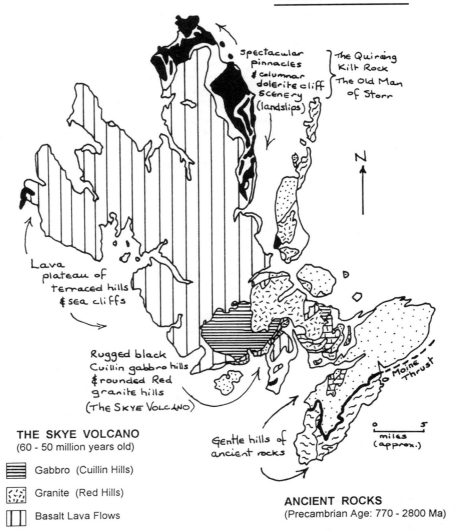

spectacular
pinnacles
& columnar
dolerite cliff
scenery
(landslips)

The Quiraing
Kilt Rock
The Old Man
of Storr

N

Lava
plateau of
terraced hills
& sea cliffs

Rugged black
Cuillin gabbro hills
& rounded Red
granite hills
(The SKYE VOLCANO)

Moine
Thrust

Gentle hills of
ancient rocks

0   5
miles
(approx.)

THE SKYE VOLCANO
(60 - 50 million years old)

▤ Gabbro (Cuillin Hills)

▨ Granite (Red Hills)

▥ Basalt Lava Flows

■ Dolerite Sills

DESERT & MARINE SEDIMENTS
(90 - 550 million years old)

☐ Cretaceous chalk (90 Ma)
Jurassic & Triassic sandstones,
shales, limestones (fossils) (230 - 150 Ma)
▦ Cambrian & Ordovician limestones
and marbles (550 - 470 Ma)

ANCIENT ROCKS
(Precambrian Age: 770 - 2800 Ma)

▦ Torridonian sandstones
(1100 - 770 Ma)
▨ Moine schists
(1100 - 770 Ma)
▨ Lewisian schists and gneiss
(2800 - 1700 Ma)

(Ma = million years old)

Over these eons of time, the ancient rocks of Sleat were once part of a very different landmass from the Scotland we recognise today. Scotland as such did not exist, and what is now the Sleat peninsula was part of a large continent which included parts of north-west Scotland, Canada and Greenland. This huge landmass was also much closer to the equator than Skye today, and was surrounded by a warm shallow sea. The muds and sediments on this sea bed, deposited 550 - 470 million years ago, form the Cambrian limestones seen around Broardford and in Strath. Much later, parts of these limestones were baked into decorative marble by the heat of the Red Hills granite. The marble has been worked in the past and is currently quarried at Torrin on the road to Elgol. Disused small quarries with their spoil heaps can be seen on the hillside of Ben Suardal above Cill Chriosd deserted village. Classic limestone, or karst, scenery is well shown in Strathaird on the track to Suisinish. Both this route, and the walk to Cill Chriosd village are described in the Walks Guide.

DESERT LANDSCAPE TO MARINE ENVIRONMENT

Over the period 470 - 270 million years ago dramatic changes occurred in the landscape across the Earth's surface. Plants evolved and colonised the land, rain forests developed and the large coal deposits of the world were formed. On Skye any rocks which formed during this time have been eroded away or buried leaving no clues as to what happened to Skye over this time. However, by the time the next group of rocks were formed the landscape had again changed to a large, hot arid desert which covered much of Scotland. The warm seas which surrounded the continent gradually flooded the desert sands and covered them in marine muds and sediments. These seas were teaming with life, and the rocks are full of the fossilised remains of these creatures. This all happened in the Jurassic period, about 100 million years ago, and produced the most fossiliferous rocks in the Hebrides. These are exposed around Broadford and in Trotternish. Examples of ammonites, gastropods, corals and belemnites are common, but in these sediments some large fossils have also been found showing Skye had its own "Jurassic Park" creatures. The remains of a plesiosaur (what many people consider the Loch Ness Monster to look like) have recently been found in Jurassic sediments near Staffin and another example was also found on Raasay in rocks of the same age. The fragments of the Staffin example are in the Hunterian Museum, Glasgow. Thin coal seams also formed in Jurassic rocks, though these are not of economic value.

Following another period of erosion, Skye was again submerged in a shallow sea which covered most of Britain. In this sea the large chalk deposits of England were deposited, but in Skye only a few thin sediments of Cretaceous age (90 million years old) remain. Any thick deposits of these rocks were removed in another long period of uplift and erosion of the land surface, this time in a humid, sub-tropical climate as Skye was then closer to the equator than today. The Mediterranean climate and 20 million years of relatively peaceful erosion of the landscape was broken by violent, explosive eruptions. The most extensive period of volcanic eruptions ever seen in NW Europe had begun. It was to last for 12 million years.

THE SKYE VOLCANO

Throughout north-west Scotland and in the Atlantic Ocean eruptions commenced and volcanoes formed about 60 million years ago. This sudden onset of violent activity was brought about by tensions in the Earth's crust caused by the opening and spreading of what is now the Atlantic Ocean. Over the next 12 million years a series of volcanoes developed on the western seaboard from Northern Ireland to Skye and out west to St Kilda. The islands of Mull, Arran, Rum and Skye represent the fossil remains or foundations of some of these volcanoes. This volcanic period started with a series of explosive eruptions which covered the area with thick ash deposits. Fracturing of the crust along lines or fissures allowed molten rock to escape, pouring over the land surface as lava flows which solidified to basalt rock. Initially there was no cone-shaped central volcano, and lavas continued to pour from the fissures covering large areas and increasing in thickness. Some individual lava flows were massive examples over 200 feet thick. The centres of such thick flows are very hard and often cooled slowly forming columnar structures similar (though often not so well defined) as those seen in the sills of Trotternish which will be described below. Eruption though is not a continuous affair, and in the periods of calm red soils formed on the top of the flow. These red bands can often been seen in cliffs made up of several (up to a dozen) lava flows in the northern and north-west of the island, and the relative softness of these layers and the tops of the flows gives rise to the distinctive stepped appearance of the cliffs and hills (e.g. MacLeod's Tables). Volcanic ash is not usually found between the flows, only at the base of the first flow. This implies that eruptions in Skye were not usually violent once volcanic activity had started, and lava simply poured steadily and relatively quietly from the fissures and vents covering the island.

As the volcanic area developed, a central volcano formed sitting over a large area, or chamber, of molten rock (magma). The gabbro of the Cuillin Hills are the solidified remnants of this huge magma chamber. When walking in the Cuillin one is actually in the bowels of a massive volcano 60 million years old. The sheer size and 1000+ °C temperature of this huge mass of molten rock produced sufficient heat to melt parts of the surrounding rocks of the Earth's crust. This new batch of molten rock solidified over time to form the granites of the Red Hills. In some areas granite and gabbro magma may have mixed to form complex intrusions. Glen Sligachan marks the boundary between gabbro and granite masses and when traversing this glen to Loch Coruisk the walker is following the margins of magma chamber on the right, and molten crustal rocks on the left. All this took place at depths of perhaps a mile or more while at the surface, vents on the central volcano were erupting more lava. The volcano lasted for about 10 million years, but over the last 50 million years the cone shape has been eroded away until all that is left today is part of the base or foundations of the volcano - the magma chamber.

As volcanic activity ceased, the molten rocks began to cool and solidify. At the surface, lava flows cool quickly and form fine-grained rocks (basalt). At depth, cooling and solidification take longer, giving time for larger crystals to form. The magma which formed the basalt lava flows is the same as that which formed the gabbro of the Cuillin Hills - the differences in appearance and properties of these rocks are due to differences in the cooling rate of the magma which produces crystals of different size. The ridge of the Cuillin is jagged and uneven, and this is partly due to the gabbro being cut by angled sheets or dykes of basalt or dolerite, which form slippery ledges and blades in the ridge. The molten rock which forms these dykes was squeezed up between cracks which formed as the gabbro solidified. In a similar way, molten rock was squeezed between the Jurassic sediments on the Trotternish peninsula and this cooled to form horizontal bands of dolerite rock, often showing well-formed columnar structures. These are classically shown at The Kilt Rock where the vertical, columnar dolerite sill overlies the more sloping Jurassic sediments. The spectacular coastal cliffs of eastern Trotternish are similarly capped by the sill, and form a dramatic backdrop to the hydro-electric station at Bearreraig Bay. The sill is harder than the local sediments and is responsible for the waterfalls on the east coast, such as at the Lealt Gorge and the Loch Mealt Falls.

THE ICE AGE

Global warming and cooling are not new phenomena in the geologic past. The last two million years have seen several episodes of climate fluctuation, which in the extreme have created periods of extensive glaciation. Each new episode of glacial activity sweeps away soils and the remains of earlier glacial episodes, and further scours the landscape. There have been several occasions over this two-million year period when the climate has cooled sufficiently to let mountain glaciers form. The first widespread glaciation took place in the early Pleistocene about two million years ago, and it is probably at this time that Skye became an island. The final period of widespread glaciation commenced 26,000 years ago and lasted for 13,000 years. Most of Skye was entirely covered except for part of the Cuillin ridge, the Red Hills and the high parts of the Trotternish escarpment. Ice moved across from the Scottish mainland but was directed north and west by the Red Hills and Cuillin mountains. In Trotternish, ice sheets abutted against the escarpment but did not cover the ridge. Instead, fingers of ice created the bealachs between peaks and moved west forming wide U-shaped valleys (e.g. Beinn Edra above Glen Uig). Meanwhile, on the Cuillin local ice caps formed and moved into the valleys in radial patterns from the mountains. The last of the glaciers melted 10,000 years ago when the climate warmed rapidly. As they retreated they left behind debris or moraines, later reworked by melt waters into a distinctive hummocky landscape as seen in Glen Sligachan and Glen Varragill. The screes on the Red Hills are the result of freeze-thaw frost shattering during glacial episodes, while the corries of the Cuillin show areas where localised ice fields formed. Deep rock basins were also cut by the ice. A good example is the basin occupied by Loch Coruisk, this loch fills a depression which was cut to a depth of 100 feet below present-day sea level.

As glaciers melt the weight of the mass of ice on the land is released and coastlines start to rise out of the sea; however, sea-levels can also rise as the melt water enters the sea. It is a balancing act as to which process dominates and depends as much on global ice melting as on local land uplift. These fluctuations result in a series of fossil or raised beaches which mark old coastlines. In Skye there are two sets of raised beaches, one at 50-100 feet above present sea level which formed about 14,000 years ago; Broadford is built on this beach. The second around 6,000 year old, and is up to 30 feet above sea level. It is this latter beach which often contains caves.

LANDSLIDES

Some of the most famous features of the Skye landscape, notably The Old Man of Storr and The Quiraing, have formed as a result of landslides. The Trotternish escarpment with its pinnacles and rock blocks formed from thick basalt lavas which slipped on the underlying Jurassic sediments. It was the sheer weight of the lavas, which in places were up to 4000 feet thick, that caused the softer sediments to give way, and blocks of the escarpment rotated and slipped towards the coast. This slipping occurred before and after glaciation, but the earlier blocks have been rounded and smoothed by the ice. Blocks of lava which slipped after the ice melted have been left to weather into pinnacles forming the famous landscape so distinctive to Skye. The sketch overleaf of the Quiraing shows the view seen today from near the car park on the Staffin - Uig road, and illustrates how the pinnacles and mounds relate to the fallen and rotated blocks of pre- and post-Ice Age landslides.

Other landslides have occurred elsewhere in Skye. Although less grand than the eastern Trotternish examples, those in Glen Uig are worth driving through. Here, the miniature mounds and pinnacles have made the area known as The Fairy Glen.

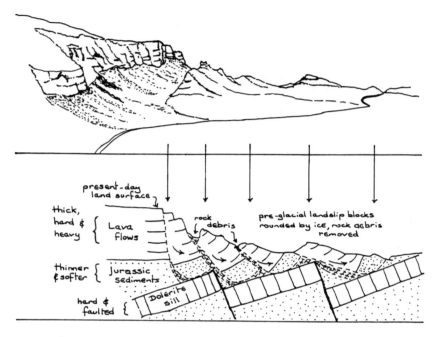

present-day
land surface

thick,
hard & { Lava
heavy { Flows

rock
debris

pre-glacial landslip blocks
rounded by ice, rock debris
removed

thinner { Jurassic
& softer { Sediments

hard & { Dolerite
faulted { Sill

The Quiraing Landslide.

BIBLIOGRAPHY

Arnold, Wendy 1988 *The Historic Hotels of Scotland: A Select Guide* Thames and Hudson

Bain, Robert *The Clans and Tartans of Scotland* Collins, Glasgow

Bell, J.J. 1948 *The Glory of Scotland* George G. Harrap & Co. Ltd, London. First published 1932.

Birks, H.J.B. 1973 *Past and Present Vegetation of the Isle of Skye* Cambridge University Press

Blackie, J.S. 1882 *Altavona* Edinburgh

Blackie, J.S. 1885 *The Scottish Highlander and the Land Laws* London

Booth, David & Perrott, David 1981 *Islands of Britain* Guideway/Windward

Boswell, James 1785 *The Journal of a Tour to the Hebrides with Samuel Johnson*

Buchanan, Robert 1873 *The Hebrid Isles*

Cockburn, Lord 1842 *Circuit Journeys*

Cooper, Derek 1970 *Skye* Routledge & Kegan Paul, London

Cooper, Derek 1979 *Road To The Isles: Travellers In The Hebrides 1770-1914* Routledge & Kegan Paul

Cooper, T. Sidney, R.A. 1890 *My Life*

Craig, David 1992 *On The Crofters' Trail* First published 1990, Jonathon Cape, London

Daniell, William 1813-23 *A Voyage Round Great Britain*

Darling, F. Fraser & Boyd, J. Morton 1964 *The Highlands and Islands* Collins, London

De Saussure, Necker 1882 *A Voyage To The Hebrides*

Geikie, Sir Archibald 1904 *Scottish Reminiscences*

Gordon, Seton 1949 *Highways and Byways in the Central Highlands* MacMillan & Co, Ltd, London, first published 1948

Gordon, Seton 1971 *Highland Summer* Cassell, London

Jackson, Michael 1991 *Malt Whisky Companion* First published 1989. Dorling Kindersley, London

Jameson, Robert 1800 *Mineralogy of the Scottish Isles* 2 Volumes

Johnson, Samuel 1775 *A Journey to the Western Islands of Scotland*

Knox, John 1787 *A Tour Through the Highlands of Scotland and the Hebride Isles in 1776*

Lamont, Rev. D. 1913 *Strath: In Isle of Skye* Archibald Sinclair, Glasgow

MacCaskill, Lady 1852 *Twelve Days in Skye* London

MacCulloch, J.A. 1910 *The Misty Isle of Skye* Oliphant

MacDonald, Lady of the Isles 1929 *All The Days of My Life* John Murray

MacGregor, Alasdair Alpin 1929 *Summer Days Among The Western Isles* T. Nelson & Sons Ltd, T.C. & E.C. Jack Ltd, Edinburgh and London

MacGregor, Alasdair Alpin 1947 *The Peat-Fire Flame: Folk Tales and Traditions of the Highlands & Islands* The Ettrick Press, Edinburgh & London, first published 1937.

MacGregor, Alasdair Alpin 1948 *Behold The Hebrides!* The Ettrick Press Ltd, Edinburgh & London, first published in 1925.

MacGregor, Alasdair Alpin 1953 *Skye and the Inner Hebrides* Robert Hale Ltd, London

MacGregor, Alasdair Alpin 1969 *The Farthest Hebrides* Michael Joseph, London

MacKenzie, Alexander 1883 *History of the Highland Clearances* First published by A. & W. MacKenzie of Inverness, reprinted 1991 by The Mercat Press, Edinburgh

MacKie, Dr Euan W. 1975 *Scotland: An Archaeological Guide* Faber & Faber Ltd, London

MacLean, Malcolm & Carrell, Christopher (eds) 1986 *As an Fhearann: From The Land* Mainstream Publishing (Edinburgh), an Lanntair (Stornoway), Third Eye Centre (Glasgow)

Martin Martin 1703 *Description of the Western Islands of Scotland*

Miket, R. & Roberts, D.L. 1990 *The Mediaeval Castles of Skye & Lochalsh* MacLean Press, Isle of Skye

Miller, Hugh 1858 *The Cruise of the Betsy* Edinburgh

Mitchell, Joseph 1883-4 *Reminiscences of My Life In The Highlands* Two volumes, reprinted 1971

Monro, Dean c.1549 *A Description of the Western Isles of Scotland, called Hybrides* Reprinted Stirling 1934

Morton, H.V. 1930 *In Search of Scotland* Methuen & Co, London, first published 1929

Munro, R.W. 1961 *Monro's Western Isles of Scotland* Oliver & Boyd

Murray, W.H. 1985 *The Companion Guide To The West Highlands of Scotland* Collins, London, first published 1968.

Napier Commission *Report on the Highlands and Islands and Evidence taken by HM Commissioners of Inquiry into the condition of Crofters in the Highlands and Islands, 1883, 1884*

"Nauticus" 1884 *Nauticus In Scotland*

Nicolson, James R. 1975 *Beyond the Great Glen* David & Charles, London

O'Dell, A.C. & Walton, K. 1962 *The Highlands and Islands of Scotland* Thomas Nelson & Sons Ltd

Pennant, Thomas 1774-5 *A Tour in Scotland and Voyage to the Hebrides*

Prebble, John 1969 *The Highland Clearances* Penguin Books, first published 1963 by Martin Secker & Warburg Ltd.

Ratcliffe, Derek 1977 *Highland Flora* Highlands and Islands Development Board

Ritchie, Graham & Anna 1985 *Scotland: Archaeology and Early History* Thames & Hudson, first published 1981

Ross, Donald 1854 *Real Scottish Grievances*

Sandison, Bruce 1988 *Game Fishing In Scotland: The Complete Angler's Guide* Reprinted 1990, Mainstream Publishing

Scott, Sir Walter *Diary Kept on board the Lighthouse Yacht 1814*, reprinted in *Memoirs of the Life of Sir Walter Scott, Bart.* by J.G. Lockhart, 1836

Scott-Moncrieff, George 1961 *The Scottish Islands* First published 1952, Oliver & Boyd, Edinburgh and London

Seton, Gordon 1951 *Highlands of Scotland* Robert Hale Ltd, London

Shea, Michael 1981 *Britain's Offshore Islands* Country Life Books

Sillar, F.C. & Meyler, Ruth 1973 *Skye* David & Charles, Newton Abbot

Smith, Alexander 1865 *A Summer In Skye* Reprinted 1912, Sampson Low, Marston & Co. Ltd, London

Smith, Rev. Charles Lesingham 1837 *Excursions Through the Highlands and Isles of Scotland*

Smith, Sheenah 1988 *Horatio McCulloch 1805-1867* Glasgow Museums and Art Galleries

Steel, Tom 1980 *The Life and Death of St Kilda* Fontana/Collins, first published in 1975

Stott, Louis 1987 *The Waterfalls of Scotland* Aberdeen University Press

Sutherland, Halliday 1939 *Herbridean Journey* Geofrey Bles, London

Swire, Otta F. 1952 *Skye: The Island and Its Legends* Oxford University Press

Thomson, Derick S. (ed) 1983 *The Companion To Gaelic Scotland* Blackwell Reference

Walker, J. Hubert 1948 *On Hills of the North* Oliver & Boyd, Edinburgh & London

INDEX